The Communication of
Emotional Meaning

THE COMMUNICATION OF EMOTIONAL MEANING

Joel R. Davitz, Ph.D.

with

MICHAEL BELDOCH, PH.D.
SIDNEY BLAU, PH.D.
LILLY DIMITROVSKY, PH.D.
EUGENE A. LEVITT, PH.D.
PHYLLIS KEMPNER LEVY, PH.D.
STEVEN MATTIS, B.S.
JOHN LE B. TURNER, PH.D.

DEPARTMENT OF PSYCHOLOGICAL FOUNDATIONS AND SERVICES
TEACHERS COLLEGE, COLUMBIA UNIVERSITY

GREENWOOD PRESS, PUBLISHERS
WESTPORT, CONNECTICUT

Library of Congress Cataloging in Publication Data

Davitz, Joel Robert.
  The communication of emotional meaning.

  Reprint of the 1964 ed. published by Mcgraw-Hill, New
York, in series: McGraw-Hill series in psychology.
  Bibliography: p.
  Includes index.
  1. Expression. 2. Emotions. 3. Interpersonal
communication. I. Beldoch, Michael, joint author.
II. Title.
[BF591.D36 1976]   152.4'2   75-31360
ISBN 0-8371-8527-0

Originally published in 1964 by McGraw-Hill Book
Company, New York

Reprinted with the permission of McGraw-Hill Book
Company

Reprinted in 1976 by Greenwood Press, Inc.,
51 Riverside Avenue, Westport, CT 06880

Library of Congress catalog card number 75-31360
ISBN 0-8371-8527-0

Printed in the United States of America

10 9 8 7 6 5 4 3 2

PREFACE AND ACKNOWLEDGMENTS

The primary purpose of this book is to present a series of researches concerned with emotional communication. Beginning with an early interest in the clinician's task of recognizing emotional expressions in the psychotherapeutic interview, the research developed along several lines of investigation dealing with a variety of problems relevant to general psychology. In a sense, the studies reported in this volume represent an initial stage in a series of ongoing researches, and one of the chief goals of this book is to stimulate further work by other researchers interested in problems of emotional communication.

It would be impossible to acknowledge the hundreds of subjects, the many consultants and colleagues who contributed in one way or another to the present volume. However, it is a pleasure to express our appreciation to a number of people most closely concerned with our research activities and with the preparation of the final manuscript. In particular, we would like to express our appreciation to Laurance F. Shaffer who participated actively in the planning, execution, and final presentation of many of the studies reported here. In addition to the specific help he offered in many of the individual studies, in his role as chairman of the clinical psychology training program at Teachers College, Columbia University, Professor Shaffer encouraged and reinforced the kind of intellectual atmosphere that fostered exploration into new psychological problem areas. All of us who have worked closely with Professor Shaffer value this experience as one of the most significant and rewarding aspects of our professional careers.

Throughout our work, a number of colleagues participated and consulted with us on various problems involved in the research. These include Professors Millie Almy, Louis Forsdale, Arthur Jersild, Kenneth Herrold, Rosalea Schonbar, and Edward J. Shoben, Jr. We also owe a special debt of gratitude to Professor Rosedith Sitgreaves for her generous help in the statistical analyses of our data.

In the preparation of the final manuscript, we are particularly grateful to Professors Harry Harlow and William Kessen. Professor Harlow read an earlier draft of the book, and his astute critical comments led to major revisions that substantially improved the final presentation. Professor Kessen also read an earlier draft, and with extraordinary care and thoughtfulness made numerous suggestions that were incorporated in the final version.

Finally, to my wife, Dr. Lois Davitz, I extend my deepest appreciation for her many significant suggestions in the formulation of research problems and for her profound support throughout our work.

Joel R. Davitz

CONTENTS

1

Introduction

Joel R. Davitz

This research began in the spring of 1958 with a small exploratory study of vocal communication. As this initial work was done, we hardly expected the first study to grow into a long-term project. In fact, we had been working in this general area for some time before realizing that something like a consistent line of research was gradually developing. The contents of this book, therefore, grew in a loosely organized way, unencumbered for the most part by an explicit overall plan. We thus enjoyed the liberties of nontheoretical freedom following leads that seemed "interesting" rather than "theoretically meaningful," with the rationale (or rationalization) that true discovery was more likely to lie along roads of interest than along any major theoretical road we were likely to plan. At this time, however, with the first publication of a substantial part of our work, it may be useful to describe something of how we began our work and how it progressed.

Tracing the impulses that lead to research is a difficult, if not impossible, task. I suspect that most research in the social sciences has roots somewhere in the personal life of the researcher, though these roots are rarely reported in published papers. Perhaps such personal histories have no scientific value. They might even disrupt the main purposes of scientific communication. Thus, reports of experiments should indeed be prefaced by clear-cut theoretical, or at least pseudotheoretical, rationales, rather than by personal accounts of how the person became interested in doing the work. But the research described in this book did not begin with any explicit theoretical view, much less a theoretical rationale, so prefacing our account of what we've done with a nicely devised theory of emotion or of communication would be something less than honest.

My interest in emotional communication and emotional sensitivity began at least as early as my first practicum experience in clinical psychology. While I was a graduate student, I was encouraged, in one way or another, to be "sensitive," to "empathize," to "understand" how the other person felt. And I can trace my first feelings of confusion about clinical practice to the problem of learning how to go about being "sensitive, empathic, and emotionally understanding." Unfortunately, nothing in the psychological literature I read seemed to help very much; those who wrote about the problem told me to listen with my "third ear," to "let myself go," to react "spontaneously and intuitively," and finally, to undergo psychoanalysis.

Like most clinical graduate students, I eventually learned to behave in a way that seemed, to my supervisors, relatively sensitive to the feelings of others. And gradually, as I continued my clinical work, the problem of how to be or become sensitive to emotional communication receded, for I apparently felt that in some mysterious way I had become reasonably empathic, appropriately intuitive, and emotionally sensitive.

The problem came to the fore again when I assumed the role of supervisor, when it became my task, in turn, to encourage student clinicians to be sensitive to how their patients were feeling. I am not sure of the basis of my judgments about students' insensitivity, but rarely did I have much doubt about instances of insensitivity. These judgments, of course, may have reflected not much more than disagreement between my supervisees' opinion and my own, though one likes to believe that training and experience make some difference in the validity of opinions in these matters. At any rate, I found myself echoing the words of my own supervisors and the writers I had read as a graduate student, telling my supervisees to "listen with the third ear," "to let themselves go," to react "spontaneously and intuitively," and if possible, "to go into analysis." Most of this advice was taken with seriousness and respect, but occasionally I noticed that some of my students reacted to this advice with a gleam of confusion. Probably more than anything else, these nonverbal expressions of confusion led to our research, for if no one had been confused or discomfited by my earnest advice, I would probably have continued my supervisory chores in standard fashion.

This is not to say that the research reported here does much to clarify the problems faced by a clinician or his supervisor; like most researchers, we soon became intrigued with problems quite divorced from our original, more practical concern. However, the difficulties encountered in a clinical setting were the major impetus to our initial work, and while we have little to offer the practicing clinician or supervisor at this stage of ignorance, we hopefully believe that greater understanding of the general problems involved in emotional communication will eventually have some practical, clinical feedback. At the moment, we can only note that emotional communication presents problems which can be investigated fruitfully by empirical means. On the basis of our present research, we know a few interesting facts that are beginning to make sense in some interrelated ways. But perhaps more important, the mysteries of the intuitive third ear have become somewhat less mysterious as our work has progressed, and we are confident that as work is continued along this line, the mysteries and confusions will eventually be resolved.

Most of the research reported in this book concerns nonverbal modes of communicating emotional meanings. This reflects my early experience of supervising students in a counseling practicum. None of the students had difficulty understanding the words clients said; often, the student clinician could give almost verbatim reports of what happened in an interview, and interpret the words of the client in any of several theoretical systems. Thus it didn't seem to be the words that were missed when a client's feelings were misunderstood; rather, what was missed seemed to be a function of the nonverbal aspects of the client's communication. Since much of the supervision was based on tape recordings of interviews, I began more and more to emphasize "how" a client said something, instead of "what" was said, for the emotional meaning carried by the form of speech, rather than by its content, seemed to cause the primary difficulties in communication.

This recurrent concern in practicum supervision led to our first study in this area (Davitz & Davitz, 1959a). In trying to sensitize student therapists to this kind of communication, I began to identify various emotional states in terms of certain vocal characteristics; e.g. the quivering voice of anxiety, the harshness of anger, etc. But from time to time, I was pushed to provide evidence for my dicta about the vocal characteristics which defined various emotional meanings, and, eventually, I realized that these dicta were based on little more than personal experience and opinion. This realization, brought home in countless instances within the supervisory setting, stimulated our first cautious, and in some ways, trivial study. Essentially, we asked speakers to express a variety of emotional meanings while reciting the alphabet; these recitations were recorded, and listeners were then asked to identify the feelings being expressed. This was hardly a revolutionary or novel idea—though unaware of it at the time, we were replicating an elementary study previously reported several times in the literature. Nevertheless, being happily naïve in this area, we were excited by our results, undoubtedly more excited and more encouraged to go on than if we had read a report of the same experiment done by someone else.

Like those who had preceded us, we found that emotional meanings were communicated nonverbally far beyond chance expectation. This did not surprise us, but it did encourage us, because even with the gross, relatively uncontrolled procedures we used, the results coincided with common sense and common experience. Moreover, this study, pristine as it was, gave us our first hint that a phenomenon shrouded in the mysteries of clinical folklore could be investigated by laboratory procedures.

Our first study supported the general notion that emotional meanings could be communicated reliably by content-free speech; but, in addition to the obvious fact that almost everyone performed beyond chance, the data showed striking individual differences among speakers in their ability to express feelings, among listeners in their ability to identify feelings expressed, and among feelings in their susceptibility to accurate vocal communication. Thus, unaware that others had made the same discovery several times before we had come to it, we had "discovered" a clinically interesting phenomenon that was measurable in a research setting, and which obviously involved a wide range of individual differences along several dimensions.

Beginning with the observation of individual differences, we decided first to investigate differences among various feelings (Davitz & Davitz, 1959b). As I currently reread this second study, I feel it is not unlike some other psychological research papers that demonstrate the obvious with considerable rigor and almost manage to obscure their obviousness by remarkable verbiage. Nevertheless, in terms of the overall research program, it served an important purpose, for we obtained moderately positive results that seemed to make sense. Nothing is as encouraging at the beginning of research as sensible, moderately positive results. We found that feelings rated as subjectively similar to each other were more difficult to discriminate in vocal expressions than were feelings rated subjectively dissimilar. Thus, other things being equal, expressions of joy and cheerfulness were more difficult to discriminate from each other than, for example, expressions of joy and disgust—hardly an overwhelming finding. We also found that in pairs of similar feelings, the one described subjectively as "stronger" is more accurately communicated, while valence (pleasantness-unpleasantness of the feeling) and activity level (activity-passivity rating of the feeling) per se are independent of accuracy of communication.

As I worked on this research, I talked about it with students and colleagues. My enthusiasm and confidence in its implications undoubtedly exceeded the bounds warranted by our initial findings, but partly as a result of this enthusiasm, and partly as a function of the intrinsic interest in the questions raised, a number of students began to work with me on related problems of emotional communication and emotional sensitivity. A number of these studies were done as doctoral dissertations at Teachers College, Columbia University, and are reported in several chapters of this book. Also, numerous minor studies were conducted by students as part of their research training in the clinical psychology program at Teachers College; several of these are reported in Chapter 11, "Minor Studies and Some Hypotheses." As in any long-term project, many exploratory pilot studies were done, and not all of these deserve being reported. I have therefore selected only those which seem most promising in the sense of opening up new areas for exploration, suggesting problems or techniques which seem likely to pay off with new knowledge about interesting questions.

Among the doctoral theses reported here, John Turner's study of schizophrenic patients was the first research done as a dissertation. The work I was doing at the time led to a discussion of emotional sensitivity among various clinical groups. We recalled that some writers had described some psychoses as a disorder of affect; others had characterized schizophrenia as a disorder of communication. We reasoned, therefore, that schizophrenia might appropriately be considered a disorder in the communication of affect. This led to Turner's study of emotional sensitivity among schizophrenic patients.

As we talked about various problems related to the general area of emotional communication, the special interests of each person played an important part in determining his view of the most important problem to be investigated. An excellent illustration of this "personal bent" is the work of Michael Beldoch, who investigated the interrelationships among various modes of emotional communication. Perhaps more than any of the rest of us engaged in this work, Beldoch came to this research with a wide range of experience in a variety of the arts. He had been a professional photographer, was and is, an excellent painter, had been actively interested in the theater, and for years, in a variety of ways, had been concerned with one or another of the arts. Thus, he focused on interrelating sensitivity in different modes of expression, posing the question, "Is there a general factor of sensitivity, or are people sensitive to one mode of expression without being especially sensitive in other modes?"

Phyllis Levy's work reflects a more direct, clinically oriented focus. Levy began with the psychoanalytic notion that self-understanding is a prerequisite of understanding others. Widely accepted in the folklore of clinical psychology, this notion was probably first presented systematically in the work of Freud, who, of course, required the psychoanalyst to first understand himself before analyzing others. In one form or another, this general proposition of a positive relation between self-understanding and understanding others has been accepted by most current schools of thought in clinical psychology. Obviously, our research did not deal with the kind of understanding or the kind of material that Freud was concerned with; but neglecting, for the moment, the basis of Freud's view, it seemed reasonable to test the generality of the proposition that self-understanding and the understanding of others are positively related. As an added fillip, Levy also considered the ability to express emotional meanings, and thus designed her study of the interrelationships among: (1) ability to understand expressions of others; (2) ability to understand one's own expressions; and (3) ability to express *to* others.

In line with my early interest in trying to help student therapists identify vocal cues of specific emotional meanings, I began to study auditory characteristics of various vocal expressions that reliably communicated particular meanings. At the outset of this study, I thought of analyzing the vocal expressions in terms of the physical characteristics of speech sounds, and frankly, I was intrigued with the picture of a research enterprise conducted in white laboratory coats and with a great deal of complex electronic equipment. But before the picture became too persuasive, I realized that my primary interest concerned the auditory cues of speech which could be discriminated by a human listener, for the clinician, in most instances, is a human listener rather than an electronic device. I therefore pursued this investigation by relating auditory cues judged by human listeners to several dimensions of emotional, or connotative, meaning, with the aim of discovering lawful relations between subjective aspects of emotional meaning and auditory characteristics that communicate these meanings.

At about the same time I was engaged in studying auditory cues of vocal expressions, Sidney Blau became interested in working with blind persons. One of the persistent bits of folklore in the literature about the blind is the notion of auditory compensation. That is, blind people were thought to compensate for their visual disability by increased sensitivity in other modes of perception, particularly the auditory mode. This proposition seemed relevant to our investigations of vocal expression, and so, beginning with a bit of folklore, Blau developed his study of "An Ear for an Eye," discovering, in the process of his research, a heretofore neglected but potentially very important variable, the tendency to selectively attend or inattend to emotional meanings.

Starting from a somewhat different point of view, Levitt observed that almost all of our research concerned the "receiving" or understanding of emotional messages. This emphasis reflected our initial interest in the clinician's task of understanding his client. The communication process, however, involves both sending and receiving messages, and any understanding of the total process would require information about both aspects of communication. In reviewing the literature, Levitt discovered a considerable amount of work concerned with facial expression, though some of the studies seemed to contradict each other. Despite common experience, some writers seemed to think that emotional meanings could *not* be communicated by facial expression; others thought facial expression was an excellent mode of communication. In most cases, previous researchers had used still photographs to investigate communication via the facial mode, while everyday facial expression obviously involves movement and change, cues which could not be expressed in a single still photograph. Therefore, Levitt proposed using sound motion pictures, comparing parallel expressions in the vocal and the facial modes. In a sense, Levitt's study of the relation between modes of expression supplements Beldoch's study of modes of receiving emotional meanings, and it is interesting to note that both obtained similar results.

In every research we did, a wide range of individual differences in ability to understand the meanings expressed always characterized our data. I became interested in these differences from the viewpoint of personality, asking the question, "What kinds of people are sensitive to emotional expressions?" For nearly a year, I investigated this problem with almost no success. Whenever I could gather a suitable number of subjects, I administered a vocal test of emotional sensitivity and any of a large variety of tests designed to measure personality variables. Perhaps because of my early reading in clinical psychology, I was convinced that personality variables played an important role in determining emotional sensitivity; after all, it was the psychoanalytically oriented personality theorists who seemed to pay most attention to problems of emotional sensitivity, and while they never described the sensitive person in measurable personality terms, finding the appropriate personality dimensions seemed only a matter of time. Some of the null fruits of this search are reported in Chapter 5, "Personality, Perceptual, and Cognitive Correlates of Emotional Sensitivity," a paper which incontrovertibly demonstrates my failure to find personality correlates.

Repeated frustration in the personality area finally led to a major revision in conceptualizing emotional sensitivity. I began to think in terms of perceptual and cognitive variables, trying to describe the communication process as a series of perceptual and cognitive events. This shifted the focus of research, and the shift was duly reinforced by subsequent results. Thus the data led us away from an earlier concern with personality variables related to sensitivity and suggested a conceptualization of sensitivity in terms of perceptual and cognitive factors.

Lilly Dimitrovsky's primary professional interest before entering clinical psychology was child development, and she brought to our work a developmental point of view that none of us had been concerned with up to the time she began her research. The value of this point of view, and the important findings to which it led, are reported in Chapter 6 on the development of sensitivity in children.

Finally, after working in this area for several years, I realized that in everyday life emotional meanings are communicated by verbal as well as nonverbal means. This led to our study of metaphors, the development of a test to measure ability to identify verbal expressions of emotion, and a preliminary investigation of the relationship between verbal and nonverbal modes of communication.

The present volume summarizes our work up to the summer of 1962, covering the results of about four years of research in this area. At any one time, there were perhaps four or five of us working on related studies, but there was never any formal structure of the group, either in terms of an overall theoretical framework or an administrative organization characteristic of integrated research projects. Of course there was a good deal of informal interaction among those who were working on studies at about the same time, and this interaction undoubtedly is reflected in the general line of investigation that gradually developed. However, independence of the individual researcher has been the consistent keynote of how we've worked.

This independence, and the absence of a general theoretical structure, has its advantages and disadvantages. The ideas that led to each study were not derived from some hypothetico-deductive model; thus, each researcher was free to explore any question that seemed interesting to him, unrestricted by explicit a priori notions of what was important. Because of this, we were freer to make discoveries, to open up new lines of investigation, though all of us hoped that eventually our findings would be integrated within a systematic theory. From my own point of view, this sort of strategy is particularly appropriate at the beginning of research in a given area; it provides an opportunity or setting for discovery, emphasizes hunches, questions, and new ideas without the restraints sometimes imposed by more formal theories.

But this approach to research must also pay a price, and probably the major price is what seems, in retrospect, to be a good deal of wasted effort in directions that never pay off, or, on problems that later appear to be trivial. I see no solution to this problem, no way of cutting the inevitable price of ignorance, for at the beginning of research, there is almost no basis for deciding what is trivial and what will become important. For example, in Blau's study of the blind, we were at first bothered by the tendency of blind subjects to "overwrite" their answers when identifying common, everyday sounds. This seemed to be a trivial nuisance for scoring the accuracy of their identifications, but later, as we began to examine these "overwritten" answers, we discovered what seemed to be a common characteristic among these answers, viz. a tendency to "hear" affective, emotional meanings in sounds that presumably were not intended to express such meanings. This led to our hunch about the blind person's "reaction sensitivity" to emotion, or "affect attentiveness," the tendency to listen for emotional meanings in auditory stimuli. This variable turned out to be one of the most interesting studied, and led to what might be the most important finding in Blau's research.

On the other hand, I spent a good deal of time searching, without a systematic rationale, for personality correlates of emotional sensitivity, assuming that such correlates must exist but never finding anything stable enough to be replicated. This sort of "blind empiricism" led us up numerous dead ends before we dropped that line of investigation. Our empirical point of view, therefore, left us free to discover new ideas, but also left us free to waste considerable time and effort. We've not been in any special hurry, however, and the findings we have to date seem encouraging enough to warrant further exploration of merely "interesting" ideas, before focusing on the development of a systematic theory in the hypothetico-deductive model.

This does not mean we have not attempted to formulate and organize our findings in some consistent fashion; each of the papers offers some preliminary theoretical speculations, though the discussions tend to be at a minor level in the sense of trying to account for a relatively limited range of phenomena investigated by each specific study. Moreover, in Chapter 13, "Summary and Speculations," I have tried to organize our findings in terms of some major questions about emotional communication and emotional sensitivity, but this attempt hardly deserves the name of a "theory" in the formal sense that characterizes, for example, some learning theories and even some theories of personality.

The absence of an overall theory does lead to occasional confusion in terminology. In most cases, we've tried not to coin new words, recognizing that the use of words previously used in other contexts runs the risk of semantic, as well as conceptual, confusion. For example, the term "emotional sensitivity" has previously been used by many writers to refer to vastly different phenomena; we have used the term with specific reference to the ability of subjects to identify emotional meanings expressed in various modes of communication. But certainly, in everyday life, functioning at an emotionally sensitive level requires not only ability of the sort we presumably measure, but also motivation for "being sensitive." Nevertheless, risking this kind of confusion, and possibly, in our own thinking, overloading the meaning of terms we've used, we prefer writing in a relatively nontechnical, nonspecialized language with a primary emphasis on empirical, operational definitions of common terms. As our empirical knowledge about the events of emotional communication increases, probably a specialized vocabulary will have to be developed, but at the present time there seems to be little real need for using such a vocabulary. Current psychological writing has enough jargon without our adding to a reader's burden.

One major change, however, has occurred during the history of our work, and this change reflects some clarification in our thinking about the central phenomenon we have been investigating. The first study published was entitled, "The Communication of Feelings by Content-Free Speech." This seemed to describe what we had investigated, but I found that others misinterpreted our work because of the phrase, "Communication of Feelings." We were studying a laboratory situation in which speakers were asked to express feelings by reciting the alphabet; and listeners were asked to identify these feelings on the basis of hearing the tape recordings. Certainly we did not expect, or intend, the speakers actually to experience the feelings they expressed, or to react in any physiological way that might characterize an emotional state. Similarly, we did not expect the vocal expressions to elicit specific emotional reactions in the listeners. We were not concerned, and never have been concerned, with the interesting problem of actually eliciting emotional reactions by some form of interpersonal communication. We have been concerned primarily with a *communication* process, with problems related to whether or not one person understands a particular kind of meaning expressed by another person—regardless of the actual emotional state of either person. Thus, the emotional expressions are indeed artificial, in that they are elicited by specific instructions in a laboratory setting and probably have little to do with the actual emotional state of the person expressing the emotional meaning. Moreover, the responses to these stimuli are also artificial, in that we typically ask the subject to label an expression in terms of its emotional meaning rather than react to another person who is actually "feeling" the emotion. But our concern has been with the communication process per se, with one person understanding (as measured by a labeling response) the emotional *meaning* of another person's expression. We have devised some criteria for defining when communication occurs (e.g., we say a given vocal item communicates a specific emotional meaning when a plurality of listeners respond in a category of emotional meaning which agrees with the speaker's intent), and within that definition, we have tried to remain consistent. Hoping to clarify the nature of our intent, however, we have changed our early terminology from "the communication of feelings," to the clumsier "communication of emotional meanings," emphasizing communication of one kind of meaning as our focal point of interest.

This book represents only a beginning of research in this area, a beginning prefaced by the work of others on related problems. We are currently engaged in a number of studies following some of the lines suggested by papers in this volume. As indicated earlier, we do not presume to answer many of the practical problems encountered by clinical psychologists, psychiatrists, social workers, communication specialists, and others concerned with human interactions that almost inevitably involve the communication of emotional meanings. But by presenting our work from our own, undoubtedly biased and limited point of view, we hope to stimulate and encourage others to pursue this important line of psychological investigation.

2

A review of research concerned with facial and vocal expressions of emotion

Joel R. Davitz[1]

Beginning with Darwin's investigations reported in 1896 (*The expression of the emotions in men and animals*), the majority of studies concerned with nonverbal, emotional communication have involved facial expression. Early studies in this area were concerned primarily with demonstrating that facial expressions do indeed convey emotional meaning, and as knowledge about facial communication gradually increased, investigators became concerned with somewhat more subtle and complex problems such as those dealt with in Schlosberg's well-known analysis of dimensions of expression (1952; 1954). In recent years, however, researchers have become increasingly interested in various aspects of vocal communication, and while these investigations in some respects parallel earlier studies of facial expression, the results of these two lines of research have not been systematically organized and related to each other. In introducing our own research, therefore, which is concerned with both modes of communication, it may be useful to summarize the findings of previous research as a basis for relating earlier investigations to the studies reported in subsequent chapters.

FACIAL EXPRESSIONS

On the basis of data obtained by a variety of experimental techniques, almost all researchers have concluded that feelings can be communi-

[1] I would like to express my appreciation to Zanvel Klein for his generous help in the preparation of this chapter.

cated accurately by facial expression alone. But while there is general agreement that facial expressions communicate feelings beyond chance expectancy, there are wide differences in accuracy reported in the literature. These differences probably are a function of the stimulus material used, the kinds of discriminations required in the experimental procedure, the categories of emotional meaning considered in a research, and individual differences in ability among those who express feelings and those who are asked to identify the expressions. It is therefore impossible to specify with any precision the level of accuracy with which facial expressions are recognized. Sometimes, even using the same stimulus material, different results are reported. Langfeld (1918a; 1918b), for example, presented 11 judges with the 105 Rudolph pictures, which are retouched photographs, resembling drawings, of a heavily bearded German actor. Judges ranged in accuracy of identification from 17 to 58 per cent, with laughter, anger, fear, and hatred most frequently identified. In a subsequent study using 14 of the "reputedly best" Rudolph pictures, and crediting for partially correct responses, Allport (1924) obtained an average accuracy of between 45 and 50 per cent.

Only two writers, Landis (1929b) and Sherman (1927a), have dissented from the general conclusion that facial cues accurately communicate feelings. It is difficult to interpret Landis' position, however, because the data he presented in his own research apparently contradict his conclusion. He reported, for instance, that judges were able to make correct identifications in 48 per cent of the cases, which is far beyond chance expectation for his experimental design. Perhaps Landis' position is noteworthy, nevertheless, to underscore the more general finding that nonverbal emotional communication rarely approaches perfect accuracy. Thus, in any mode of expression, nonverbal cues account for only part of the variance in accuracy of communication.

Sherman's point of view is based on data quite different from those considered in other studies (1927a). Sherman investigated the ability of adults to judge the emotions conveyed by facial expressions of human neonates, and his results demonstrate that such judgments cannot be made reliably. In light of other developmental data, it seems reasonable to assume that the behavioral reactions of neonates to any strong stimulus are too diffuse and gross to permit distinctive responses that convey unequivocal information, but as shown by a study reported by Goodenough (1931), apparently sufficient maturation occurs during the first 10 months of human life to allow the infant to produce identifiable facial responses. Goodenough's judges matched eight still photographs of an infant with paragraphs describing the conditions under which the responses were emitted, and her findings indicate that judges were correct approximately half the time.

Methods of Recording Expressions

Despite the obvious limitations of using posed photographs of a single person a substantial number of studies have used this technique in obtaining their stimulus materials. Among the most frequently used pictures are those developed by Feleky (1914; 1922), who posed for 86 photographs, attempting in each to express an emotion. Her results indicate relatively high accuracy in communicating surprise, laughter, disgust, and horror. These findings were further supported by Kanner (1931) who used 18 of the Feleky pictures, and found that all the photographs were identified accurately about 50 per cent of the time, with expressions of surprise, fear, and horror most frequently recognized. Goodenough and Tinker (1931), also using the Feleky pictures, found results quite similar to those reported by Kanner in terms of the kinds of feelings most easily communicated. Nevertheless, these findings can hardly be generalized to expressions of other persons. Most studies in this area recognize the need to sample judges, but if one is to generalize about the communication process, both people who *express* and people who *identify* the expressions must adequately be sampled. Just as Kanner (1931) obtained a sample of 409 judges to identify expressions, it would seem equally necessary to obtain a sufficient sample of persons who express emotions. Otherwise, one's conclusions are limited to the single person who provided the set of facial expressions. We can therefore conclude that Feleky was particularly apt in posing expressions of surprise, fear, and horror, but we have no idea of whether this is a function of Feleky's unique expressive abilities or if this indeed represents a more general phenomenon.

Other investigators have used a similar technique with a set of pictures developed by Ruckmick (Ruckmick, 1921; 1936; Gates, 1923; May, 1938; Hanawalt, 1944), and clearly the same limitations relevant to the Feleky pictures apply to studies using the Ruckmick set. But perhaps even more critical than the sampling problem is the artificiality of the stimulus materials used, represented at the extreme by a series of studies using the Piderit model developed by Boring and Titchener (1923). The stimulus in this case is the profile of a head about 18 inches high with a number of interchangeable brows, eyes, noses, and mouths. Using this model, Buzby (1924) constructed six faces which presumably expressed different emotions, and these stimuli were used to investigate accuracy of identification in studies by Buzby as well as by Fernberger (1927; 1928). Generalization of their results, however, is severely limited, for though the Piderit profiles may be an interesting teaching aid, the model is a rather unfortunate caricature of the human face and does not present a stimulus comparable to that in normal human interaction (Frois-Wittman, 1930).

To reduce artificiality of their stimuli, a number of investigators have used photographs of unposed, spontaneous facial expressions (Schulze, 1912; Munn, 1940; Hanawalt, 1944), and it is interesting to note that in terms of accuracy of communication, there are no consistent differences between the results obtained with posed and unposed pictures. Communication necessarily involves shared interpretations of more or less conventional cues; without such conventions one could hardly expect one person to understand another. It seems reasonable, therefore, to assume that the cues which communicate meaning in posed pictures are similar to, and in fact based on, cues observed in normal, everyday facial expression. Unless one were to assume a special, artificial facial "language" specific to the theater or the psychological laboratory, one must conclude that the relatively accurate communication reported in most studies is a function of knowledge shared, at least implicitly, by those persons who communicate with each other.

An important limitation of still photographs is the loss of information possibly conveyed by *changes* in facial expression over time. It is therefore remarkable that so little research has utilized motion pictures, though an early study by Dusenberry and Knower (1938) and a subsequent study by Coleman (1949) provide promising methodological leads in this direction.

Cues Aiding in Recognition

In view of the differences in stimulus materials used by various researchers and the particular limitations of most techniques, it is not surprising that investigations of the role played by particular muscle groups and facial regions in emotional expression have provided equivocal, and sometimes, contradictory evidence. For example, Buzby (1924), using Piderit profiles, concluded that the eye and brow are more important than the mouth in conveying feelings; Ruckmick (1921), on the other hand, using two different sets of photographs, concluded that the lower half of the face provided the dominant cues used in emotional communication. In contrast to these writers, both Dunlap (1927) and Hanawalt (1942; 1944) proposed that the relative importance of a particular facial area is a function of the emotion expressed. Dunlap suggested that the mouth area conveys best those feelings that are either extremely pleasant or unpleasant; Hanawalt suggested that the mouth region is more important in conveying happiness while the eyes and brow are more important in communicating surprise and fear.

The evidence in support of associating one facial cue with a particular category of feeling obviously is not clear-cut. In fact, Frois-Wittman (1930) has suggested that *no* emotional expression is characterized by specific contraction of one muscle or muscle group; rather, the significance of any given muscular movement depends upon the total pattern of response typifying certain emotional reactions. Thus, in the communication of most feelings, it is not the specific movement of the eyes or the mouth, but the overall pattern of cues which communicates emotional meaning. Moreover, as Coleman (1949) has suggested, the pattern of expression seems to vary somewhat among different individuals, partly as a function of the emotion expressed.

Perhaps the most promising approach to classifying facial expressions is suggested by Schlosberg's analysis (1952; 1954) in terms of dimensions of emotion. Beginning with the six-step scale developed by Woodworth (1938), Schlosberg initially obtained data which suggested two dimensions of facial expression, pleasantness-unpleasantness and attention-rejection (1952). These dimensions seemed comparable to the blue-yellow and red-green axes of the color surface, which suggested a possible third dimension paralleling visual brightness. Subsequent research supported this view, and in 1954, Schlosberg presented a description of facial expressions in terms of the three dimensions of pleasantness-unpleasantness, attention-rejection, and level of activation. Thus, instead of searching for facial cues associated with specific categories of emotion, it may be more profitable to investigate cues associated with dimensions of emotional meaning such as those proposed either by Schlosberg or suggested by the research of Osgood, et al. (1957). The results of a study in this direction concerned with vocal expression are reported in Chapter 8, and indeed this line of investigation seems much more promising than previous attempts to isolate cues of specific feeling states.

Previous research has failed to define the specific facial cues or pattern of facial movements which consistently communicate emotional meaning, but several studies agree that knowledge of the situation in which an emotion is expressed significantly increases accuracy of communication (Munn, 1940; Vinacke, 1949; Cline, 1956; Frijda, 1958). These findings are consistent with the results reported by Hunt, et al. (1958), Rump (1960), and more recently by Schachter and Singer (1962), which conclusively demonstrate that emotional states are defined, in part, by situational cues. As Frijda has suggested (1958), perhaps facial cues define the more general category of emotional expression (e.g., positive versus negative; active versus passive), while situational cues determine the more specific and subtle discriminations within a general category (e.g., anger versus impatience; satisfaction versus contentment).

In almost all of the studies reported in this area, the person who expressed feelings as the stimulus material was a stranger to the judges who were asked to identify the meanings expressed. Therefore, the accurate judgments must have been based on relatively widely shared cues. But undoubtedly there are individual differences in emotional expression, idiosyncratic facial movements whose meaning could be interpreted only by a person who had had relatively long experience with the communicator and was familiar with the subtle, minimal cues of his feeling state. Thus, other things being equal, familiarity with the communicator should lead to increased accuracy of communication. This view has been presented by Hebb (1946), and echoed by a number of subsequent writers (Arnold, 1960; Asch, 1952; Bruner & Tagiuri, 1954; Woodworth & Schlosberg, 1954); but unfortunately, there is almost no empirical evidence with human subjects in support of this hypothesis.

Innate and Acquired Determinants of Communication

Two lines of investigation are relevant in estimating the degree to which innate and acquired factors differentially influence emotional communication; the first concerns cross-cultural communication and the second concerns the expressions of congenitally blind persons.

If emotional communication depends primarily on learned patterns of expression and interpretation, one might reasonably expect that persons from different cultures, who presumably experience varying conditions of learning, would have considerable difficulty in communicating with each other. This is obviously true for verbal communication between persons who speak different languages, but the evidence for cross-cultural differences in nonverbal communication is not nearly as clear cut.

For example, May (1938) presented 44 Caucasian Americans and 10 Chinese with pictures of Chinese and American subjects expressing different feelings. Interpretation of the results is confounded both by the small number of Chinese judges and by the fact that all of the Chinese judges had lived in the United States for some time; nevertheless, the data show that while each group was superior to the other in recognizing expressions used by members of its own culture, there was also considerable success in identifying the meaning of expressions made by persons in the opposite group. Therefore, there must have been substantial similarities in the communication patterns in the two cultural groups.

The results obtained by Vinacke (1949) even more strongly emphasize the similarities rather than differences between racial groups. He showed photographs of spontaneous emotional reactions of Caucasian subjects to Chinese, Japanese, and Caucasian judges. Within each of the groups, female judges, in comparison to the males, showed greater agreement in interpreting the emotional meaning of the pictures, but the difference among groups was no greater than that between sexes in any single group.

Similarly, Triandis and Lambert (1958) found that Greek college students rated a series of facial expressions of emotion along the dimensions of pleasantness, attention, and tension in essentially the same way American students had performed the task in an earlier study (Engen, Levy, and Schlosberg, 1958).

And finally, in direct contradiction to the assumption of special *difficulties* in cross-cultural communication, Dickey and Knower (1941) reported a study in which Mexican adolescents were in fact superior to their American counterparts in interpreting a variety of emotions portrayed by two American actors.

The results of these few studies can hardly be considered conclusive, but while differences between cultures in nonverbal emotional communication may be found, certain facial expressions are universally meaningful. This point of view was suggested by Asch (1952), who wrote:

The accounts of ethnologists are in agreement that there is a fund of expressions that occur in human societies without exception. Crying in pain and weeping in sorrow are universal; fear gives rise generally to trembling and pallor. Laughter and smiling are general expressions of joy and happiness. It is probable that the identities cover a wider region, including reactions of surprise, boredom, and puzzlement. We may therefore speak of certain invariants in emotional expresison, though they have not been adequately described (p. 195).

The limited amount of cross-cultural research thus far reported in the literature suggests that a substantial amount of the variance in emotional communication is accounted for by innate factors independent of learning. Currently available evidence does not provide a rigorous basis for defining those aspects of expression which are acquired and those which are innate, but the evidence indicates that at least some expressive facial patterns are not learned, their emergence depending primarily on physical maturation. This conclusion is further supported by studies of congenitally blind subjects, whose opportunities for learning facial expression by imitation are obviously limited. Studies by Goodenough

(1932), Thompson (1941), and Fulcher (1942) demonstrate marked similarities between emotional expressions of blind and sighted, though the work of Fulcher, as well as Dumas (1932), suggests that blind persons tend to be relatively limited in their repetoire of spontaneous expressions and do not show the same degree of increased differentiation of expression typically found among sighted children as they grow older. Thus, there appears to be an interaction of innate and acquired factors in the development of emotional expression, such that, "a native pattern develops to a certain level, and then it fails to develop further unless it is integrated into learned behavior" (Woodworth & Schlosberg, 1954, p. 131).

Studies of the blind have been concerned with the *expression* of emotion, but the total communication process also involves the *recognition* of the emotional meaning expressed. Although common observation suggests that even very young infants may react differentially to varying emotional expressions, there is no research available which deals with innate, perhaps temperamental, variables related to the recognition aspects of the communication process. We therefore do not know how innate factors influence emotional sensitivity, but there is some research indicating that learning plays an important role in the process of identifying facial expression. Several studies, including those reported by Allport (1924), Guilford (1929), and Jenness (1932b), report that brief periods of training lead to increased accuracy of identifications. If communication inevitably involves a knowledge of social conventions, learning undoubtedly influences the ability to recognize emotional meanings. But other than the few studies of very brief and limited training procedures, research has thus far failed to specify the effects of particular kinds of learning experiences or the ways in which learning interacts with other factors in determining emotional sensitivity.

Individual Differences in Communication

Notwithstanding folklore beliefs about the efficacy of women's intuition, the research evidence about sex differences in sensitivity to facial expression is consistently contradictory. Allport (1924) and Guilford (1929), for example, found no reliable differences between men and women in judging the Rudolph pictures; but Jenness (1932a), who essentially replicated the earlier studies, found women to be significantly more accurate. A series of studies with the Piderit models showed a similar history of contradiction: Buzby (1924) reported women as slightly better judges, while subsequent replications by Jarden and Fernberger (1926) and by Fernberger (1927; 1928), found no consistent differences.

Coleman (1949) found no differences between male and female judges in his study, and in an earlier investigation of children reported by Gates (1923), boys and girls performed at about the same level of accuracy. However, Kellogg and Eagleson's (1931) replication of Gates' study with Negro children reported that girls were superior to boys. Vinacke (1949) discovered that women showed higher inter-judge agreement about the meaning of candid pictures presumably depicting expressions of feeling, and Weisberger (1956) found female college students superior to their male peers in judging the Ruckmick and Carmichael-Roberts pictures. Weisberger's finding, however, might well be accounted for by the higher linguistic ability of his female sample.

This pattern of inconsistent results suggests that variables other than those controlled by the experimenters are operating differentially in the several studies reviewed, and it seems most likely that variables associated with sex of the judge interact with other factors in the communication process to influence accuracy of recognition. Levy and Schlosberg (1960), for instance, found that women were superior to men in judging pictures of a woman expressing feelings. Thus, apparent differences between men and women in emotional sensitivity may be in part a function of the sex of the person expressing the feelings. Or perhaps men and women differ in the kinds of feelings to which they are especially sensitive or insensitive; if current stereotypes have any validity, one might expect women to attend, and be particularly sensitive, to expressions of interpersonal feelings such as affection, while men might pay greater attention to and be relatively more accurate in identifying expressions of more active feelings such as anger. These speculations certainly are not based on rigorous evidence; nonetheless, investigations focused on these kinds of possible interactions probably are of greater value than the replication of relatively uncontrolled studies designed merely to determine whether or not men and women differ in terms of some general measure of emotional sensitivity.

In contrast to the contradictory findings about sex differences, most researchers have found a low, but positive, correlation between the ability to identify facial expressions and various measures of intelligence. For example, in 1931, Kanner reported a correlation of .21; twenty-five years later, using somewhat different measures of emotional sensitivity and verbal ability, Weisberger (1956) reported a correlation of .20. These data, however, do not provide a basis for interpreting the role of intelligence in the process of identifying emotional expressions; they merely suggest that measures of intellectual ability, or some correlate of this ability, account for some small part of the variance in sensitivity. On the basis of previous data, it is difficult to estimate the magnitude of the relationship between intelligence and sensitivity in the general population, for factors such as range of intelligence in any sample influence the size of the correlation obtained. Weisberger's sample of college students clearly is not a random sample of the general population and one would expect the relatively restricted intellectual range represented by such a sample to limit the size of a correlation obtained with almost any variable. Only one study reported to date has dealt with samples widely different in intellectual ability; Levy, Orr, and Rosenzweig (1960) compared the pleasant-unpleasant ratings made by college students and mental retardates of a series of photographs of facial expressions. The mean ratings of the two groups did not differ significantly. Thus, in so far as gross judgments about the relative pleasantness of facial expressions is concerned, marked differences in intellectual ability appear to be independent of responses to emotional stimuli. But pleasantness represents only a single dimension along which emotional states may vary, and the more complex task of accurately identifying emotional meanings within a multidimensional matrix such as that described by Osgood, et al. (1957), may indeed require a good deal of intellectual ability.

Almost nothing appears in the experimental literature relevant to the relationship between sensitivity to facial expression and either the judge's personality or his emotional state at the time he makes his judgments. This *absence* of research focused on personality variables is remarkable in light of the considerable clinical lore concerned with the personality of the sensitive clinician, but perhaps this gap in the research is accounted for by the fact that most of the studies of facial expression were conducted before the more recent interest in personality research.

Two studies touch upon this general problem. Anecdotally, Ruckmick (1921) reported that identifications changed from day to day as an apparent function of the judges' moods, but in an attempt to investigate this hypothesis more rigorously, he found that exposing the judges to somewhat stressful experiences, such as scolding, had only slight effects on their subsequent judgments.

In a more recent study, Levy, Orr, and Rosenzweig (1960) compared the ratings of facial expressions on a pleasant-unpleasant scale made by 50 acutely psychotic males and 96 normal college students previously studied by Engen, Levy, and Schlosberg (1958). The two groups made similar judgments, with no consistent differences between mean ratings, though the ratings made by the psychotic group were more variable than those made by the sample of college students.

With these exceptions, this area of investigation has generally been neglected. Bruner and Tagiuri (1954), in their discussion of social perception, comment, "That the state of the judge may have a profound effect on his perception of emotion is, of course, a truism of psychopathology" (p. 639). But like other truisms, questions about emotional communication as a function of either personality variables or more temporary characteristics of the judge are still to be investigated.

VOCAL EXPRESSIONS

To investigate the communication of emotional meaning by vocal expression, three major techniques have been used to eliminate or control the verbal information conveyed by speech. In some studies, speakers attempt to express feelings merely by reciting the alphabet or counting, for example, from one to nine, assuming that neither letters nor numerals carry verbal information relevant to emotional communication (Davitz & Davitz, 1959a; Dusenberry & Knower, 1939; Knower, 1941; 1945; Pfaff, 1953; Thompson & Bradway, 1950). Other researchers have utilized standard verbal content that presumably is emotionally neutral; speakers recite the same few sentences while trying to express different feelings, so that whatever emotional meaning is communicated depends upon vocal rather than verbal cues (Fairbanks & Pronevost, 1939; Pollack, et al., 1960). In recent years, a number of studies have capitalized on electronic filtering techniques which substantially decrease the verbal content of tape recorded utterances without destroying the simultaneous emotional communication carried by certain vocal characteristics of the speech (Soskin & Kauffman, 1954a; Soskin & Kauffman, 1954b; Soskin & Kauffman, 1961; Starkweather, 1956).

Regardless of the technique used, all studies of adults thus far reported in the literature agree that emotional meanings can be communicated accurately by vocal expression. This seems like a fairly obvious hypothesis supported by common, everyday experience, but a large proportion of studies in this area have been designed to test and to retest this observation. A detailed description of each of these studies would be repetitive, and would serve little purpose but to demonstrate that in some respects, at least, the results of research in this area can be remarkably consistent. It may be useful, however, to consider one representative study at this point, not because it is unusually informative, but because it illustrates the findings reported in most other related studies.

Davitz and Davitz (1959a) instructed each of eight speakers to express 10 different feelings by reciting parts of the alphabet. These vocal expressions were tape recorded, and the recordings were played to

30 judges, who were given a list of 10 feelings and asked to identify the emotional meaning conveyed by each expression. Like all other studies in the area, Davitz and Davitz found that on the average, feelings were communicated far beyond chance expectation. However, speakers varied markedly in the accuracy with which their vocal expressions were recognized; one speaker's expressions were identified correctly in only 23 per cent of the cases, while another speaker communicated accurately well over 50 per cent of the time. Listeners, too, showed a wide range of differences, varying in accuracy from only 20 per cent to nearly 50 per cent correct. And finally, as most other studies have reported, feelings clearly differed in the accuracy with which they were communicated; anger, for example, was communicated accurately over 63 per cent of the time, while pride was identified correctly in only 20 per cent of the cases.

Differences in the ease or accuracy of communicating various feelings have been reported in several studies. Pfaff (1953), for example, found that of nine categories of feeling which he investigated, joy and hate were most accurately communicated, while shame and love were the most difficult to recognize. These kinds of differences are consistently mentioned in the literature, but only one relatively minor study has focused specifically on an attempt to account for this phenomenon. Beginning with the observation that identifying an emotional expression is essentially a problem in discrimination, Davitz and Davitz (1959b) reasoned that subjective similarity of the feelings portrayed should be inversely related to the ease of discriminating among expressions of these feelings. Thus, it would seem reasonable to expect greater difficulty in discriminating between anger and impatience than between anger and sadness. The results of their research generally support this position, though the data demonstrate that subjective similarity among feelings accounts for only a small part of the variance in accuracy of communication. Davitz and Davitz also report that given expressions of two similar feelings, such as anger and impatience, the subjectively stronger of the two feelings is communicated more accurately. Beyond these preliminary findings, the literature provides no answer to the question of why various feelings are communicated with differential accuracy.

Vocal Cues of Emotional Meaning

The research has not been especially productive in defining the vocal cues which convey specific emotional meanings. Undoubtedly this is partly a function of the complex technical difficulties involved in establishing reliable measures of vocal characteristics (Scott, 1958; Dittman

& Wynne, 1961). Nevertheless, a limited number of studies have investigated this general problem.

The results of an early study by Dusenberry and Knower (1939) suggest that the sequential pattern of speech provides important cues for recognition of emotional meaning. Testing this hypothesis in a later, more carefully designed study, Knower (1941) compared recordings of vocal expressions played backwards with those played in normal sequence; he found that the reversed expressions were recognized beyond chance expectation, but the accuracy of the judgments was greatly impaired. He therefore concluded that the sequential pattern of speech was a significant aspect of emotional expression, but subsequent research has by and large failed to follow up this lead in defining the particular sequences of vocal cues which are associated with the communication of various meanings.

If the sequence of cues is an important component of speech which carries emotional meaning the next step in research would seem to be specifying the vocal characteristics which are involved in this sequential pattern. Two studies suggest that rate, pitch, and the time of pauses in a vocal utterance are consistently related to the meanings expressed. Fairbanks and Hoaglin (1941) reported that feelings such as anger, grief, and contempt may be differentiated in terms of rate, ratio of pause time to phonation time, and aspects of pitch such as range and rate of change. For example, anger tends to be expressed by a relatively fast rate; grief, by a high ratio of pause to phonation time; and fear, by relatively high pitch. Similarly, Skinner (1935) found that pitch reliably differentiated expressions of happiness and sadness; the pitch of happy expressions was appreciably higher than that of either sadness or emotionally neutral utterances.

Despite these findings, feelings apparently can be communicated accurately even with marked reduction in the range and specificity of the vocal stimulus. Knower (1941), for example, found that even when speakers whispered, which eliminates the fundamental frequency of the normal voice, the accuracy of listeners was over four times that expected by chance. Pollack, Rubenstein, and Horowitz (1960) also reported that the emotional meanings expressed by samples of whispered speech played under increasing signal-to-noise ratios were identified at above chance levels. Perhaps even more striking, Pollack, et al. found that emotional communication was possible with speech samples as short as 60 milliseconds.

Thus, the research to date offers a few, limited clues about vocal characteristics of emotional expression, but these clues have not been consistently helpful in identifying speech correlates of particular feeling states. For example, a series of studies concerned with identifying vocal characteristics associated with anxiety has produced inconsistent and even contradictory results which at best suggest wide individual differences in vocal expressions of anxious people (Eldred & Price, 1958; Krause, 1961; Ruesch & Prestwood, 1949; Sauer & Marcuse, 1957).

Undoubtedly a major difficulty in this area is the technical problem of describing speech. Perhaps recently developed methods of micro-linguistic analysis such as those presented by Pittenger and Smith (1957) might be used profitably, though the research reported by Dittman and Wynne (1961), which investigated both linguistic and paralinguistic aspects of vocal expression, is not encouraging in this regard. A more promising line of research is suggested by Hargreaves and Stark-weather (1961), who have used spectographic records of speech to identify vocal qualities relevant to emotional communication. Studies using electromechanical methods of analyzing speech surely would be an important step toward defining the vocal cues of feeling. But in addition to such studies, it would also be imperative to investigate the auditory cues which can be discriminated by listeners, rather than by electronic devices, for in the final analysis, the cues heard by listeners must carry the emotional meanings involved in interpersonal, vocal communication.

Correlates of Sensitivity to Vocal Expression

Research focused on factors related to accuracy of recognizing vocal expressions is even more limited than that concerned with the parallel problem in the area of facial expression. There are, nonetheless, a few studies whose results suggest some correlates of sensitivity to vocal expression.

Gates (1927) noted that both age and intelligence of children were positively related to accuracy of identifying expressions of one speaker, but unfortunately, only a brief abstract of her research has been published so that it is difficult to fully assess and interpret her results. Pfaff (1953) also reported a positive relationship between intelligence and sensitivity to vocal expressions, though factors such as socioeconomic class of his subjects were neither statistically nor experimentally controlled, so that the positive results he reports for intelligence could possibly be a function of other uncontrolled variables.

As in the investigations of facial expression, the limited evidence about sex differences in ability to recognize vocal expressions is contradictory. Dusenberry and Knower (1939) found that women in their sample were superior to men in the accuracy of their judgments, but the difference was not statistically significant. Pfaff (1953) reported a difference significant beyond the .001 level, in the direction of greater accuracy for college women in comparison to an equivalent sample of men. But Fay and Middleton (1940), on the other hand, failed to find reliable differences in sensitivity between men and women.

The literature provides no evidence about sensitivity to vocal expressions as a function of personality variables, but Pfaff (1953) has reported that amount of speech training is positively related to sensitivity, while the severity of the judges own speech problems is negatively related to accuracy of recognition.

In considering accuracy of recognition, one must not overlook differences among speakers in their ability to convey particular feelings, a phenomenon noted by several investigators (Davitz & Davitz, 1959a; Dusenberry & Knower, 1939; Fairbanks & Pronevost, 1939; Knower, 1945). Kramer (1962a, pp. 17–18) has reviewed some of the literature on the inability of certain psychiatric groups to show appropriate vocal affect, but there is no experimental evidence concerned primarily with individual differences among speakers in their ability to express feelings.

Of special interest to clinicians and therapists is the observation by Soskin (1953) that both therapist and patient may disrupt emotional communication by sending messages in the verbal channel that are incongruent with those in the vocal channel. That affective communication in the word-free channel is, in fact, disrupted by a conflicting emotional message delivered verbally has been demonstrated by Kauffman (1954).

DISCUSSION

An inordinate amount of effort seems to have been devoted in previous research to demonstrating that nonverbal, emotional communication occurs, but having demonstrated this phenomenon with appreciable success, studies in this field have not been especially productive in following up the inumerable leads suggested both by everyday experience and by earlier work. Perhaps this failure to develop a cumulative body of knowledge focused on a limited range of problems is a consequence of the peculiar bimodal history of research in this area. A substantial number of studies concerned with emotional communication were conducted in the 1920s and thirties; then, probably as a function of other demands during the war years, there was a sharp decrease of activity in this area which continued until the past few years. During the 1950s and early sixties, researchers once again became interested in the general topic of emotional communication, but in many instances there was a considerable methodological as well as conceptual gulf between the

earlier and later work, and an unnecessary repetition of previous research. This is nicely illustrated by the first study in this area reported
by Davitz and Davitz (1959a), who essentially replicated earlier studies
of the same general problem. Certainly some repetition is desirable and
necessary in scientific endeavor, but replication without awareness is a
clumsy way of building a consistent science. In this light, one of the
chief purposes that this review might serve is to bring together the relevant research within the areas of facial and vocal expression, so that
researchers may proceed with some firmer basis in earlier findings.

These findings, unfortunately, are not extensive. Beyond demonstrating the fundamental fact that feelings can be conveyed effectively in
nonverbal modes, we know relatively little about the particular cues
which communicate these meanings. Both age and intelligence seem to
be related positively to the ability of judges to identify emotional expressions, but certainly chronological age per se cannot account reasonably
for increased sensitivity, and the role of intelligence in emotional communication is at present unclear. The studies concerned with sex differences present a confusing set of contradictions, and investigations of
other possible correlates of sensitivity, such as dimensions of personality,
are practically nonexistent.

At this point it might be worthwhile to comment briefly on the variety
of methods and experimental designs used by various researchers. Earlier
workers, of course, were handicapped by technical limitations in recording either facial or vocal expressions. Recent developments in providing
relatively inexpensive methods for obtaining motion pictures and tape
recordings, plus the increasing availability of electronic devices for both
modulating emotional expression (e.g., Soskin & Kauffman, 1954a) as
well as analyzing various aspects of the stimulus (e.g., Hargreaves &
Starkweather, 1961), should lead to rapid advances in understanding
the more mechanical components of the communication process. The
diversity of techniques which characterizes research in this area, such as
the various methods of eliminating meaningful verbal content from
vocal expression, has undoubtedly inhibited a steadily progressive ac-
cumulation of knowledge; but, in a sense, this diversity has its own advantage, for if essentially the same results are obtained with somewhat
different methods, one might have greater faith in the generality of the
findings. Therefore, while technological advances should reasonably
result in more precise methods and greater standardization of procedures,
one might also hope that the intrinsic richness of the substantive problems is not sacrificed for the sake of standardized methodology. Obviously some greater degree of order, some greater sense of sequential
development must be brought to programs of investigation in this area.

But just as obviously, the need for order and logical sequence of investigation must be balanced by "shots in the dark" that may lead to productive and fruitful lines of research.

The studies reported in the remainder of this volume hopefully represent something of a balance between a logical sequence of questions and occasional, unrelated hunches. We have studied certain standard psychological problems, such as the developmental pattern of emotional sensitivity and possible personality, perceptual, and cognitive correlates of sensitivity. These might fairly be considered reasonable extensions of earlier work, providing some answers to questions posed in the past. But in addition, from time to time we have explored apparently novel lines of research, such as the interrelationships among various abilities involved in the communication process. Thus, we hoped to base our work on previous knowledge as well as to venture along new paths of investigation.

3

Sensitivity to expression of emotional meaning in three modes of communication

Michael Beldoch

Although previous studies have identified individual differences in ability to recognize emotional expressions, each of these researches has been concerned with only a single mode of communication. Thus, for example, Davitz and Davitz (1959a) reported a wide range of accuracy in identifying vocal expressions, but there is no evidence about the relationship of sensitivity to vocal messages and sensitivity in other modes of communication. The present study, therefore, was designed to investigate the interrelationships among abilities to identify nonverbal emotional expressions in three modes of communication: vocal, musical, and graphic.

At the outset of this research, there was no substantial basis for making any specific prediction about the interrelationships of sensitivity in the three modes studied. Perhaps, like intelligence, emotional sensitivity might be characterized by a general factor which operated in a variety of media, as Spearman's g seems to account for some part of the variance in most intellectual tasks. On the other hand, it was just as reasonable to predict that emotional sensitivity was a specific function of the particular mode of expression, so that measures of sensitivity to vocal cues would be independent of sensitivity to either musical or graphic communications. This research was thus designed as a cross-validation study in an effort to define, with reasonable confidence, the particular pattern of emotional sensitivities which exist in relation to the various modes of nonverbal expression.

PROCEDURE

In measuring abilities to identify expressions of emotional meaning via different media, there was initially the dual problem of determining whether or not ability in each of the modes is a stable characteristic and of developing a reliable measure for each mode.

Speech Instrument

Previous work (Davitz & Davitz, 1959b; Fairbanks & Pronevost, 1939) using vocal communication provided important guides in developing the measure to assess sensitivity to vocal expression. Three male and two female speakers tape-recorded recitations of the same three-sentence paragraph in an attempt to communicate twelve different emotions: admiration; affection; amusement; anger; boredom; despair; disgust; fear; impatience; joy; love; worship. The paragraph, "I am going out now. I won't be back all afternoon. If anyone calls, just tell them I'm not here," was selected for its apparent neutrality so far as specific emotional content was concerned.

The 12 emotions as communicated by the five speakers constituted a pool of 60 items from which the final items for the vocal test were selected. Two criteria were established for determining whether or not a given expression communicated the intended emotional meaning: (1) the number of listeners who identified the item correctly, in terms of speaker's intention, had to exceed that which would be expected by chance at the .01 level; (2) a plurality of listeners had to respond in the category of meaning intended by the speaker.

The total pool of 60 items were played to 58 subjects (Ss) on two separate occasions one week apart. They were provided with the list of emotions and were told that each emotional meaning could appear once, more than once, or not at all. On the basis of these data, an item analysis of responses to the 60 items was carried out, utilizing the two criteria for selecting items. The final instrument consisted of 37 of the original 60 items, involving 10 of the 12 categories of emotional meaning. Affection and worship were dropped from the final instrument because not enough identifications of these emotions were obtained to warrant inclusion in the final instrument. Of the 37 items finally selected, the 58 Ss correctly identified a mean of 22.2 on the first test and 24.2 on the retest, with a test-retest correlation for total accuracy of .74.

Graphic Art Instrument

The steps followed in developing a reliable measure of communication via the vocal mode served as a model for the construction of the instruments for other modalities. Artists were asked to create abstract representations of the 10 emotions used in the speech tape, and to avoid using obvious kinds of symbolization such as heart shapes to convey love, etc. The art work was shown on two separate occasions one week apart to samples similar in composition to those used in developing the speech instrument. After item analysis to eliminate paintings and drawings which did not communicate the artist's intention the final graphic art instrument consisted of 26 samples of colored art work and 24 pencil line drawings, all free from any content cues or obvious symbolization. Test-retest correlation for this instrument was .48.

Music Instrument

The music instrument was developed in a manner similar to the speech instrument. Musicians were asked to create and tape record on the instrument of their choice short compositions, 10 to 20 seconds in length, each attempting to communicate one of the 10 emotions. The 50-item tape was then played to 26 Ss and replayed to 20 of the Ss one week later. Following the procedure and criteria described in the development of the speech instrument, an item analysis of the 48 papers yielded 26 items, and a rescoring of the papers according to these items yielded a test-retest correlation of .52 ($N = 20; p < .05$).

Procedure for Principal Study

The final presentation included a tape recording of 37 items of content-standard speech, a 26-item tape of recorded original musical selections, and an opaque projection of 50 graphic items, 26 in color and 24 in pencil. The test-retest correlations derived from the preliminary study were relatively low according to usual psychometric criteria. However, estimates of internal consistency based on split-half reliability coefficients for the experimental sample of 89 Ss were somewhat higher. These coefficients were: .75 for speech, .67 for music, and .62 for art.

In addition to these instruments, a 40-item vocabulary test (Thorndike, 1942) was administered to obtain an estimate of verbal intelligence. A 300-item Adjective Check List, developed by Harrison Gough, was completed by all Ss in the final sample in an attempt to identify some of the self-reported personality correlates of the traits measured by the art, music, and speech instruments. Finally, the subjects answered a questionnaire relevant to their background, training, and interest in drama, music, and painting.

Subjects

The subjects of the principal study were 89 men and women students attending Teachers College, Columbia University. For the purpose of the cross-validation design they were divided randomly into two groups.

Group A contained 45 subjects; group B 44 subjects. Group A consisted of 23 males ($\overline{X}$ age = 29.35) and 22 females ($\overline{X}$ age = 32.95); group B consisted of 20 males ($\overline{X}$ age = 31.07) and 24 females ($\overline{X}$ age = 34.63). Vocabulary scores for groups A and B were not significantly different (group A, $\overline{X}$ = 24.21, SD = 5.68; group B, $\overline{X}$ = 24.83, SD = 5.70; t = .49, p > .05).

RESULTS

This study concerned itself with interrelationships among abilities to identify emotional meanings expressed in different media, and the relationship of self-reported personality characteristics as well as various background factors to the several measures of emotional sensitivity.

Correlations among Media

Table 3-1 presents the product moment correlations obtained between scores on the speech and music, speech and art, and music and art instruments for groups A and B. From this table it can be seen that there is a clearly positive interrelationship among scores representing responses to the three media. The design of this study required the testing of hypotheses generated by group A by cross-validation on group B. The results for group B were analyzed by product moment correlations using one-tailed tests of significance since direction could now be predicted. As indicated in Table 3-1, the results of this analysis

Table 3-1. Intercorrelations among Scores on Speech, Music, and Art Instruments

Group and variable	Music	Art
Group A[a]		
Speech	.64**	.56**
Music		.53**
Group B[b]		
Speech	.43**	.27*
Music		.55**

[a] Two-tailed tests.   * Significant at .05.
[b] One-tailed tests.   ** Significant at .01.

support the initial finding that scores in all three media are positively interrelated.

Instruments

The relationship of verbal intelligence and ability to identify expressions of feelings was investigated by product moment correlations between scores on the vocabulary test and scores on each test of emotional sensitivity. As indicated in Table 3-2, verbal intelligence is positively related to scores in all three media for both groups A and B.

Table 3-2. Correlations of Vocabulary Scores
with Separate Media and Total Score

Variable	Correlation with vocabulary	
	Group A[a]	Group B[b]
Speech	.46**	.31*
Music	.32*	.47**
Art	.41**	.69**
Total	.50**	.62**

[a] Two-tailed tests.   * Significant at .05.
[b] One-tailed tests.   ** Significant at .01.

Since there were significant correlations between each of the separate media and the vocabulary scores, it was decided to compute partial correlations between the three media, holding the effects of the vocabulary scores constant.

As indicated in Table 3-3, controlling for verbal intelligence, the correlations between speech and music and between music and art are

Table 3-3. Partial Correlations between
Media, Controlling for the Effects of Verbal
Intelligence

Group and variable	Music	Art
Group A[a]		
Speech	.59**	.46**
Music		.46**
Group B[b]		
Speech	.34*	.08
Music		.38**

[a] Two-tailed tests.   * Significant at .05.
[b] One-tailed tests.   ** Significant at .01.

significant for both group A and group B. However, the positive relationship between speech and art, though significant for group A, was not supported by the cross-validation.

Relationship to Self-reported Sensitivity

Forty of the 45 subjects in group A completed a six-step rating scale included in the general questionnaire Ss filled out as part of the research procedure. This item read, "I am (very, quite, fairly, moderately, a bit, not at all) sensitive to other peoples' emotional expressions." Ss were instructed to check the word or words in the brackets that best described their own sensitivity. The distribution of responses to the rating scale was such that by combining the number of subjects who responded to this item by checking either "very" or "quite," and by combining the number of respondents who checked any of the other alternatives, a median test analysis of the results for the separate media and for the total score was possible. The results indicated that total scores as well as scores on the speech and graphic art instruments are positively related to self-reported emotional sensitivity, but scores on the music instrument are independent of self-reported sensitivity.

Another attempt to measure self-reported personality correlates of ability to identify emotional expression was investigated by means of a 300-item Adjective Check List. This list was administered to all subjects in an attempt to find out if Ss who scored above the median on the combined speech, music, and art instruments checked different adjectives than those who scored below the median. An item analysis of the 300 adjectives based on group A yielded two adjectives which were significantly more often checked by high scorers: leisurely and outgoing. Five adjectives were significantly more often checked by low scorers: aggressive, interests narrow, painstaking, simple, and thrifty. However, when these seven adjectives were cross-validated on group B, none of the seven were significant at the .05 level.

Effect of Training and Background

An attempt was made to evaluate the effects of training, current interest in, and degree of reported enjoyment received from the various media on scores on the art, music, and speech instruments. Answers to items on the questionnaire eliciting information about these areas were subjected to chi-square analysis. Of the nine analyses done, only one was significant at the .05 level. Such a finding could easily be due to chance in that the probability of finding one hypothesis out of nine confirmed at the .05 level when all of the hypotheses are drawn from a single common source is between .30 and .40 (Sakoda, et al., 1954).

Therefore, it would seem warranted to conclude that training, current interest in, and degree of enjoyment received from the various media do not significantly affect scores on the art, music, or speech instruments.

Two additional analyses of the data were carried out. Table 3-4 lists the mean scores for men and women on the speech, music, and art

Table 3-4. Means and Standard Deviations for Men and Women, and Significances of Sex Differences

Instrument	Men		Women		t	p
	Mean	SD	Mean	SD		
Speech	20.7	4.0	19.6	5.7	.97	> .05
Music	12.3	2.8	11.3	3.5	1.38	> .05
Art	13.7	4.7	13.9	5.0	.16	> .05
Total	46.8	8.1	44.8	12.5	.85	> .05

instruments and for total scores. No significant differences between the sexes were obtained for any set of scores.

DISCUSSION

At the outset of this study there was no information available upon which to base a prediction about the relationships among abilities to identify the communication of emotional meaning in various media. It is now evident that there exists a general ability to identify emotional communications which transcends a given medium of expression. Thus, those individuals who better identify emotional expressions in content-standard speech also tend to identify expressions more accurately in graphic and musical modes. Ability to identify nonverbal emotional expressions, therefore, is a relatively stable human characteristic which can be measured with some reliability and which generalizes over specific modes of communication.

However, a finding of equal, or perhaps greater, importance emerges from the study in relation to the operation carried out to control for intelligence. Verbal intelligence was related to all three measures of the ability to identify emotional expressions, although partialling out verbal intelligence did not eliminate all of the significant intercorrelations among the measures. Thus, although verbal intelligence is positively related to the ability to identify emotions expressed in the three media, verbal intelligence alone does not account for the common variance among the three measures of sensitivity.

Intelligence in this study was measured by a vocabulary test. The ability to identify the intended emotion, on the other hand, was measured by three content-standard or content-free tests. But both kinds of measures involved responding to symbolic stimuli. On the vocabulary test, of course, the Ss responded to linguistic symbols; in the tests of emotional sensitivity, the Ss responded to vocal, graphic, and musical symbols. Regardless of the test, however, Ss were required to understand the symbolic meaning of each item, i.e. to identify the meaning of each vocabularly item in terms of a multiple choice among several words, and to identify the meaning of each vocal, musical, and graphic item in terms of a multiple choice of 10 different feelings. Thus, all of the measures involved symbolic processes, and the results might best be conceptualized in terms of a general theory of symbolization.

Discursive and Nondiscursive Symbols

The theory of symbolic processes developed by Susanne Langer (1942; 1953) seems particularly appropriate to this study in view of her distinction between discursive and nondiscursive symbols, for this distinction may clarify the relationship between verbal intelligence and the ability to identify emotional expressions.

A knowledge of word meanings, according to Langer's theory, is a knowledge of discursive symbols, which correlate names or concepts and things, are verifiable, duplicable, and have a defined syntax and order. Nondiscursive symbols, on the other hand, depend upon personal perceptions, on intuition, and on direct insight for understanding. They cannot be verified or duplicated, do not have "dictionary meanings," and do not have a socially defined syntax and order.

Miss Langer interprets art as communication in the nondiscursive mode. The artist is concerned with the expression of feelings even though he may not at the moment of expression actually be experiencing the emotion in question; specifically, he creates forms symbolic of human feeling. Although it would be unreasonable to assume that the persons in this study who produced the vocal, graphic, and musical items were creating symbols which would generally be recognized as art objects, in the sense that they did indeed produce forms that communicated emotional meanings, one might assume a parallel between the nondiscursive symbols of Langer's theory of art and items contained in our three tests of emotional sensitivity. Thus, the three tests of ability to identify intended emotions seem to fall within the realm of nondiscursive symbols, for they involved expressions of feeling on the basis of formal, or content-free properties of each mode of communication. In contrast, the measure of verbal intelligence would seem to involve, according to Langer's view, discursive symbolization. Therefore, the correlations between verbal intelligence and the three measures of ability to identify expression of emotion may reflect a relationship between abilities to deal with symbols both in the discursive and nondiscursive modes of communication. If this interpretation is valid, the results suggest that these two kinds of symbolic ability are positively related, but have considerable independent variance, and both kinds of ability may very well be involved in the communication of emotional meanings in everyday, human interaction.

Conceptualizing the ability to identify communication of emotions in terms of a symbolic ability, related to but different from, the usual measures of intelligence, may help rescue the concept of "emotional sensitivity" from the mysterious, and perhaps unknowable realm of empathy, "third ears," and other notions which have been proposed to account for observed differences in ability to identify communications of feeling. For in terms of this point of view, emotional sensitivity involves symbolic processes which can be investigated empirically, with the aim of discovering the general principles of "emotional intelligence" in perhaps much the same way as psychologists have discovered the principles underlying discursive intellectual functioning. Langer cogently emphasized throughout her work that nondiscursive symbolization is governed by a logic, a set of principles, which is different from that of discursive symbolization, but is not theoretically any more mysterious, unknowable, or less open to empirical investigation. If emotional sensitivity, therefore, can legitimately be accounted for in terms of nondiscursive symbolization, the task of research is to discover the psychological principles of this kind of ability, just as Spearman, Thurstone, and others have discovered the principles of discursive intelligence.

Correlates of Sensitivity

Psychologists are already familiar with many of the correlates of discursive symbolic ability; most of what is measured when a subject is given a standard test of intelligence concerns this area of symbolic behavior. But what are the correlates of nondiscursive symbolic activity?

The fact that high-scoring Ss describe themselves as more sensitive than low-scoring Ss probably reflects the more or less accurate feedback as a consequence of correctly responding to emotional communication in everyday life. Awareness of one's own emotional sensitivity or insensitivity probably is an important aspect of interpersonal adjustment. The results of this study do not support the familiar and popular notion about the superiority of women's intuition; men and women did not differ significantly on any of the music, art, or speech measures or on the total sensitivity score. Nor did training or background courses in the three media contribute to success in identifying the communication of feelings in the media. In addition, the attempt to isolate relatively gross personality variables as they relate to this ability met with largely null results.

Potential Value of the Measurement of Nondiscursive Symbols

Although the broad personality factors presumably tapped by the Adjective Check List do not identify correlates of ability in the non-discursive area, the consistently null results at least serve to direct attention to other approaches. In fact, the theoretical conclusions based on the present study suggest a radically different research attack, for if the ability to identify emotions is a function of the ability to deal with non-discursive symbols, it would seem potentially more valuable to investigate cognitive characteristics. For example, nondiscursive symbolization presumably deals with abstract relations among aspects of a particular communication. Therefore, one would expect a substantial positive relationship between a measure of abstract ability and a measure of emotional sensitivity. By means of such an investigation, one might determine the degree to which ability to identify feelings is saturated by a general symbolic factor, and the extent to which this ability is independent of such a general factor.

Perceptual abilities represent another potentially meaningful set of variables in charting the components of sensitivity to nondiscursive symbols. Nondiscursive symbols have to do with the interrelationships among elements within a symbol, the relationships of aspects of the formal properties of the stimulus. For example, in speech, the characteristics of loudness, pitch, timbre, and rate comprise a complex pattern of interrelationships, i.e., pitch in relation to loudness, timbre in relation to rate, etc. If ability in the nondiscursive mode depends at all upon acuity in the relevant medium, it must be thought of not only in terms of noticing or responding to differences in absolute amounts of stimulus energy, but also in terms of the ability to notice and respond to *changes* in the amounts of stimulus and to the relationships among the formal properties of the symbol. An abstract painting may be understood, in so far as its communication of feelings is concerned, in terms of the viewer's ability to respond to the subtle changing gradations in hue or value of a color, in the direction of a line, or in the more complex relationship that might exist between, say, a softly curving line of decreasingly intense color as it comes in contact with a harshly executed angle of flaring, intense color.

One of the interesting advantages of considering sensitivity to the communication of emotions as an ability to make sense of nondiscursive symbols is in relation to some of the findings of Holt and Luborsky (1958) at the Menninger Foundation. There, the attempt to identify significant and useful predictors of success in clinical psychiatry met with disappointing results; the major personality measures functioned very poorly as predictors of such skill. Is it possible that clinical skill often referred to as one's "clinical sensitivity," may be more readily predicted by tests of ability in the nondiscursive mode than by the usual personality tests?

It would seem, then, that where previous psychological investigators have treated symbolic activity primarily within a discursive orientation, this research supports the view that there are two related, but different, symbolic activities, one having to do with discursive symbols, the other with nondiscursive symbols. Since it is likely that most of our cognitive and conceptual activities in the normal course of living are in response to stimuli that are partly nondiscursive in nature, it is important to increase our understanding of cognitive and conceptual function and malfunction as they relate to ability in the nondiscursive mode.

SUMMARY

It was the central purpose of this study to examine by means of a cross-validation design the interrelationships that exist among abilities to identify the communication of feelings in different media.

Although there has been considerable interest through the years in the ability to identify emotional communication in a variety of media, there has been no research on the interrelationships that exist among abilities to identify such communications in different media. It was the central purpose of this study to examine such realtionships by means of a cross-validation design.

Tape recordings of male and female speakers reciting the same neutral paragraph in an attempt to communicate various emotional states were presented to evening college students on two separate occasions. Item analyses of responses to the tapes were conducted and a final tape developed which included only items which were more often identified as the speaker's intended emotion than any other choice. A similar technique was used with recordings of musical phrases created and played by musicians in an attempt to communicate the same emotions. Abstract art created by artists to convey these emotions was shown by opaque projection to still another group of evening students and the same criteria used to select items that successfully communicated the artists' intention. Reliability coefficients for each instrument were in the .60s and .70s, indicating that the measures in the three media were internally consistent.

The final study presented to 89 men and women graduate students in Teachers College tape recorded speech selections and musical phrases, opaque projections of abstract art, a 300-item Adjective Check List, and a questionnaire which elicited background information with regard to the *S*s training, participation in and enjoyment derived from the separate media. A six-step self-report scale of sensitivity to other peoples' emotional expressions and a 40-word vocabulary test as a measure of intelligence completed the materials used in this study.

Significant intercorrelations were obtained among the abilities to identify the expression of feelings in all three media. Vocabulary scores also correlated significantly with ability in all three modes and with total score, although when controlling for vocabulary scores, two of the three significant relationships among abilities in the three media remained significant. Background training or current interest in the arts did not contribute to success with any of the instruments. None of the adjectives on the check list discriminated between high and low scorers on the sensitivity measures, but self-reported sensitivity did distinguish between groups, the high scorers describing themselves as more sensitive than the low scorers.

The results of the study were discussed in terms of Langer's distinction between discursive and nondiscursive symbolic activity. Intelligence is most often measured by tasks in the discursive mode, such as knowing the meaning of words. Nondiscursive symbols, on the other hand, are communicated by their formal properties, and are the kind used by artists and in the process of intuition. This research suggests that abilities in the discursive and nondiscursive modes have some common variance, but that they are in many ways independent of each other. The implications for further research focus on understanding the correlates of ability in the nondiscursive mode, especially as they may relate to cognitive and conceptual function and malfunction.

4

The ability to express
and perceive vocal
communications of feeling

Phyllis Kempner Levy

Research in the area of vocal communication of feelings has shown that verbal expressions of various feelings can be discriminated with a degree of specificity beyond chance expectancy (Dusenbury & Knower, 1939; Fairbanks & Provenost, 1939). The existence of individual differences in ability to express emotions and in ability to identify feelings expressed by others has also been demonstrated (Davitz & Davitz, 1959; Dusenbury & Knower, 1939; Fairbanks & Provenost, 1939; Gates, 1927; Turner, Chapter 10). However, certain aspects of the communication process, such as the *relationship* between the expression and perception of feelings, have received little attention. A single study (Knower, 1945) relating skill in transmitting and understanding vocal expression reported a correlation of .55 between these two abilities. Knower, however, in this examination of the relationship between expression and perception, limited his definition of perception to identification of the emotional productions of other persons only.

Consideration of research in the area of social perception suggests that, in addition to perception of others, a second aspect of perception may be distinguished, namely, perception of one's self. Although certain older studies seem to have found a marked relationship between perception of self and perception of others, they have been severely and cogently criticized for lack of control of response bias and stereotypy (Cronbach, 1950; Cronbach 1955; Gage & Cronbach, 1955). Nonetheless, despite the methodological and conceptual imperfections of these

43

studies, and despite the fact that they have dealt primarily with the perception of personality traits, there remains a suspicion that there may be a relationship between the ability to perceive oneself and others which may be applicable to the vocal communication process.

It appears possible, therefore, to distinguish two aspects of the perceptual process in communication of emotions: perception of the emotional expressions of others and perception of one's own expressions. These, in turn, may be distinguished from the expressive aspect of the communication process. Examination of the relationship among these three components of the vocal communication process was the major focus of the present study. Furthermore, although no relationship has previously been established between ability to express emotions and ability to perceive one's own expressions, it was believed that, if the other variables do in fact interrelate positively among themselves, it would raise the possibility that a general factor might underlie all three. Such a general factor might operate much like g in intelligence, whereby, although separate abilities play their roles, one unitary ability underlies a variety of discrete abilities.

Thus, demonstration of the possible existence of a general ability to communicate feelings would necessitate showing (1) that the two variables, ability to express emotions to others and to identify one's own expressions, covary; (2) that the ability to perceive the emotional expressions of others and the ability to perceive one's own emotional expressions, the relationship between which had heretofore been suggested but not experimentally demonstrated by past research, also covary; and (3) that it is possible to replicate Knower's findings of a relationship, which he found to be only moderate, between ability to express emotions and ability to perceive emotional expressions of others. It was therefore hypothesized that the three communication abilities—expression, perception of self, and perception of others—would be positively intercorrelated.

Another issue investigated in the present study was the question of possible sex differences in the ability to communicate feelings. The existing literature in this area, which appears to be limited to two studies, has investigated only the aspect of the communication process concerned with the perception of others. Furthermore, the findings reported are somewhat contradictory. Pfaff (1954) found female college students more capable of interpreting vocal expressions of feeling than male college students, whereas high school students showed no sex differences. Dusenbury and Knower (1939), on the other hand, reported that, although women did tend to be better judges of vocal expressions of feeling than men, the differences were not significant.

When these results, which in and of themselves are neither consistent nor clear-cut, were considered in conjunction with the familiar popular notion that women are both more "intuitive" and more emotionally expressive than men, the possibility was suggested that sex differences in favor of women might exist in the vocal communication process. This speculation formed the basis of the final prediction of the present study, namely, that women would show greater accuracy than men in all three communication abilities.

METHOD

Operational Definitions

Ability to Identify Vocally Expressed Feelings of Others. A 37-item content-standard speech instrument developed by Beldoch (Chapter 3) was used to measure ability to identify vocally expressed feelings of others. The instrument consists of tape-recorded recitations of 10 emotions: admiration, amusement, anger, boredom, despair, disgust, fear, impatience, joy, and love. The tape, which has a test-retest reliability of .74, was played for all Ss, their task being the identification of the feeling expressed in each item. Ability to identify vocally expressed feelings of others was then defined as the total number of feelings correctly identified, and the resulting scores were called "other-perception" scores.

Ability to Express Feelings Vocally to Others. Tape recordings of content-standard vocal expressions of feeling obtained from the Ss themselves were used to measure ability to express feelings vocally to others. Ss were asked to recite a three-sentence paragraph, differing only slightly from the one used by Beldoch, in an attempt to convey each of the 10 emotions used in the Beldoch instrument. Each emotion was recited twice, resulting in 20 emotion items recorded by each S. The recorded items obtained in this manner were played to judges who were asked to identify the feeling being expressed in each item. Ability to express feelings to others (referred to as "expression" score) was measured by the mean number of correct identifications made by the judges for each S.

Ability to Identify Own Feelings Expressed Vocally. The tape recordings obtained from the Ss themselves were used to measure ability to identify one's own expressions. From one to two weeks after the recordings were collected, each S listened to his own 20-item tape and was asked to identify the feeling being expressed in each item. Ability to identify one's own feelings expressed vocally, referred to as "self-perception" score, was defined as the total number of his own emotional expressions correctly identified by each S.

Subjects

Seventy-seven graduate students (33 male, 44 female) served as Ss. Twenty-six of the Ss were Negro and 51 were Caucasian. The age range for the total sample was 21 to 51 and the mean age was 32.37 years. In order to obtain information on a number of variables which it was believed might affect performance on the three measures under investigation, an identifying data sheet, which included questions regarding major field, occupation, native language, presence of a speech or hearing defect, language training, and dramatic training, was filled out by each S. Although it was assumed that the sample was fairly homogeneous with respect to educational level and intelligence because of the population from which it was drawn, the Vocabulary Test-GT (Thorndike, 1942) was nevertheless administered to the Ss in order to obtain more reliable information about intelligence. With a possible score of 40, the range of scores for the total sample was 14 to 37 (Mean = 25, SD = 5.39).

Judges

Ten white adults (three male, seven female), relatively comparable to the Ss in educational level and socioeconomic background, were used as judges. One of the judges was a first-year graduate student in clinical psychology; the other nine judges were in fields unrelated to psychology. All judges spoke English as their native language, were under forty years of age, and claimed no hearing defects.

Procedure

Two days after administration of the identifying data sheet and the Vocabulary Test-GT, tape recordings of the Ss' expressions of feeling were obtained. Each S was alone in a room during the recording period and was instructed to recite the same three-sentence paragraph in an attempt to convey each of the 10 different emotions *twice*. The content-standard paragraph was "I am going away on a trip. I will be gone all summer long. If anyone wants to reach me, give them my address." Following the period during which the Ss received the instructions, they were presented with 21 5 by 8 index cards each containing the name of one emotion (with the exception of the first card which was "normal conversation") and a short paragraph describing a situation in which the emotion might be expressed. Ss were asked to read *only* the three-sentence paragraph in the emotional tone specified; they were told that the accompanying description on each card was simply to help them "get in the mood." The same procedure was followed with the "normal conversation" card. The 20 emotion cards were composed of two sets of the same 10 feelings and the order of presentation of the emotions was randomized within sets of 10.

Approximately one week after collection of the Ss' expressions of feeling, the Beldoch instrument was administered. It was played during a class period and the Ss therefore heard it in a group situation. Ss were instructed to listen to the tape and to identify, by filling in an answer sheet, the feeling being expressed in each item.

Approximately one week after administration of the Beldoch instrument (and thus from about one to two weeks after the original recording of their expressions), Ss were asked to identify their own expressions of feeling. During the listening procedure each S was alone in one of the rooms previously used for the recording sessions.

The reliability of the Ss' judgments of the two sets of emotion items was determined by computing the split-half reliability coefficient between the first and second 10 items. A correlation coefficient of .65 was obtained for the two sets of emotions items, resulting in a reliability coefficient of .79 after application of the Spearman-Brown formula. The means and dispersions of the two halves of the test were similar: the mean of the first 10 items was 5.03 (SD = 2.77), and of the second 10 items, 5.43 (SD = 2.75).

The Ss' expressions were then presented to 10 judges. Because of the tedious nature of the task of judging 20 emotion items for each of 77 Ss, the judges were divided into three groups, A, B, and C. The number of judges in each group was: Group A, five judges (two male, three female); group B, two judges (both female); group C, three judges, (one male, two female). Originally, group B included four judges (two male, two female), but the two male judges did not complete the judging procedure and their judgments were therefore omitted from the tabulation of results.

Group A judged the emotion items of 26 Ss; group B judged the emotion items of 26 other Ss; and group C judged those of the remaining 25 Ss. The assignment of Ss to the groups of judges was done in a random manner. In addition, six Ss were randomly selected from the 26 assigned to group A, and their productions were judged by all 10 of the judges.

Prior to listening to the Ss' productions, the judges were administered the Beldoch instrument, both to give them training and to provide a rough measure of their ability to identify vocally expressed feelings of others. The mean number of items correctly identified (out of a possible 37) was compared by inspection for the three groups of judges in order to provide an estimate of the similarity among means, and they appeared comparable.[1]

Intragroup agreement among judges in each group was measured by correlating the number of correct identifications of feeling made by each judge for each *S* with the number correctly identified by every other judge in the group. Table 4-1 presents these data. The mean correla-

Table 4-1. Intragroup Agreement among Judges on the Number of Correct Identifications of Feeling Made for Each Subject[a]

Group	Judges	1	2	3	4	5
	1	—	.76	.66	.79	.81
	2		—	.69	.82	.74
A	3			—	.63	.73
	4				—	.71
	5					—
	6	—	.90			
B	7		—			
	8	—	.76	.82		
C	9		—	.87		
	10			—		

[a] $N = 26$ for groups A and B; $N = 25$ for group C.

tion for each group of judges was .74 for group A, .90 for group B, and .82 for group C.

A Kendall coefficient of concordance was used to measure intergroup judge agreement. This analysis yielded a *W* of .72, a value which permits the conclusion that the judges were applying essentially the same standard in judging the subjects under study.

RESULTS

Product-moment correlations were used to examine the interrelationships among the three communication abilities. Table 4-2 presents these correlations, as well as product-moment correlations of the three communication variables with vocabulary score and with age. Partial cor-

[1] The raw score of one of the judges in group B was considerably higher than the scores of the other nine judges, which in turn elevated the mean score of group B. This may be explained, however, in terms of the fact that the judge in question was one of the speakers on the Beldoch instrument. Taking this fact into consideration, comparison of the means of the three groups of judges suggests that the groups are comparable with respect to ability to identify the expressions of feelings of others.

relations among three ability measures, controlling for the effect of vocabulary score and for the effect of age, are also presented in Table 4-2.

Table 4-2. Product-moment Correlations among the Three Ability Measures and Partial Correlations Controlling for Vocabulary Score and Age

Variables correlated	N^a	r	Partial r, controlling vocab. score[b]	Partial r, controlling age[c]
Self-percept—other-percept	74	.59**	.48**	.59**
Other-percept—expression	75	.63**	.55**	.64**
Self-percept—expression	76	.74**	.69**	—

[a] The Ns for the correlations vary slightly due to the fact that not all the scores were available for all the Ss.
[b] Correlations of vocabulary score with major variables were: .46** with self-perception, .46** with other perception, and .39** with expression.
[c] Correlations of age with major variables were: $-.13$ with self-perception, $-.34**$ with other perception, and $-.08$ with expression.
** Significant beyond the .01 level, two-tailed test.

It may be seen that there are significant positive relationships among the three communication abilities—self-perception, other perception, and expression—permitting the conclusion that the stated hypotheses concerning the interrelationships of the variables under study were confirmed.

Since previous research has shown that ability to identify vocal expressions of feeling of others increases with IQ, an attempt was made to determine the relation of verbal intelligence to the three communication abilities. As examination of Table 4-2 (cf. footnote) reveals, a positive relationship was found to exist between verbal intelligence and performance on each of the three experimental measures, and therefore, partial correlations among scores on the three ability measures were computed, controlling for the effect of vocabularly score. Since all three of the partial correlations were found to be significant, it may be concluded that, despite the positive relation of verbal intelligence to each of the communication abilities, the hypothesized relationships among the three abilities are sustained even when intelligence is controlled.

The relationship of age to the experimental variables was examined statistically, for age has also been shown to be a factor influencing ability to understand vocal expressions of feeling of others (Gates,

1927; Turner, Chapter 10). Although age was not found to be related to ability to identify one's own expressions of feeling or ability to express feelings to others, a significant inverse relationship was obtained with ability to identify the expressions of feelings of others (Table 4-2).

Because of this significant negative correlation, partial correlations between other-perception scores and expression scores were computed, controlling for the effect of age. Since, as inspection of the tabled findings reveals, the difference between the partial correlations and the original zero-order correlations between these variables is negligible, it is possible to conclude that, although age has an inverse relationship with ability to identify the expressions of feelings of others, this relationship does not alter the previously established relationships between ability to identify expressions of others and the other two communication abilities.

Sex differences in the three communication abilities were tested by means of t tests. The means and standard deviations for males and females on the three ability measures, Vocabulary Test-GT, and age are presented in Table 4-3. As examination of the means and standard

Table 4-3. Means and Standard Deviations for Males and Females on Three Ability Measures, Vocabulary Test-GT, and Age[a]

Group	Self-percept M	SD	Other percept M	SD	Expression M	SD	Vocabulary M	SD	Age M	SD
Males	10.31	4.58	20.31	3.85	8.41	3.45	24.84	5.22	29.91	5.27
Females	10.57	5.27	19.64	5.51	8.66	3.43	25.12	5.56	34.21	8.66

[a] For self-perception, other perception, and expression comparisons, $N = 32$ for males, $N = 42$ for females. For vocabulary score and age comparisons, $N = 32$ for males, $N = 43$ for females.

deviations suggests, no significant differences were found between males and females on any of the three communication variables. Thus, the hypotheses concerning sex differences were not confirmed.

In order to determine the effects, if any, of verbal intelligence on the tests of hypotheses concerning sex differences, the vocabulary scores of males and females were compared. Inspection of the means and standard deviations of the two groups (Table 4-3) reveals that the two groups in the sample had almost identical vocabulary scores, thereby ruling out any effect of intelligence as measured in this study.

Age differences between men and women in the sample were also examined, in order to determine whether the effect of age might be obscuring sex differences in the three communication abilities. The women in the sample were found to be older than the men, and since age was seen to be inversely related to the other-perception measure, an analysis of covariance was computed, controlling for the effect of age. The F ratio was not found to be significant and it was therefore concluded that even when the effect of age is held constant, there are no significant differences between men and women in other-perception ability.

Since the sample included both Negro and white Ss, post hoc exploration of racial differences in the major variables was possible. The analysis of the data by races must be regarded as highly tentative, however, because there is no evidence that the white and Negro Ss in the sample are representative of their races, and furthermore, this study made no predictions concerning the effects of racial or cultural differences on the vocal communication process.

The effect of the racial variable was examined by comparing by inspection the scores of Negro and white Ss on each of the three ability measures. Differences in favor of whites seemed apparent on each of the three measures. These differences persisted even when sample differences in intelligence were controlled, suggesting that differences in performance on the experimental measures cannot be attributed to differences in vocabulary score. Of course, no conclusions can be drawn from these tentative findings until further investigation of a more controlled nature is done.

DISCUSSION

Since it was possible to demonstrate that the three aspects of the vocal communication process—self-perception, other perception, and expression—share a significant amount of variance, it no longer would seem sufficient to consider them only as separate, discrete abilities. Rather, it would appear that underlying these three abilities is a general "communication factor," such that, although each of the separate abilities continues to account for a considerable amount of individual variance, a significant degree of overlap among the three is present. Thus, those individuals in the present study who showed greater accuracy in any one of the three abilities also tended to show greater accuracy in the other two. To put it somewhat differently, one may say that the ability to communicate is composed of a general factor plus at least three specific abilities. Thus, the major hypotheses of the study are confirmed.

Although significant positive relationships were found between each of the three communication abilities and verbal intelligence, suggesting that some of the variance shared by the three experimental variables is caused by the common relationship of these with intelligence, partial correlations among the three ability measures demonstrated that, when the variance because of intelligence is controlled, the correlations among the three abilities remain significant. Similarly, age was seen to have a significant inverse relationship with the other-perception measure. Again, partial correlations between the other-perception measure and each of the remaining two communication measures, controlling for the effect of age, revealed that age differences among the Ss had a negligible effect on the original hypothesized relationships among the communication abilities.

The concept of a general communication ability is also consistent with the findings of two other studies. In an investigation of the ability to identify expressions of feeling in three different media, Beldoch (Chapter 3) found positive interrelationships among the abilities to identify feelings expressed vocally, graphically, and musically. He concluded from these results that a general ability to identify emotional communication exists which transcends a given medium of expression. And, in a study presently in progress, Levitt (Chapter 7) has obtained a significantly positive relationship between the ability to express feelings vocally and the ability to express feelings through facial expression, suggesting the possibility that the ability to express feelings transcends mode of expression. Such results, taken together with those of the present study, give rise to the hypothesis that the communication of feeling, regardless of the medium through which it occurs or its manner of expression, and regardless of the particular aspect of the process in question, demands certain stable and uniform ways of organizing and responding to internal and environmental cues. The response to such cues would seem to operate in a consistent, characteristic fashion in individuals, transcending both contextual and content changes. Thus, it would seem likely that those individuals who demonstrate a high degree of accuracy in one aspect of the comunication process, or through one medium or mode of expression, will show corresponding accuracy in other aspects of the process and through other media or expressive modes.

Consideration of the existence of a general communication factor leads one to question what the correlates or components of such an ability might be. Some of Beldoch's findings, in the investigation previously referred to, bear on this question. He found that background training, current interest in, or degree of enjoyment received from various media did not significantly affect scores on the art, music, or speech instruments. In addition, an adjective check list failed to yield any items which successfully discriminated between high and low scoring Ss on the combined score for the three instruments. Further,

Davitz obtained similar results; none of the scales on a number of standard paper-and-pencil personality tests were responded to in a significantly different manner by Ss scoring high or low on the identification of feeling measures used by Beldoch (Davitz, Chapter 5).

The results of these studies imply at least two possible conclusions, either (1) that the ability to communicate feelings is not a function of, nor related to, gross personality differences, or (2) that the ability to communicate feelings is not related to the type of personality variables tapped by standard paper-and-pencil tests used for assessment purposes, but might very well be related to dimensions of personality when conceptualized and measured in other ways. Beldoch and Davitz appear to subscribe to the first conclusion. Beldoch, for example, following a theory of symbolic processes developed by Susanne Langer (1942), proposes that the ability to identify feelings falls within the realm of "nondiscursive symbolization." Beldoch therefore suggests that a research approach involving investigation of specific cognitive and perceptual abilities would have more potential value than attempts to investigate broad personality traits. Davitz also views the ability to communicate feelings as a symbolic process and thus is investigating the symbolic correlates of the ability to identify feelings by analyzing the receiving aspects of the vocal communication process into what might be called its "symbolic components" and measuring each of these components separately.

Although both Beldoch and Davitz were unsuccessful in their attempts to isolate personality correlates of the ability to identify feelings, it does not yet seem appropriate to totally abandon this approach to the study of the ability to communicate feelings. It is quite possible, for example, that personality inventories, because they are designed to measure trait dimensions of personality rather than structural variables, and because they are based on self-report, do not successfully tap the variables relevant to the ability to communicate feelings. Projective techniques would therefore seem to offer an alternative means of investigating and generating hypotheses regarding the personality correlates of the ability under study. Certainly it would seem important to attempt to determine whether any such relationships exist before entirely abandoning the investigation of personality dimensions related to the communication process.

In fact, one may question whether the proposed separation of cognitive functions from personality dimensions is feasible at all (cf. Rapaport, 1945). Another possible approach to the issue is one which is based on the essential inseparability of personality and cognitive dimensions. Thus the concept of "cognitive attitude" is applicable here, where cognitive attitude is defined by Klein (1960, p. 107) in the following manner:

A cognitive attitude describes a way of organizing a transmitted array of information . . . . They [cognitive attitudes] have the status of intervening variables and define rules by which perception, memory, and other basic qualitative forms of experience are shaped . . . .

A cognitive attitude is triggered by a *situation* [italics his], a requirement to adapt, not simply by a physical stimulus.

A number of cognitive attitudes, such as "sharpening," "leveling," and "scanning," have been experimentally isolated (Klein, 1960). The relevance of these attitudes to the study of the ability to communicate feelings would seem to lie in the fact that many of the abilities which would appear to be necessary for accuracy in vocal communication—such as ability to focus attention selectively, to process information from a variety of stimuli and to organize it, to respond to the noncontent aspects of stimulus fields, and so on—would appear to be the very functions to which the concept of cognitive attitude addresses itself. For example, one might expect a "sharpener," whose tendency it is to be hyperaware of perceptual nuances, to be better at identifying his own and other's expressions of emotion than an individual who is a "leveler" and tends not to differentiate well between successive stimuli, or one who is a "scanner" and takes a coldly searching attitude. These issues, then, would seem to bear further study.

The fact that the prediction concerning sex differences favoring women in the three communication abilities was not substantiated in the present study is not inconsistent with some previous findings (Dusenbury & Knower, 1939; Pfaff, 1954). Nonetheless, although the majority of available evidence appears to support the assumption that there are no differences between men and women in ability to communicate feelings vocally, the lack of complete consistency in the findings reported (Pfaff, 1954) leaves the question as yet unsettled. In addition, the findings of the present study, as well as those of Dusenbury and Knower, and Pfaff, would seem to call strongly into question the notion, so long popular among laymen and psychologists alike (cf., for example, Smith, 1961), that women are both more "intuitive" and more emotionally expressive than men. If they are more expressive, they certainly do not seem to be better able to communicate accurately what it is they are expressing.

It has already been pointed out that the racial differences obtained in this study must be regarded as suggestive and tentative rather than conclusive. Space does not permit detailed speculation about what factors might account for these differences nor is it the purpose of this study to do so. One possibility is that the differences are "pseudo-differences," reflecting differences in the use and comprehension of language rather than differences between races. This speculation is suggested by the fact that the geographical distribution of the Ss in this study was such that the majority of the Negro Ss came from the South, whereas the majority of the white Ss were Northerners. However, it was not possible to analyze the data for regional differences, since the sample included only one Northern Negro and only seven Southern whites.

SUMMARY

The present study examined the relationship between the ability to express and to perceive vocal communications of feeling. The variables investigated were: (1) expression, or ability to express feelings vocally to others; (2) other perception, or ability to identify feelings expressed vocally by others; (3) self-perception, or ability to identify one's own vocal expressions of feeling; and (4) sex differences related to these variables. It was hypothesized that the three ability variables are positively intercorrelated and that women show greater accuracy in these abilities than men.

Operational definitions of the three communication abilities were formulated and the measures of the experimental variables were based on these definitions. The measures employed content-standard speech.

Significant positive intercorrelations were obtained among the three communication abilities and, despite a significant relationship which was found between verbal intelligence and each of the three abilities, the original significant intercorrelations among the three abilities were sustained when the effect of intelligence was controlled. Similarly, although age was found to be inversely related to other perception, this relationship did not alter the previously established relationships between other perception and the remaining two communication abilities. Contrary to the hypothesis, however, no significant sex differences were found in performance on the three experimental measures.

The results of the study were discussed in terms of a general communication factor which might underlie the three separate communication abilities. The question was raised of what the correlates or components of such a general ability might be. It was suggested that, although other studies in the area have so far found no relationships with personality variables, a somewhat different approach to such an investigation could prove fruitful. Several suggestions for future research were offered. The lack of significant sex differences was mentioned as calling into question the popular notion that women are both more "intuitive" and more emotionally expressive than men.

5

Personality, perceptual, and cognitive correlates of emotional sensitivity

Joel R. Davitz

This chapter reports two studies concerned with possible correlates of the ability to identify vocal expressions of emotional meanings. The first study deals with personality variables, the second with perceptual and cognitive variables.

PERSONALITY VARIABLES

Although the folklore of clinical psychology abounds in hunches about the personality of an emotionally sensitive person, at the beginning of this study there was no rigorous theory or previous research which suggested reasonable hypotheses about specific personality correlates of emotional sensitivity. Therefore, rather than investigate a restricted range of personality variables, the study was designed as a cross-validation research, first exploring possible relations between emotional sensitivity and a large number of personality measures, with the aim of discovering hypotheses about specific variables which could then be cross-validated with a second sample.

Method

A battery of personality tests was administered to a large group of subjects (*S*s) and their ability to identify vocal expressions of emotional meaning was measured. The total group was divided into two subgroups

57

on a random basis, the data analyzed for group 1 and the results cross-validated with the data of group 2.

Subjects

The Ss were 80 graduate students enrolled in a summer course at Teachers College, Columbia University. Group 1 consisted of 22 males and 18 females, 14 Negro and 26 white Ss, with a mean age of 31.9 years and a range from 22 to 50 years. Group 2 consisted of 24 males and 16 females, 11 Negro and 29 white Ss, with a mean age of 31.3 years and a range from 20 to 51 years.

Personality Measures

A battery of personality tests was selected to measure a variety of personality variables. Although all of the tests were self-report, paper-and-pencil questionnaires, according to the rationales underlying construction of the tests, and usual interpretations of the results, the battery presumably tapped a variety of interrelated areas of personality functioning. Included were: (1) the Guilford-Zimmerman Temperament Survey; (2) the Allport-Vernon-Lindzey Study of Values; (3) the Edwards Personal Preference Schedule; (4) the Psychaesthenia and Hysteria scales of the MMPI.

The Guilford-Zimmerman Temperament Survey measures 10 personality traits identified through factor analysis. These traits include: general activity, restraint, ascendance, sociability, emotional stability, objectivity, friendliness, thoughtfulness, personal relations (tolerance, cooperativeness), and masculinity-femininity.

The Allport-Vernon-Lindzey Study of Values measures theoretically derived, basic interests or values, including: theoretical, economic, aesthetic, social, political, and religious.

The Edwards Personal Preference Schedule (EPPS) was designed to measure 15 needs defined in terms of Murray's conceptualization of motivation. These needs are: achievement, deference, order, exhibitionism, autonomy, affection, intraception, nurturance, change, endurance, heterosexuality, and aggression.

The Hysteria (Hy) and Psychaesthenia (Pt) scales of the MMPI probably are the two scales of the MMPI most frequently used in recent psychological research. The MMPI, of course, was developed empirically on the basis of psychiatric diagnoses; however, these particular scales, Pt and Hy, have been used fruitfully in many previous studies of nonclinical samples. The Pt scale concerns self-reported symptoms usually associated with anxiety, and the Hy scale deals with personality characteristics theoretically associated with the clinical syndrome of hysteria.

The four sets of personality measures had the advantages and disadvantages of most personality questionnaires. They provided reliable, objective, efficient measures of a wide range of personality variables, though they presumably did not tap some of the more dynamic aspects of functioning emphasized, for example, by most psychoanalytic theorists. As instruments for an initial, exploratory research, however, they seemed particularly appropriate and useful. If personality variables are at all related to emotional sensitivity, one would reasonably expect some evidence of these relationships to be indicated by at least some aspects of this battery.

Ability to identify vocal expressions of emotional meaning was measured by responses to a tape recording developed by Beldoch, and subsequently used by both Levy and Blau. The recording involves 37 expressions of 10 different categories of emotional meanings. Beldoch reports a test-retest reliability of .74. This measure is described more fully in Chapter 3.

RESULTS

A total of 33 personality variables were measured, and the correlation of each of these with the measure of emotional sensitivity was computed for data of group 1. Of the 33 correlations obtained, three differed significantly from zero. These involved heterosexuality ($r = .34$) and aggression ($r = .42$) as measured by the EPPS, and general activity ($r = .39$) as measured by the Guilford-Zimmerman Temperament Survey. These results obviously could be accounted for by chance, and indeed, upon cross-validation, none of the correlations involving these variables achieved statistical significance. Therefore, the results of this research indicate that the 33 personality variables measured by the various instruments are independent of the ability to identify vocal expressions of emotional meaning.[1]

DISCUSSION

The null results obviously do not support a general hypothesis that specific kinds of people, as described by various personality tests, are especially sensitive or insensitive to expressions of emotional meaning.

[1] In a subsequent study, the Dogmatism and Opinionation scales developed by Rokeach (1960) and a measure of ability to identify vocal expressions of emotional meaning was administered to 61 Ss. Correlation coefficients were computed between the measure of emotional sensitivity and scores on the two scales. These correlations did not differ significantly from zero.

The absence of positive results cannot be accounted for by unreliability of the specific measures used, although it is possible that other personality variables measured by other techniques might indeed be related to emotional sensitivity. For example, variables presumably tapped by performance on various projective techniques might be investigated, though the results of a small pilot study by Harriet Field are not encouraging in this respect.[2]

Taken at face value, these results mean that many different measures of personality variables have nothing to do with whether or not a person is sensitive to other people's emotional expressions. Thus, emotionally sensitive persons might very well have different patterns of needs and values, and display widely divergent personality traits. At any rate, if personality correlates of emotional sensitivity are to be found, a radically different approach must be made to the measurement of personality characteristics, and perhaps a different conceptualization of personality used as the basis of the research. The present shotgun procedure using questionnaire techniques clearly is not a profitable line for further investigation.

PERCEPTUAL AND COGNITIVE CORRELATES

The null results obtained in the study of personality variables led to a reformulation of the search for correlates of emotional sensitivity. Rather than focus on personality characteristics, an attempt was made to identify the perceptual and cognitive processes likely to be involved in recognizing the emotional meaning of a vocal expression. This was done largely on a common-sense basis, stemming from the experimenter's own experience in listening to the recordings and his observation of, and discussion with, many subjects in previous related studies.

---

[2] Field administered the Rorschach, selected TAT cards, and a measure of ability to identify vocal expressions of emotional meanings to 22 Ss. The Rorschach protocols were scored for total movement (M) responses, total form (F) responses, the ratio of number of M responses to total number of responses $(M/R \%)$, and the ratio of number of F responses to total number of responses $(F/R \%)$. The TAT protocols were rated on a five-point scale of emotional elaboration. This scale was developed by Terry (1952). The correlation between each projective variable and the measure of emotional sensitivity was computed; none of these correlations were significantly different from zero. Obviously, the results of this study cannot be generalized with much confidence. The small number of Ss, the relatively few projective variables studied, and the atomistic analysis of the Rorschach data manifestly limit the generality of the conclusions; nevertheless, the results are consistent with those obtained by questionnaire techniques and do not offer much promise for further research of this sort.

Beginning with the vocal expression itself, it seemed obvious that emotional meaning must be conveyed by the auditory cues of vocal expressions. Indeed, an earlier study identified some of these cues (Chapter 8). Therefore, in order to understand the meanings expressed, it was assumed that the listener must first be able to discriminate the auditory cues which carry these meanings. A totally deaf person is unable to understand the emotional meanings vocally expressed simply because he cannot perceive the auditory stimuli. Although ordinary communication probably does not require extremely high ability, some minimal capacity for making auditory discriminations would seem to be a requisite for the kind of emotional sensitivity measured in this research.

Hearing the vocal cues of expression might be necessary for understanding, but it did not seem a sufficient basis for identifying the meanings expressed. In one pattern or another, the nonverbal characteristics of speech, tone, timbre, inflection, etc., combine to represent symbolically a specific emotional meaning, and though the exact pattern of cues associated with various meanings cannot be defined with great precision, it is obvious that these patterns of interrelated vocal characteristics are complex, symbolic stimuli. Therefore, to respond appropriately to these stimuli, to "understand" and identify the meanings expressed by these complex, nonverbal symbols, a listener presumably must have the cognitive ability to deal with abstract symbols, to perceive and meaningfully organize the numerous, subtle, nonverbal characteristics which comprise a vocal symbol with emotional meaning.

Having perceived and somehow organized the vocal stimulus, a listener is required to interpret its emotional meaning. Although there is no explicit, standardized dictionary defining emotions in terms of vocal cues, reliable communication would seem unlikely without at least some implicit knowledge, on the listener's part, of the more or less conventional vocal cues of emotional meaning. This does not imply that a listener is aware of his implicit dictionary of emotional meanings, no more than the reader is constantly aware of the vocabulary he is using while reading this page. But just as reading ability is a function of vocabulary knowledge, it also seems likely that the ability to interpret emotional meanings of vocal messages is a function of knowledge about vocal characteristics commonly associated with various emotional expressions.

Finally, in our test situation, the subject is required to name or label the feeling expressed, a verbal response similar to that employed in the usual vocabulary tests, and probably involving the same sort of verbal ability. Thus, it was reasoned that verbal ability would be likely to be associated with ability to identify emotional meanings.

Subjects

The Ss were 61 graduate students enrolled at Teachers College, Columbia University. Among these Ss were 38 females and 23 males, with a mean age of 32.0 years and a range from 22 to 52 years.

Measures

Measures of the following variables were obtained for each S: (1) ability to make auditory discriminations; (2) abstract symbolic ability; (3) knowledge of vocal characteristics of emotional expressions; (4) verbal intelligence; (5) ability to identify vocal expressions of emotional meanings.

Auditory Discrimination. Ability to differentiate auditory stimuli was measured by four tests of the Seashore Measures of Musical Talents. These included tests of ability to discriminate sounds in terms of the following dimensions: (1) pitch, (2) loudness, (3) time, and (4) timbre. Although the sounds used in these tests were not produced vocally, and thus were qualitatively different from the sounds contained on the recording of vocal expressions, the Seashore tests presumably tap a more or less general auditory ability along each of the specified dimensions of pitch, loudness, etc. Moreover, pitch, loudness, time, and timbre were found to be important characteristics of vocal expressions in a previous research (Chapter 8), and finally, the Seashore measures had the merit of considerable previous standardization.

Abstract Symbolic Ability. The ability to deal with abstract symbols was measured by the Progressive Matrices test developed by Raven (1947). Designed as a measure of Spearman's g factor, the test consists of 60 abstract designs, from each of which a part has been removed. The S is required to select the missing part from several alternatives, and the task involves the eduction of various logical relations within the abstract material.

Knowledge of Vocal Characteristics. Before obtaining the measure of emotional sensitivity, each S was asked to describe what a voice sounds like when expressing each of the eight emotional meanings contained in the tape recording used to measure sensitivity. These descriptions were scored against the key presented in Table 5-1. Five judges listened to the five expressions of each emotional meaning contained in the test, and then gave an overall rating of the five expressions on a five-point scale for the dimensions of loudness, pitch, timbre, and rate of speech. The judges also were asked to describe the speech in terms of inflection, rhythm, and enunciation. After independent judgments, differences in ratings were resolved by discussion, and the consensus of the group

Table 5-1. Characteristics of Vocal Expressions Contained in the Test of Emotional Sensitivity

Feeling	Loudness	Pitch	Timbre	Rate	Inflection	Rhythm	Enunciation
Affection	Soft	Low	Resonant	Slow	Steady and slight upward	Regular	Slurred
Anger	Loud	High	Blaring	Fast	Irregular up and down	Irregular	Clipped
Boredom	Moderate to low	Moderate to low	Moderately resonant	Moderately slow	Monotone or gradually falling	...	Somewhat slurred
Cheerfulness	Moderately high	Moderately high	Moderately blaring	Moderately fast	Up and down; overall upward	Regular	
Impatience	Normal	Normal to moderately high	Moderately blaring	Moderately fast	Slight upward	...	Somewhat clipped
Joy	Loud	High	Moderately blaring	Fast	Upward	Regular	
Sadness	Soft	Low	Resonant	Slow	Downward	Irregular pauses	Slurred
Satisfaction	Normal	Normal	Somewhat resonant	Normal	Slight upward	Regular	Somewhat slurred

63

of judges was used as the key for scoring. The descriptions written by the 61 Ss were scored independently by two judges, one point scored for each correct characteristic noted and a half-point subtracted for an incorrect characteristic. High agreement between the two scorers was indicated by a correlation of .88 for the entire sample of 61 Ss, and the mean of the two scores assigned by the judges was used as the measure of knowledge of vocal characteristics.

Verbal Intelligence. A 40-item vocabulary test developed by Thorndike (1942) was used as the measure of verbal intelligence.

Emotional Sensitivity. The ability to identify vocal expressions of emotional meaning was measured by a 45-item tape recording of expressions of eight different emotional meanings plus five nonemotional or neutral items. Using a content-standard technique described by Beldoch (Chapter 3), speakers expressed each of the following emotional meanings: affection, anger, boredom, cheerfulness, impatience, joy, sadness, and satisfaction. In addition, each speaker recorded a neutral expression. In a preliminary study, a total sample of 190 items were identified by 73 Ss. Items were accepted for the next step in developing the test if a plurality of listeners' responses agreed with the meaning intended by the speaker. These items were then played to a sample of 91 Ss, and on the basis of an item analysis, the five most discriminating items for each category of meaning were selected. Thus, the final recording was comprised of 45 items, five in each category of emotional meaning and five neutral items. A test-retest reliability of .82 was obtained for the final test with a sample of 38 Ss.

Results

Scores on the five measures were intercorrelated; partial correlations were computed; and finally, a multiple correlation of the several predictor variables against the criterion variable of emotional sensitivity was computed.

The matrix of correlations is presented in Table 5-2. As indicated in the table, the correlation of each of the four predictor variables with the criterion measure of emotional sensitivity was significantly different from zero at the .01 level. In addition, all of the predictor variables were positively interrelated, as shown by the low, but statistically significant, correlations among the predictor variables. Therefore, partial correlations were computed and are summarized in Table 5-3. As would be expected on the basis of the low positive intercorrelations, the partial correlations are somewhat smaller than the correlations in the zero-order matrix presented in Table 5-2; however, all the partial correlations are statistically significant at or beyond the .05 level.

Since each of the predictor variables was positively related to the criterion variable, a multiple correlation combining the weights of the four predictor variables was computed. The beta weight for each of the four predictor variables was: (1) verbal intelligence, .19; (2) abstract ability, .13; (3) auditory ability, .18; (4) knowledge, .35. The multiple

Table 5-2. Intercorrelations of Verbal Intelligence, Abstract Ability, Auditory Ability, Knowledge of Vocal Characteristics, and Emotional Sensitivity

	Verbal	Abstract	Auditory	Knowledge
Verbal intelligence				
Abstract ability	.26*			
Auditory ability	.30*	.30*		
Knowledge	.27*	.30*	.31*	
Emotional sensitivity	.37**	.34**	.39**	.50**

* Significant at .05.
** Significant at .01.

Table 5-3. Partial Correlations of Predictor and Criterion Variables

	Partial correlation with emotional sensitivity		
	Controlling verbal intelligence	Controlling abstract ability	Controlling auditory ability
Abstract ability	.26*		
Auditory ability	.29*	.31*	
Knowledge	.44**	.43**	.43**

* Significant at .05.
** Significant at .01.

correlation with ability to identify expressions of emotional meaning was .60, significant beyond the .01 level.[3]

[3] In a subsequent study, Beverly Elkan found further evidence of a relationship between another perceptual variable and sensitivity to nonverbal emotional expressions. Elkan administered the 45-item tape of vocal expressions and the Gottschaldt Embedded Figures Test to 32 Ss. The Embedded Figures Test requires an S to identify given linear patterns within increasingly complex backgrounds, and presumably taps the ability to discriminate figure from ground in a visual task. The correlation between performances on the two tasks was .47, significant beyond the .01 level. Controlling for verbal intelligence, measured by the Thorndike Vocabulary Test, a partial correlation of .45 ($p < .01$) was obtained. These results are consistent with a perceptual-cognitive interpretation of emotional sensitivity. In the content-standard vocal task of identifying emotional meanings, the listener must discriminate the vocal "figure" from the verbal "ground," and the Embedded Figures Test apparently measures, in a visual mode, a perceptual ability which plays some role in the auditory task involved in responding to vocal expressions.

DISCUSSION

In striking contrast to the study of personality variables, the investigation of perceptual and cognitive correlates yielded consistently positive results. The correlations indeed are modest; no single variable, possibly excepting knowledge of vocal characteristics, accounts for a great deal of the variance. But considered together, ability to discriminate auditory cues, verbal intelligence, abstract symbolic ability, and knowledge of vocal characteristics account for nearly 40 per cent of the variance in ability to identify vocal expressions of emotional meaning. Of course much of the variance remains unaccounted for, but the line of research suggested by this study is clearly more promising than the study of possible personality correlates of emotional sensitivity.

The findings lend credence to a conceptualization of emotional sensitivity in terms of complex stimuli, intervening perceptual and symbolic processes, and subsequent verbal responses. Some previous theoretical discussions of emotional sensitivity have involved mysterious terms such as the "third ear," and other obscure hypothetical constructs without measurable referents; unfortunately, such conceptualizations have hindered, rather than promoted meaningful empirical research in this area. This does not mean that the present research has resolved all problems, that all differences can be accounted for by the few variables considered in this study. Obviously, this is not the case. Moreover, some of the characteristics of so-called "intuitive behavior," such as immediate, or at least very rapid, recognition, seem to describe the behavior of subjects who make correct responses to the experimental tape. Certainly suggestions from any point of view need to be considered in planning further research, but the results of this study support the view that emotional sensitivity can be conceptualized fruitfully in terms amenable to experimental investigation.

Inspection of the scatter plot of each of the correlations reveals a fairly consistent pattern for the several variables studied: in each instance, some minimal level of perceptual or cognitive ability is required for successful performance on the test of emotional sensitivity, while scores above this minimal level are relatively independent within the upper range of the criterion measure. For example, the capacity to make very fine distinctions among auditory stimuli is not always related to very high scores on the emotional sensitivity tape; but without minimal ability to make fairly gross auditory discriminations, recognition of the vocal expressions tends to be very low. Thus, the low, positive correlations obtained reflect this gross difference, rather than a consistently linear relationship along the entire range of both variables involved in any single correlation. The most appropriate conceptualization, therefore, would seem to be a multivariable model in which a specific level of functioning in each of several, relatively independent dimensions is required for adequate communication. Thus, despite high verbal intelligence, high abstract symbolic ability, and a great deal of knowledge about vocal characteristics, a person who cannot discriminate the auditory cues of the voice could not be sensitive to vocal expressions. It would therefore seem that each of several diverse abilities and skills is a necessary, but not sufficient, condition of emotional sensitivity.

The highest zero-order correlation involved emotional sensitivity and knowledge of vocal characteristics. This, of course, underscores the cognitive aspects of the recognition task; however, this finding does not necessarily support a problem-solving, so-called "intellectual," view of emotional sensitivity. As noted earlier, vocabulary knowledge is positively correlated with reading ability, though the process of reading, particularly for the practiced reader, probably bears little relation to the sort of problem-solving process typically considered in psychological research. It is possible, of course, that some third variable may account for the correlation between knowledge of vocal characteristics and emotional sensitivity; or, emotional sensitivity may be an antecedent, rather than consequence, of knowledge. Only further experimental, in contrast to correlational, research can resolve this issue. In my opinion, knowledge probably does play an important part in the process of identifying emotional expressions, though it probably operates rapidly and without the subject's awareness. At this stage of ignorance, however, this is merely an opinion open for empirical investigation.

This research has identified some of the perceptual and cognitive correlates of emotional sensitivity, but like all correlational studies, the results can offer only a tentative basis for making guesses about the actual processes involved. The study at least identifies some of the variables which may operate in the process of identifying emotional expressions, and a next step in this area of research is to investigate the process of communication in an experimentally controlled, rather than correlational, study.

SUMMARY

Two studies concerned with possible correlates of the ability to identify vocal expressions of emotional meanings were reported in this paper. In the first study, 33 personality variables were investigated; none of these were reliably correlated with the measure of emotional sensitivity. In the second study, four perceptual and cognitive variables were investigated. These were: (1) auditory ability; (2) abstract symbolic ability; (3) verbal intelligence; and (4) knowledge of vocal characteristics of emotional expressions. Each of these variables was found to be positively related to a measure of ability to identify vocal expressions of emotional meanings, and a multiple correlation of .60 was obtained between a combination of all four variables and the measure of emotional sensitivity. The results were discussed in terms of a conceptualization of emotional communication in terms of a symbolic process, and leads for research concerned with the process of communication were suggested.

6

The ability to identify the emotional meaning of vocal expressions at successive age levels

Lilly Dimitrovsky[1]

The ability of adults to identify the emotional meaning of vocal expressions has been demonstrated in a number of studies (Chapter 2), but little is known about the development of emotional sensitivity during early childhood. In the only experimental study dealing with this problem, Georgina Gates (1927) tested children from grades three through eight using a recording of the alphabet recited to express each of nine different emotional meanings. Gates found that the ability to identify the emotional expressions was positively related to age, grade, school experience, and intelligence. Unfortunately, however, only a very brief summary report of·this study was published, and the original data are no longer available.[2] The present study, therefore, was designed to replicate, in part, Gates' earlier research, and to explore additional questions relevant to the development of emotional sensitivity from ages five through twelve.

This research focused on the following specific questions: (1) Does the ability to identify the emotional meaning of vocal expressions increase with chronological age? (2) Does the ability to recognize various emotional meanings develop differentially? For example, does the ability to recognize anger develop differently from the ability to recognize sadness, love, or happiness? (3) What kinds of errors are typically made by children in identifying emotional expressions, and is there any

[1] This research was supported by U.S.P.H.S. Fellowship Grant No. MF-17,892.
[2] Personal communication from Prof. Arthur Gates.

difference in the pattern of errors made at successive age levels? (4) Is there any difference between boys and girls in the development of emotional sensitivity? (5) What is the relation between emotional sensitivity and verbal intelligence among children?

METHOD

In order to minimize the effect of increasing verbal ability with age, the procedures used in this study involved simply labeled categories of emotional meaning that were likely to be familiar to even fairly young children. Thus, the general procedure was to ask children at successive age levels to identify the emotional meaning of vocal expressions by selecting one of the following four choices: (1) anger, (2) happiness, (3) love, and (4) sadness.

Subjects

*S*s were 14 children of each sex at each year level between the ages of five and twelve, a total of 224 children. They were selected from a larger school population on the basis of their having the most recent birthdays. Thus, for example, the five-year-olds were 5-0, 5-1, 5-2, and 5-3. In only a few cases was it necessary to include a child whose birthday was four months past in order to obtain the necessary number of *S*s for a particular age group. No child whose IQ was known on the basis of school records to be below 90 was included in the sample. The community from which the *S*s were sampled is a small town in central New Jersey and is relatively homogeneous in terms of socioeconomic status. Accordingly, almost all of the *S*s were children of skilled workers.

Instruments

Three instruments were used in the research: (1) a test of ability to identify the emotional meaning of vocal expressions; (2) a set of stick figure drawings designed to aid the children in remembering the four categories of emotional meaning; (3) the Ammons Full-Range Picture Vocabulary Test (Form A).

Vocal Expressions. Twenty-four items were selected from the recordings of vocal expressions obtained by Beldoch (Chapter 3) and Davitz (Chapter 5) in the development of their tests of sensitivity to vocal expression. In each case, the speaker recited a standard paragraph of verbal content while vocally expressing either anger, happiness, love, or sadness. All of the speakers were adults. Twelve items involved male speakers, and 12, female speakers. Among the 12 items by male speakers, there were three that expressed each of the four emotional meanings, and these items were arranged in a randomized order. The same pattern was followed for the female speakers. For a fuller discussion of the standardization of these items, see Chapters 3 and 5.

Stick Figure Drawings. In related studies of adults, a list of emotions usually is presented to the listener, and he is asked to identify the emotional meaning of an item by scanning the list and writing the name of the emotion he thinks is expressed by that item. But with young children, an experimental task involving either reading or writing obviously could not be used. Therefore, the children were asked to respond by pointing to one of four stick figure drawings that represented the categories of emotional meaning. There were two sets of drawings, one set depicting a sad man, a happy man, an angry man, and two drawings of a loving man with a child. The second set consisted of corresponding pictures of women. Two drawings depicting love were used because this category of emotional meaning was the most difficult to represent pictorially, and each child was asked to select the one from each set that looked as though the adult loved the child more. Before using these drawings in the emotional identification task, the children were trained to associate each of the four drawings in a set with the appropriate emotional word. The drawings were so obvious that almost all of the children immediately associated the proper emotional meaning with each drawing, and all *S*s reached a satisfactory criterion of correct identification after a short period of preliminary training. The figure drawings used are presented in Figure 6-1.

Ammons Full-Range Picture Vocabulary Test. In order to obtain an estimate of verbal intelligence within a relatively short testing time, Form A of the Ammons Full-Range Picture Vocabulary Test was used. Evidence in support of the validity, reliability, and appropriateness for the ages studied is reviewed in the test manual.

Procedure

All *S*s were seen individually. In order to accustom them to listening to tape recordings, they were initially asked to participate in a very simple identification task. They listened to a recording of three speakers and were asked to say whether the person talking was a man, woman, or child. These items were extremely obvious, almost assuring success.

*S*s were then shown the two pictures of the loving men and were asked to choose which of these looked as though he loved the child more. The picture chosen was then placed in front of the *S*s together with the pictures of the sad, happy, and angry men. *S*s were asked to point to the sad man, the happy man, etc. This was repeated until all of the drawings were correctly identified twice consecutively.

*S*s were then instructed as follows: "You are going to hear different men say the same thing in different ways. Some will sound happy, some sad, some angry, and some loving. Listen to each one and point to the man that it sounds like. Does it sound like the happy man, the sad man, the angry man, or the loving man?

| Happy | Sad | Angry | Loving | Loving |

| Happy | Sad | Angry | Loving | Loving |

Fig. 6-1. Stick figure drawings representing the four categories of emotional meaning.

The recording of the male speakers was then played and *S*s made the 12 choices.

A similar procedure was followed for the drawings of the women and the recordings of the female speakers.

For half of the *S*s of each sex at each year level the recording of the male voices was played first and that of the female voices second. For the other half of the *S*s the order was reversed.

Ss were then administered Form A of the Ammons Full-Range Picture Vocabulary Test.

For the purpose of reliability studies, four Ss of each sex at each year level, a total of 64, were retested on the recordings of vocal expressions one week after the original testing.

RESULTS

The data reveal that with chronological age there is gradual, but steadily progressive increase in ability to identify the emotional meaning of vocal expressions. An analysis of variance (Table 6-1) shows this

Table 6-1. Analysis of Variance for Ss of Different Ages and Sexes in Terms of Accuracy of Response to Vocal Expressions of Emotional Meaning

Source of variation	Sum of squares	df	Mean square	F ratio
Age of Ss	103.55	7	14.79	33.61***
Sex of Ss	3.38	1	3.38	7.68**
Age $\times$ sex of Ss	3.43	7	0.49	1.11
Ss within groups	92.12	208	0.44	
Emotion	254.34	3	84.78	188.40***
Emotion $\times$ age of Ss	15.17	21	0.72	1.60
Emotion $\times$ sex of Ss	0.80	3	0.27	0.60
Emotion $\times$ age $\times$ sex of Ss	5.49	21	0.26	0.58
Emotion $\times$ Ss within groups	278.01	624	0.45	
Sex of speaker	1.87	1	1.87	6.23*
Sex of speaker $\times$ age of Ss	2.77	7	0.40	1.33
Sex of speaker $\times$ sex of Ss	0.02	1	0.02	0.07
Sex of speaker $\times$ age of sex of Ss	3.00	7	0.43	1.43
Sex of speaker Ss within groups	63.30	208	0.30	
Emotion $\times$ sex of speaker	27.14	3	9.05	36.20***
Emotion $\times$ sex of speaker $\times$ age of Ss	10.41	21	0.50	2.00**
Emotion $\times$ sex of speaker $\times$ sex of Ss	2.04	3	0.68	2.72*
Emotion $\times$ sex of speaker $\times$ age $\times$ sex of Ss	3.14	21	0.15	0.60
Emotion $\times$ sex of speaker $\times$ Ss within groups	155.83	624	0.25	

*** $p < .001$.
** $p < .01$.
* $p < .05$.

increase to be statistically significant beyond the .001 level. Inspection of the mean scores at the various age levels (Table 6-2) shows that the increase from age group to age group is relatively smooth; in fact, these mean scores come fairly close to falling along a straight line. While the

Table 6-2. Means and Standard Deviations of Number of Correct Identifications for Children of Different Age Levels

Age	Mean score	SD
5	8.07	2.51
6	10.00	3.51
7	11.54	2.80
8	12.82	1.94
9	14.21	2.08
10	15.11	2.53
11	15.07	1.92
12	15.68	2.76

Maximum possible score = 24.

five-year-olds do relatively poorly (mean score 8.07 out of a possible 24), a binomial estimate of probability reveals that even their performance is better than chance ($p = .01$). From a low of 8.07 for the five-year-olds, the curve rises to a high of 15.68 for the twelve-year-olds. These results are summarized graphically in Figure 6-2.

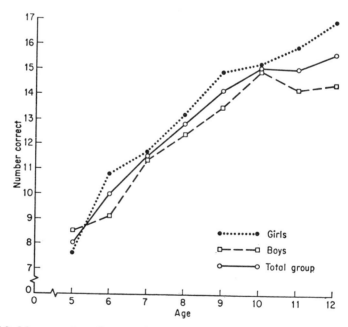

Fig. 6-2. Mean number of correct identifications at successive age levels.

Table 6-3 presents the mean percentage of identical responses, regardless of whether correct or incorrect, on test and retest for each of the age groups for the 64 Ss who were tested twice. While only 44 per cent of the responses of the five-year-olds were identical on retest, the corresponding percentage for the eight-year-olds was 70. No consistent

Table 6-3. Per Cent of Identical Responses on Test and Retest at Different Age Levels

Age	Per cent of identical responses
5	44
6	55
7	63
8	70
9	68
10	75
11	71
12	76

Table 6-4. Means and Standard Deviations of Number Correctly Identified among Children of Different Ages for Each Category of Emotional Meaning

Age	Happy	SD	Sad	SD	Angry	SD	Loving	SD
5	1.36	0.83	3.00	1.44	2.14	1.56	1.57	1.40
6	1.61	1.47	4.46	1.45	2.68	1.33	1.25	1.55
7	1.93	1.09	4.64	1.10	3.39	1.71	1.57	1.32
8	2.14	1.08	4.82	0.72	4.14	1.08	1.71	1.54
9	2.82	1.12	5.07	0.77	3.93	1.30	2.39	1.59
10	2.93	1.41	5.21	0.74	4.36	1.16	2.61	1.13
11	3.04	1.40	5.32	0.61	4.04	0.84	2.68	1.36
12	2.93	1.54	5.14	0.71	4.39	1.20	3.21	1.64

Maximum possible score = 6.

increase in stability of response was shown between the ages of eight and twelve.

Table 6-4 presents the mean scores for the combined group on the items expressive of each of the emotions. Figure 6-3 presents these data graphically for each age level. From these data it is apparent that mean rate of recognition is highest for "sad" items. "Angry," "happy," and "loving" items follow in the stated order. This order of relative difficulty is maintained at all but the five- and twelve-year levels, where "loving" items are correctly identified more often than "happy" ones. The difference between the recognition rates for "sad" and "angry" items is considerable, as is the difference between "angry" and "happy"

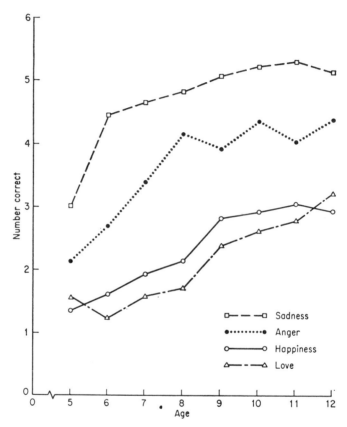

FIG. 6-3. Mean number of correct identifications of expressions of each category of emotional meaning at successive age levels.

items. An analysis of variance (Table 6-1) reveals that the difference in rate of recognition for the different emotions is significant beyond the .001 level. There is some evidence of interaction effects between age and emotion (Table 6-1). Inspection of the data reveals that, in addition to the two exceptions to the general order of difficulty, differences in the recognition rate for expressions of the four emotions are greater at some age levels than at others; however, no consistent pattern over age is apparent in the data. There is no evidence that the trends in recognition of the four emotions differ for boys and girls (Table 6-1).

Table 6-5 reveals that, in responding, Ss favored the negative emotions, saying "sad" and "angry" far more often than "loving" or "happy," regardless of the stimulus presented. While there is a definite

Table 6-5. Number of Emitted Responses in Each Category of Emotional Meaning for Each Age Group

Age	Happy			Sad			Angry			Loving		
	C[a]	I[b]	T[c]	C	I	T	C	I	T	C	I	T
5	38	88	126	84	137	221	60	135	195	44	86	130
6	45	78	123	125	156	281	75	90	165	35	68	103
7	54	76	130	130	126	256	95	87	182	44	60	104
8	60	58	118	135	114	249	116	80	196	48	61	109
9	79	46	125	142	108	250	110	67	177	67	53	120
10	82	38	120	146	101	247	122	60	182	73	50	123
11	85	35	121	149	105	254	113	54	167	75	55	130
12	82	33	115	144	104	248	123	51	174	90	45	135

[a] Correct.
[b] Incorrect.
[c] Total.

Table 6-6. Percentage of Emitted Responses Correct for Each Age Group and for the Total Group

Age	Happy	Sad	Angry	Loving
5	30.2	38.0	30.8	33.8
6	36.6	44.5	45.5	34.0
7	41.5	50.8	52.2	42.3
8	50.8	54.2	59.2	44.0
9	63.2	56.8	62.1	55.8
10	68.3	59.1	67.0	59.3
11	70.2	58.7	67.7	57.7
12	71.3	58.0	70.7	66.7
Total group	53.7	52.6	56.6	49.9

decrease in the number of errors with age, the pattern of total emitted responses remains fairly stable. In other words, approximately the same number of responses of each type are emitted at all ages, but in the older groups more of these responses are emitted appropriately.

Table 6-6 represents an attempt to control for the differential numbers of the four responses emitted. For each of the four emotional meanings, the percentage of times a response was emitted correctly was calculated. Thus, for example, the number of times five-year-olds said "sad" correctly was divided by the total number of times they said "sad" and multiplied by 100. These calculations were made for each of the age groups and for the total group. When this measure is used as the criterion, the recognition rates for the four categories of emotional meaning are fairly close.

Errors tend to be characterized by similarity along the dimension of activity, rather than valence. That is, the active emotions (anger and happiness) tend to be confused, as do the passive emotions (sadness and love) (Table 6-7). However, here too, it follows that positive emo-

Table 6-7. Frequency in Each Response Category for Each Stimulus Category for the Total Group

		Response		
Stimulus	Happy	Sad	Angry	Loving
Happy	525	205	458	156
Sad	57	1055	77	155
Angry	217	146	814	167
Loving	179	600	89	476

tions are erroneously identified as negative far more often than the reverse. Expressions of love were mistaken for sadness 600 times, whereas sadness was mistaken for love only 155 times. Similarly, happiness was erroneously identified as anger 458 times, while expressions of anger were mistaken for happiness only 217 times. These findings, of course, reflect the tendency to emit responses with negative, rather than positive, emotional meaning.

Inspection of the mean scores for boys and girls (Table 6-8) reveals that, except at the five-year level, girls do slightly better than boys.

Table 6-8. Means and Standard Deviations of Number of Correct Identifications for Boys and Girls of Different Ages

	Boys		Girls	
Age	Mean	SD	Mean	SD
5	8.50	2.74	7.64	2.27
6	9.14	3.84	10.86	3.03
7	11.43	3.01	11.64	2.68
8	12.43	1.91	13.21	1.97
9	13.50	1.99	14.93	1.98
10	15.00	2.54	15.21	2.61
11	14.21	1.93	15.93	1.54
12	14.43	2.77	16.93	2.20

Maximum possible score = 24.

Between the ages of ten and twelve, the girls' scores continue to rise, while those of the boys drop slightly. These results are summarized graphically in Figure 6-2. A consideration of the individual scores of the two sexes indicates that in five of the eight age groups more than

Table 6-9. Correlation between Verbal Intelligence and Number of Correct Identifications at Different Age Levels

Age	Correlation
5	.37*
6	.22
7	.08
8	−.11
9	−.01
10	.17
11	.03
12	−.12

*$p < .05$.

Table 6-10. Means and Standard Deviations of Number of Correct Identifications for Children of Different Ages on Male and Female Speaker Items

Age	Male speakers Means	SD	Female speakers Means	SD
5	4.11	1.93	3.96	1.37
6	5.57	2.01	4.43	2.06
7	5.79	2.06	5.75	1.90
8	6.71	1.58	6.11	1.23
9	7.25	1.38	6.96	1.55
10	7.79	1.17	7.32	1.68
11	7.89	1.07	7.18	1.56
12	7.68	1.61	8.00	1.56

Maximum possible score = 12.

70 per cent of the girls exceeded the score for the median boy. An analysis of variance shows the generally greater accuracy of the girls to be significant beyond the .01 level (Table 6-1).

A consideration of the relationship between the ability to recognize vocal expressions of feeling and verbal mental ability as measured by score on the Full-Range Picture Vocabulary Test reveals a correlation

Table 6-11. Mean Number of Correct Identifications for Boys and Girls of Different Ages on Male and Female Speaker Items for the Four Emotions

Age	Boys								Girls							
	Male voices				Female voices				Male voices				Female voices			
	H*	S	A	L	H	S	A	L	H	S	A	L	H	S	A	L
5	0.64	2.07	1.36	0.50	1.00	1.29	0.93	0.71	0.43	1.57	0.86	0.79	0.64	1.07	1.14	1.14
6	0.86	2.43	1.14	0.64	0.86	1.71	1.07	0.43	0.93	2.79	1.64	0.71	0.57	2.00	1.50	0.71
7	0.86	2.36	1.43	0.86	1.14	2.36	1.86	0.57	0.93	2.71	1.64	0.79	0.93	1.86	1.86	0.93
8	0.86	2.86	1.71	0.79	1.14	1.86	2.43	0.79	1.14	2.93	1.93	1.21	1.14	2.00	2.21	0.64
9	1.43	2.86	1.71	1.21	1.64	2.00	2.07	0.79	1.36	2.86	1.64	1.43	1.43	2.43	2.43	1.36
10	1.29	3.00	1.93	1.64	1.21	2.29	2.43	0.79	1.43	2.79	1.86	1.64	1.50	2.36	2.50	1.14
11	1.21	2.86	1.86	1.43	1.21	2.50	2.07	1.07	2.07	2.93	1.86	1.57	1.57	2.36	2.29	1.29
12	1.00	2.64	1.51	1.71	1.43	2.21	2.29	1.57	1.86	2.93	2.00	1.64	1.57	2.50	2.93	1.50

Maximum possible score = 3.
* H: Happiness
S: Sadness
A: Anger
L: Love

of .67 for the total group. This compares with a correlation of .69 between age and sensitivity to vocal expressions of feeling. Examination of the relationship between verbal intelligence and sensitivity within each age group (Table 6-9) indicates a significant correlation only at the five-year level. Table 6-10 presents the mean scores of children of different ages on items read by male speakers and by female speakers. The difference in favor of male speakers is significant beyond the .05 level (Table 6-1). When this question is more carefully examined, however, it becomes apparent that while male speakers communicate love and sadness with a greater degree of accuracy, female speakers are superior in the communication of anger (Tables 6-1 and 6-11). There are also significant interaction effects between emotion and sex of speaker and age of Ss (Table 6-1). Inspection of the data suggests that the differences between male and female speakers in communicating specific emotions are more apparent at some ages than at others. Specifically, for anger and love it would seem that such differences become greater after the age of eight.

Table 6-11 presents the mean scores for boys and girls of different ages on male and female speaker items for the four categories of emotional meaning. An analysis of variance reveals no overall difference between boys and girls in their reaction to male and female speakers, but does show interaction effects between emotion and sex of speaker and sex of subject (Table 6-1). There is some indication that the relative superiority of male speakers in communicating love is slightly greater for boys than for girls. Also, while speakers of either sex are about equally effective in communicating happiness to girls, female speakers are slightly superior in communicating it to boys.

DISCUSSION

The results of this research indicate that, between the ages of five and twelve, there is a gradual and steadily progressive increase in the ability to identify the emotional meaning of vocal expressions. This general finding is consistent with an earlier study reported by Gates (1927). It also parallels what is known concerning the development of sensitivity to facial expressions of feeling (Dashiell, 1927; Gates, 1923; Kellogg & Eagleson, 1931).

It is apparent, then, that the childhood years of five through twelve represent a period of considerable growth in sensitivity to emotional communication. However, it must also be pointed out, that by the age of five children have already undergone a fair amount of development in this area. In the present study, the five-year-olds, as a group, scored better than chance expectation, and individuals among them performed with a remarkably high degree of accuracy. The highest scoring five-year-old did considerably better than the lowest scoring twelve-year-old. Among children, as among adults, individual differences are striking.

It seems self evident that the question of sensitivity to vocal expressions of emotion during the early years of life is an important subject for further research. Observers (Buhler & Hetzer, 1935; Lewis, 1936) have pointed out that infants respond to differences in the intonation of the voice as early as the sixth month. However, little is known about functioning in this area between the ages of one and five. One question of particular interest regarding this period concerns the influence of the acquisition of language, with its emphasis on verbal content, on sensitivity to vocal communications of feeling. It has been noted (Shirley, 1933a; 1933b) that there is a cyclical relationship between linguistic development and certain aspects of motor development. Speech development is held in abeyance at the time that motor development is most rapid. One might speculate that a similar relationship could possibly hold true for the content aspect of speech and sensitivity to nonverbal vocal expressions of emotion during the early years of life. That is, as the child's verbal ability increases rapidly, growth in sensitivity to nonverbal stimuli may progress at a relatively slower rate; while subsequent development of sensitivity to nonverbal aspects of communication may be associated with relatively slower rates of increase in verbal ability.

Consistency of performance was investigated by a test-retest procedure with one week interval between testing sessions. The finding that children of age eight and over tend to have higher reliability scores than do younger children generally parallels what is known of the consistency of children's performance on other intelligence tests (Wechsler, 1949). Perhaps the more important question in this area concerns relative consistency of performance over longer periods in the life span. For example, is the child who is relatively sensitive to nonverbal emotional expressions at the age of five also relatively sensitive at ages ten or twelve, or even later, as an adult? Obviously the answer to such a question depends upon further longitudinal investigation.

The fact that children correctly identify "sad" and "angry" items more frequently than "happy" and "loving" ones at all age levels must be considered in conjunction with the related finding that, in answering, they also tend to choose the negative emotions far more often than the positive ones. If the responses "sad" and "angry" are emitted more frequently, there is, of course, a greater chance that the negative emotions will be identified correctly. This can clearly be inferred from the analysis of emitted responses correct.

The pattern of emitted responses is similar for all age groups; responses with negative emotional valence are emitted far more often than those with positive valence. The present research offers no clear-cut explanation of these findings, but the observation that children tend to respond in terms of negative, unpleasant emotional meanings is in itself of considerable psychological interest.

In this study children identified expressions of feeling by adults. The question of whether the same response tendencies are as strongly apparent when children discriminate expressions of feeling by their peers, or when adults judge emotions expressed by other adults, is a subject for further investigation. When the results presented by Davitz and Davitz (1959a) in their study of adults are analyzed in terms of the number of correct identifications of items expressive of positive and negative feelings, it becomes apparent that adults, too, correctly identify expressions of negative feelings more frequently than expressions of positive feelings. However, other data obtained from adults (Davitz, Chapter 5) suggests that normal adults do *not*, on the average, emit a greater frequency of negative, in comparison to positive, responses in identifying emotional expressions. The tendency to respond to vocal expressions in terms of negative emotional meanings, therefore, seems to be particularly characteristic of children.

Children's erroneous judgments of vocal expressions tend to be similar to the emotion intended in terms of the activity dimension of connotative meaning. These results are consistent with the findings reported by Davitz in a study of adults (Davitz, Chapter 8). These results with both adults and children would appear to be a logical consequence of the fact that loudness, timbre, pitch, and rate, the more obvious aspects of speech, are a function of the subjectively rated activity level of the feeling communicated. Thus expressions of feelings that are similar in terms of activity level are similar in terms of gross vocal cues, and therefore tend to be confused.

The fact that girls are more accurate than boys in identifying expressions of feeling fits in well with findings concerning the superiority of girls in general language development (E. A. Davis, 1937; I. P. Davis, 1938; Doran, 1907; McCarthy, 1930; F. M. Young, 1941). Speech involves the simultaneous operation of the verbal and vocal communication channels; thus, previous findings that girls tend to develop verbal skills more rapidly than boys do are consistent with the present findings in regards to vocal communication.

Cultural stereotypes present the female as sensitive and intuitive and the male as less involved with the emotional aspects of living. The issue of whether sex differences in sensitivity to the communication of feelings in children are innate or the result of cultural influences remains unsettled. However, the data of the present study include an intriguing hint which is relevant to this question and deserves further investigation. The five-year-olds were the only group in which the boys scored higher than the girls. Also, from the age of ten, the curve for the girls continues to rise, while that for the boys does not. One might speculate that at the age of six, when children begin school, and during the preadolescent years, the cultural sex role pressures are particularly strong and are reflected in performance in this area. Thus, one might expect preschool boys and girls to show little or no difference in a variable such as emotional sensitivity, but gradually with age, as the cultural expectations that a girl is sensitive and intuitive and a boy is active and "objective" play an increasingly important role in development, one would expect greater differences in the degree to which boys and girls attend to emotional stimuli and thus acquire skill in discriminating emotional expressions.

We do not know, however, on the basis of the present study whether or not there are consistent sex differences in sensitivity below the age of five or beyond twelve. Sex differences in language development have been observed from the preschool period until the age of nine and a half (E. A. Davis, 1937). It would appear that girls' superior ability to discriminate emotional communications does not span exactly the same period, although there is considerable overlap. This study obviously does not add anything to our knowledge of such functioning during the early preschool years. The results for the five-year-old group, although they can in no way be considered conclusive, suggest that sex differences in this area may not become apparent until the school years. Certainly there are indications that they continue beyond the nine and a half year level. Whether they persist into adulthood is open to question. Although the majority of relevant investigations (Beldoch, Chapter 3; Dusenbury & Knower, 1939; Levy, Chapter 4) report no significant differences between men and women, one investigator did find such differences (Pfaff, 1954). It should also be noted that investigations with adults in this area have used students, undergraduate and graduate, as subjects. The present study dealt predominantly with children of working-class parents, thus representing a population that is somewhat different in socioeconomic terms from a typical college student sample. Therefore, generalization of the differences in sensitivity between boys and girls in the present sample depends upon further investigation of children and adults from a wider socioeconomic range than has been studied heretofore.

The significant overall correlation between sensitivity and verbal intelligence is consistent with previous findings with adults (Beldoch, Chapter 3; Davitz, Chapter 5; Levy, Chapter 4; Turner, Chapter 10) and children (Gates, 1927). The fact that only one of the correlation coefficients for the individual age groups achieved significance may in part be due to the fact that the age range within each particular group is very narrow. As noted earlier, Ss were selected from a larger school population on the basis of their having the most recent birthdays, and in only a few instances was it necessary to include a child whose birthday was four months past. The single significant correlation at the five-year level suggests that, for the youngest group, verbal intelligence might have played an important role in the understanding of the instructions.

More important than the obtained difference in favor of male speakers, and indeed achieving a higher level of statistical significance, is the fact that male and female speakers differed in their ability to communicate specific emotions to children. Expressions of sadness and love were more frequently recognized when made by male speakers. Expressions of anger were more often correctly identified when made by female speakers.

Although one cannot generalize on the basis of the small number of speakers used in the present study, these findings are of interest. On the basis of reinforcement theory one might have expected that female speakers would communicate all emotions more effectively to children, since most children generally have more contact with women than with men, and therefore hear women express all emotions much more often. It is difficult to understand why this expectation was not realized. It is possible that the expression of anger, in a loud voice and with blaring timbre, contrasts more strongly with the typically, or perhaps only stereotypically, soft speaking voice of women, and is therefore more easily recognized. Similarly, the soft expressions of love and sadness may stand out more against the typically louder male voice. It is unclear also why in the case of love and anger these differences in effectiveness are less apparent at the lowest age level. Tentative and unconfirmed as they are, these results do raise the issue of sex differences in the ability to communicate specific emotions as an important subject for further investigation. Of interest too in this connection are the limited findings concerning the differential effectiveness of different sexed speakers in communicating specific emotions to subjects of different sexes. The only study dealing with the question of sex differences in vocal expressiveness, Levy's (Chapter 4) research on the relationship between the ability to express and perceive vocal communications of feeling, showed no significant differences between male and female speakers in ability to communicate emotion to adults. However, this investigation compared the sexes only in their general effectiveness of communication, and not in their ability to express specific emotions, or to communicate specific emotions to subjects of different sexes.

SUMMARY

A study of 224 children selected from a normal school population (14 of each sex at each year level between the ages of five and twelve) revealed the following results:

1. With age there is a significant increase in the ability of children to correctly identify the emotional meaning of vocal expressions.

2. Expressions of sadness are most frequently identified correctly by children. Anger, happiness, and love follow in the stated order.

3. Children give the responses "sad" and "angry" more frequently than the responses "happy" and "loving" to vocal expressions by adults. This response tendency largely accounts for the differences in rate of recognition in the four categories of emotional meaning.

4. There is no marked consistent difference in the pattern of correct or incorrect responses made by children at various age levels, from five through twelve.

5. Erroneous judgments made by children are similar to the emotional meaning intended in terms of the activity dimension of connotative meaning.

6. Girls are more accurate judges of vocal expressions of feeling than are boys.

7. The correlation between ability to recognize vocal expressions of feeling and verbal mental ability is .67 for the total group. When the corresponding correlation coefficient was calculated for each age group individually, however, it achieved significance only for the five-year-olds.

8. Male and female adult speakers in the present sample differ in the degree to which they communicate specific emotional meanings to children.

7

The relationship between abilities to express emotional meanings vocally and facially

Eugene A. Levitt

Beldoch's study of responses to vocal, graphic, and musical expressions demonstrated that individual differences in emotional sensitivity tend to be consistent across modes of communication. That is, a person able to identify the emotional meaning of vocal expressions with a relatively high degree of accuracy also tends to be accurate in identifying the meaning of graphic and musical expressions (Chapter 3).

In a related study, Levy found that a person who is accurate in *identifying* the emotional expressions of other people also tends to be accurate in *expressing* emotional meanings to others. In addition, the person who is sensitive to others' expressions is also relatively accurate in identifying the meaning of his own vocal expressions (Chapter 4).

Thus, the results of Beldoch's and Levy's studies suggest that a general factor accounts for part of the common variance in a variety of behaviors involved in emotional communication. Neither of these previous studies was concerned with the relationship between different kinds of expressive behaviors, but if there is indeed a general factor underlying various aspects of the total communication process, it would be reasonable to expect a positive relationship between abilities to *express* emotional meanings in different modes of communication. The present research, therefore, was designed to test this prediction in terms of the relationship between vocal and facial expressions. In addition, the study was also designed to compare the relative accuracy with which vocal and facial expressions communicate emotional meanings, and to investigate differences in the accuracy of communication by simultaneous vocal-facial expressions versus each mode treated independently.

Specifically, the following hypotheses were tested:

1. There is a positive relationship between the ability to express emotional meanings facially and vocally.

2. Emotional meanings are communicated more accurately by vocal expressions than by facial expressions.

3. Emotional meanings are communicated more accurately by simultaneous vocal plus facial expressions than by expressions in either mode treated independently.

METHOD

Sound motion pictures were made of the simultaneous vocal and facial emotional expressions of 50 Ss. Three sets of judges then attempted to identify the emotional meanings expressed by each S: (1) The first set of judges based their judgments on the vocal expressions obtained from the sound track of the film; (2) the second set based their judgments on viewing the facial expressions recorded on the film itself, without the sound track; and (3) the third set of judges simultaneously viewed the film and listened to the sound track, so that their judgments were based on both facial and vocal expressions. The hypotheses were then tested in terms of the accuracy with which each set of judges identified the emotional meaning expressed by each S on the basis of the sound track, the film itself, or the simultaneous sound film.

Subjects

The Ss who expressed emotional meanings recorded on the sound film were 25 male and 25 female graduate students enrolled in a general educational psychology course at Teachers College, Columbia University. The sample included only Caucasian Ss whose native language was English, and who reported no speech or hearing deficiencies, neurological defects, or gross physical handicaps. The age range in this sample was from 20 to 39 years.

Judges

The judges who identified the emotional meanings were 12 males and 12 females, ranging in age from 21 to 37 years, and were also graduate students at Teachers College selected on the basis of the same criteria established for selecting Ss whose expressions were judged.

Procedure

Sound Film Recordings. The emotional expressions were recorded by an 8-millimeter motion picture sound camera. The head and shoulders of each S were photographed in full face view, and, of course, microphone, camera, and lighting conditions were identical for all Ss throughout the collection of data.

In a brief interview immediately preceding the collection of data, the general procedure was explained to each S. A questionnaire was completed to provide a record of age, sex, area of geographical origin, and ethnic background. An estimate of verbal intelligence was obtained by means of a 40-item vocabulary test (Thorndike, 1942).

Each S was first asked to read a content-standard paragraph, similar to that used by Beldoch (Chapter 3) and Levy (Chapter 4), in a normal, conversational tone, without trying to express any particular emotional meaning. The stimulus paragraph was, "I'm going out now. I won't be back today. If anyone calls, take a message." To obviate memorization, these sentences were printed on a 2 by 3-foot card mounted on a tripod next to the camera.

After reading the stimulus paragraph in a presumably neutral fashion, Ss were instructed to read the sentences six more times, each time expressing both vocally and facially one of the following: joy, surprise, fear, disgust, anger, and contempt. To define each category of emotional meaning more fully for the Ss, descriptions of various situations in which a particular emotion might typically be experienced were presented. For example, the situation described for joy was as follows: "Imagine that you have just received a letter informing you that you have won $100,000 on the Irish sweepstakes. You had never won anything before, let alone so huge a sum of money. You're simply floating in a dream of joy, picturing the new clothes you're going to buy, the car, home, and trip to Europe."

The order in which the six kinds of emotional meaning were expressed was varied randomly among the 50 Ss. Each expression required approximately 10 to 15 seconds, so that the data for each S were recorded on somewhat less than 2 minutes of sound film.

Judgments. The basic problem of this research involved the comparison of individuals' abilities to *express* emotional meanings vocally and facially. Obviously any measure of expressiveness must involve the total communication process, which is comprised of both sending and receiving messages. It was therefore reasoned that the most appropriate measure of an individual's expressive ability was the accuracy with which other persons recognized the emotional meanings the individual intended to convey. That is, by definition, judges would tend to recognize and identify accurately the intended emotional expressions of a person with a high degree of expressive ability; while in contrast, judges would be relatively unable to identify correctly the intended emotional meanings of a person with low expressive ability. Thus an S's expressive ability was estimated by the number of correct identifications made by judges observing his emotional expressions.

The definition of expressive ability in terms of accuracy of judgments reflects the inextricable relationship between the expressive and receptive aspects of the communication process, for the information value of a given expression is a function of the accuracy with which others receive that information. For the purposes of this research, therefore, an S's expressive ability was operationally defined by the number of judges who correctly identified each of his six emotional expressions.

The hypotheses of this study involved comparisons of three modes of communication, vocal, facial, and simultaneous vocal-facial expressions. To obtain measures in each mode, three groups of judges were established: (1) group 1 based their judgments only on listening to the sound track of the film, which of course recorded the vocal expressions; (2) group 2 based their judgments only on watching the film itself, which recorded the facial expressions; and (3) group 3 based their judgments on the simultaneous vocal and facial expressions recorded by both the sound track and the film.

The 12 male and 12 female judges were divided randomly into the three judging groups, stratifying the random selection so that each group was comprised of four male and four female judges. The judges in each group were given the list of six emotional meanings expressed by each S. They were told that each S would first be presented as if he were in normal conversation, to give the judges an opportunity to hear the S's voice or see his face in a relatively neutral situation, but on each successive trial for that S he would be expressing one of the six emotional meanings. The judges were informed that an S might express any particular meaning once, more than once, or not at all, and their task as judges was to identify the emotion intended by each expression.

Operational Definition of Expressive Ability. For each S, an accuracy of expression score was defined operationally by the number of times judges correctly identified his intended emotional meaning in each mode of communication. That is, every expression of each S was scored on the basis of the number of judges who correctly identified the intended emotional meaning. For example, if an S intended to express anger, and five of the eight judges who listened to his vocal expression identified it as anger, the S's score for that vocal item was 5. On the other hand, if an S intended to express joy, and only three of the eight judges who viewed his facial expression identified it as joy, his score for that facial item was 3. In each mode of communication, vocal, facial, and simultaneous vocal-facial, an S's score on a particular expression could range from 0 to 8, and over the six expressions within each mode, the S's score could range from 0 to 48.

Comparability and Reliability of Judges. Although the hypotheses concerned expressive variables, the operational definition of these variables was in terms of judgments made in response to the expressions. It was therefore necessary to establish an empirical basis for interpreting the results in terms of individual differences among Ss in their expressive abilities rather than in terms which reflected differences among judges. Within each mode of communication, vocal or facial, the same group of judges identified the expressions of all 50 Ss. Therefore, in so far as the eight judges in each group are concerned, the individual differences in accuracy of communication within each mode can reasonably be interpreted as a valid reflection of differences in the expressive abilities of the 50 Ss. But in addition, it was also desirable to establish some empirical support for the assumption that the three groups of judges were sampled from the same population. To test this assumption, at least indirectly, the judges were first required to identify a random sample of 25 expressions in each mode of communication; that is, vocal, facial, and simultaneous vocal-facial expressions. The means and standard deviations of these sample judgments shown in Table 7-1 indicate that the three groups performed at about the same level

Table 7-1. Means and Standard Deviations of Judges on Twenty-five Sample Items in Three Communicative Modes

Group	N	Vocal Mean	SD	Facial Mean	SD	Vocal-Facial Mean	SD
Group I (vocal)	8	10.8	1.4	14.9	1.5	11.6	1.9
Group II (facial)	8	11.8	3.5	15.9	1.8	11.4	2.1
Group III (vocal-facial)	8	10.9	2.5	15.4	2.3	12.1	2.0

of accuracy in each mode; and an analysis of variance presented in Table 7-2 revealed no statistically significant differences among the three groups. The data therefore provide indirect support of the comparability of the three groups of judges.

Table 7–2. Analysis of Variance of Judges' Scores of Sample Items in Three Modes of Expression

Mode	Source of variation	df	Sum of squares	Mean square	F	p
Vocal	Between groups	2	4.74	2.37	.31	> .05
	Within groups	21	161.88	7.71		
Facial	Between groups	2	4.00	2.00	.51	> .05
	Within groups	21	81.62	3.89		
Vocal-Facial	Between groups	2	2.58	1.29	.20	> .05
	Within groups	21	132.75	6.32		

Reliability of judges was estimated by comparing scores for all 50 Ss based on four randomly selected judges with scores based on the other four judges in each group. As shown in Table 7-3, these reliability co-

Table 7-3. Split-half Reliability of Judges in Three Modes of Expression

Mode	Mean A	Mean B	SD A	SD B	Reliability coefficient[a]
Vocal	11.46	10.94	3.24	3.20	.67
Facial	13.74	12.96	4.24	3.26	.69
Vocal-Facial	13.80	14.60	3.64	3.76	.82

[a] All coefficients corrected with Spearman-Brown prophecy formula.

efficients are not high by psychometric standards, but appear to be adequate for the purposes of this research.

RESULTS

Relationship of Vocal and Facial Expressive Abilities

The range, mean, and standard deviation of expressive scores in the vocal and facial modes are shown in Table 7-4. The first hypothesis,

Table 7-4. Means and Standard Deviations of Expressive Scores

Mode	Range	Mean	SD
Vocal	7–35	22.44	5.60
Facial	15–42	27.12	6.70

Maximum possible score = 48.

which predicts a positive relationship between vocal and facial expressive abilities, was tested by means of a product moment correlation. The value obtained was .35, which is significantly different from zero beyond the .02 level. Thus, while the correlation is relatively low the data provide some support for the central hypothesis of the study. It is reasonable to conclude, therefore, that persons who are able to express emotional meanings vocally also tend to be able to express these meanings facially, though it must also be emphasized that less than 15 per cent of the variance in the two ability measures is accounted for by the correlation obtained in the present sample.

Comparative Accuracy of Communication in the Three Modes

The second and third hypotheses dealt with the relative accuracy of communication in vocal, facial, and simultaneous vocal-facial modes. To assess the accuracy of communication in each mode, the number of correct identifications made by each judge over all 50 Ss was computed. Since each judge attempted to identify six expressions for each of the 50 Ss, a judge's score could range from 0 to 300. To test the second and third hypotheses, the scores of judges in the three groups were compared to each other.

As shown in Table 7-5, an analysis of variance revealed differences among the three groups which are statistically significant beyond the .01

Table 7-5. Analysis of Variance of Scores on Three Modes of Expression

Source of variation	df	Sum of squares	Mean square	SD	F
Between groups	2	6123	3061.5		7.18*
Within groups	21	8959	426.6	20.65	

* Significant at .01.

level ($F = 7.18$). In order to test the specific predictions about the nature of the differences among the three groups, the differences between the group means, shown in Table 7-6, were examined by Scheffé's method.

The second hypothesis, which predicts that communication in the vocal mode is more accurate than that in the facial mode, was clearly not supported. In fact, the results were statistically significant in the direction opposite to that predicted; in the present sample, at least, emotional meanings were communicated much more accurately in the facial mode.

Table 7-6. Differences between Means of Judging Groups in Three Modes of Communication

Variable	Facial	Vocal-Facial	Vocal
Vocal			
Mean = 140.25	29.25*		
SD = 22.85			
Facial			
Mean = 169.50	. . .	7.88	
SD = 14.77			
Vocal-Facial			
Mean = 177.38	. . .	. . .	37.13*
SD = 19.47			

* Significant beyond .05.

The third hypothesis, which predicts that communication in the simultaneous vocal-facial mode is more accurate than in either mode considered independently, was only partially supported by the data. While emotional meanings were indeed communicated more accurately in the simultaneous vocal-facial mode than in the vocal mode alone ($p < .05$), the difference between simultaneous vocal-facial communication and facial alone was not statistically significant. In view of the results obtained in comparing vocal versus facial communication, it seems most reasonable to account for the relative superiority of the simultaneous vocal-facial mode, in comparison to the vocal mode alone, primarily as a function of the information provided by the facial expressions.

Additional Analyses

Table 7-7 summarizes the data on expressive ability for the 25 male and 25 female Ss. As indicated in the table, none of the differences in expressive ability between males and females in any of the three modes is statistically significant.

Table 7-7. Sex Differences in Emotional Expressive Ability

	Mean				
Mode	Male ($N = 25$)	Female ($N = 25$)	SD	t	p
Vocal	26.12	27.68	5.62	.23	> .05
Facial	22.92	21.64	6.79	.82	> .05
Vocal-Facial	29.16	27.48	6.80	.88	> .05

During the course of the experiment, scores for 29 *S*s were obtained on the Raven's Progressive Matrices, a measure of abstract intellectual ability previously found to be positively related to the ability to identify emotional meanings (Chapter 5). For all *S*s, data on age were recorded, and for 49 *S*s, scores on the 40-item vocabulary test developed by Thorndike (1942) were obtained. Product moment correlations were computed between the measures of expressive ability and age, vocabulary scores, and scores on the Progressive Matrices. As shown in Table 7-8, only one of the nine correlations was significantly different from

Table 7-8. Correlation Coefficients

Variable	*N*	M	SD		Expressive mode Vocal-Facial	Vocal-Facial
Age	50	28.52	5.24	−.01	−.12	−.06
Vocabulary	49	29.28	3.68	.07	.20	.28*
Raven	29	54.38	3.32	−.08	.15	.33

* Significant at .05 (two-tailed test).

zero (simultaneous vocal-facial expression by verbal intelligence), but in view of the likelihood of obtaining by chance one out of nine correlations at a statistically significant level, this result can be interpreted most reasonably as a chance finding.

The comparative effectiveness of communication of each emotion in each expressive mode was computed in terms of the number and per cent of correct identifications of each emotion. The results, summarized in Table 7-9, show that not only were there decided differences in the

Table 7-9. Number and Percentage of Correct Judgments of Each Feeling in Each Mode (400 = 100 Per Cent)

Emotion	Vocal Number	Per Cent	Facial Number	Per Cent	Vocal-Facial Number	Per Cent
Joy	168	42.00	343	85.75	325	81.25
Surprise	165	41.25	173	43.25	206	51.50
Fear	297	74.25	233	58.25	292	73.00
Disgust	136	34.00	209	52.25	206	51.50
Anger	223	55.75	250	62.50	243	60.75
Contempt	133	33.25	148	37.00	147	36.75
Total	1,122	46.75	1,356	56.50	1,419	59.13

effectiveness with which the different emotions were communicated but the degree of adequacy of communication of any specific emotion varied with the communicative mode as well. For example, joy, surprise, anger, and contempt were communicated more accurately in the facial mode, but fear was communicated much more accurately in the vocal mode. In fact, fear was the most accurately communicated category of emotional meaning in the vocal mode, while joy was clearly the category most accurately communicated in the facial mode.

DISCUSSION

Perhaps the most striking aspect of the present study, in contrast to previous experiments, is its clear-cut demonstration that emotional meanings can be communicated via the facial mode with a high degree of specificity. Previous researchers have varied in their opinions about whether or not facial expressions can serve as an effective mode of emotional communication. Undoubtedly the most pessimistic view is represented by Landis (1924a), who proposed that there is no consistent relationship between facial expression and specific feelings (1924b; 1929a; 1929b). Other researchers have also suggested that facial expression does not reliably communicate emotional meanings (Fernberger, 1928).

In view of the conclusions of the above investigators the results of the present experiment are somewhat remarkable, for the judges correctly identified over 56 per cent of the facial expressions, while on the basis of chance alone one would have expected only 17 per cent of the judgments to have been correct. It is obvious, therefore, that in the present study facial expressions served as a basis for accurate communication at a level far beyond chance expectation.

The discrepancy between the present findings and earlier ones probably can be accounted for in terms of the differences in experimental techniques. This study employed motion pictures to record facial expressions while most previous studies utilized either still photographs, models, or drawings. These latter devices are likely to eliminate nuances of expression, such as the rate of movement or the rhythm of facial changes over time that can be captured only by motion picture recordings. Thus the null results of the past may well have been a function of inadequate experimental techniques, and certainly the results of the present study would encourage the utilization of motion pictures in further investigations of facial expressions.

The results of this study lends credence to the assumption that a general factor underlies various aspects of behavior involved in emotional communication. The correlation between vocal and facial expressive abilities is indeed low, but nevertheless positive and significantly different from zero. Thus, the results of this research are consistent with the findings of Beldoch (Chapter 3) and Levy (Chapter 4), both of whom found relatively low but positive correlations among a variety of aspects of emotional communication. Beldoch found that the abilities to perceive emotional meanings expressed through several modes are interrelated; Levy found that the abilities to express and to judge vocal communications are positively related; and the present study demonstrated that expressive abilities in at least two modes go together. In almost all instances, the correlations are low, but they are consistently positive and statistically significant from zero.

If there is a general factor underlying emotional communication, how can this factor best be described and investigated? Several avenues of speculation suggest themselves. Beldoch, for example, has proposed that emotional communication can be conceptualized as a symbolic process involving symbols that Langer (1942, 1953) called "nondiscursive." If this is valid, further research designed to describe this general factor might well focus on symbolic abilities. Another possibility, not inconsistent with the symbolic approach, concerns the possible physiological or innate basis of a general ability to express and perceive emotional communication. Diamond (1957) has pointed out that babies differ widely from one another in various dimensions of temperament, manifested by individual differences in general level of sensitivity to stimulation and activity, characteristic response to frustration, amount of crying, tempo of sucking, intensity and duration of response to startle, readiness of smiling, and quality of response to disturbances. Perhaps these temperamental, and presumably innate, physiological differences are reflected in later differences in emotional expressiveness and sensitivity.

A third way of conceptualizing the possible nature of a general factor underlying the ability to communicate emotions is in terms of attitudes or values. People who are particularly interested in feelings, for one reason or another, may tend to focus a greater degree of attention on emotional communication, more readily learn the cues or symbols associated with emotional expression in a variety of modes, and, when called upon to express feelings, be more knowledgeable about the most effective manner in which to communicate specific feelings.

The data of the present study offer no compelling clues to the most rewarding avenue of further investigation of this particular problem, but obviously people differ in their ability to communicate emotional meanings and this study provides additional evidence that some part of these individual differences is common to various aspects of emotional communication. The task of further research is to account for the common variance, perhaps in terms of symbolic abilities, physiological characteristics, or attitudinal variables.

Despite some support of a general factor theory, only a small part of the variance in emotional communication can be accounted for by such a factor. The correlation obtained between vocal and facial expressive ability was only .35. By far the greater amount of variance in these two communicative modes is independent. Beldoch and Levy similarly reported positive but low correlations. As in Spearman's theory of intelligence, though it seems reasonable to postulate a general factor accounting for the common variance in emotional communication, the data also require the hypothesis of specific factors or abilities involved in specific aspects of communication. In fact, these specific factors undoubtedly account for a greater part of the variance among individuals. There appear to be people who are primarily facial expressors, others who are more adequate in the vocal mode, and still others who are equally adept in one or the other mode. Therefore, while further research may well be concerned with the commonality of abilities to communicate, perhaps even more important, at least in terms of the amount of variance accounted for, is the investigation of specific abilities involved in different kinds of emotional communication.

The prediction that feelings are more accurately communicated vocally than facially was not supported. These two modes had not previously been examined together, and the hypothesis was based on previous studies which reported equivocal support of facial expression as a mode of communicating feeling, but offered clear-cut evidence of the effectiveness of vocal communication. If the earlier negative findings related to facial communication were indeed a function of inadequate techniques used to record expression, the prediction of vocal superiority was based on faulty experimental evidence. At least in the present sample, using expressions recorded by motion pictures, facial communication was distinctly more effective than vocal communication. This part of the study certainly requires replication since the finding was statistically significant but unpredicted.

It was anticipated that simultaneous vocal-facial communication would be more effective than communication in either one of the other two modes. This prediction was only partially supported. Vocal-facial communication, while superior to vocal communication, was not more effective than facial communication alone. In view of the results, it seems likely that the facial component was primarily responsible for the superiority of vocal-facial over vocal communication. The potency of the facial mode is further supported by the fact that in four out of six emotional meanings communicated, facial expression alone communicated with slightly greater accuracy than the combined vocal-facial mode. The overall differences between these modes for the present sample is not statistically reliable, but the findings at least warrant further exploration of the optimum amount and kind of information needed for accurate communication. Perhaps the vocal cues in the vocal-facial mode contributed more noise than information to the communicative channel, and other types of cues, such as situational or postural information, might be combined with facial expression as an efficient means of communication.

A number of post hoc analyses of the data were made. Comparisons of the male and female subjects in the present sample do not support the assumption that women are more accurate expressors of emotion than are men. The correlation between verbal intelligence and accuracy of communication in the combined vocal-facial mode was statistically significant, but this was the only one of nine post hoc correlations that attained statistical significance and can be accounted for most reasonably as a chance finding. None of the other correlations involving measures of intelligence and ability to express emotional meanings was statistically significant. Therefore, intelligence, as measured either by a vocabulary test or Raven's Progressive Matrices, probably is independent of expressiveness.

Specific categories of emotional meaning were not communicated with the same degree of accuracy in the two modes studied. For example, ranking the six categories expressed in each mode from most to least accurately communicated, joy ranked highest in the facial mode and third in the vocal mode, and fear ranked first in the vocal mode and third in facial communication. Fear was the only emotion more accurately judged in the vocal than the facial mode. Apparently some emotional meanings are more easily communicated in one mode than in another. This may be a consequence of certain conventional and obvious cues associated with the expression of a particular feeling in a given mode. Joy, for example, was uniformly expressed facially by a smile; the vocal expression of fear was typically characterized by stammering, hesitance, irregularity of word spacing and rhythm, and a strained, breathy quality. These observations, however, merely offer a description of the specific data of this study and do not provide a rationale accounting for the differential accuracy with which feelings are communicated in particular modes. If further research substantiates this finding, the nature of the relationship between particular emotional meanings and various modes of communication presents an important problem for a general theory of communication.

SUMMARY

There has been widespread research in the past dealing with the efficiency of judgment of vocal and facial communication of emotion. More recently, interest has been manifested in the relationship between the abilities to identify emotional meanings expressed in various modes and the relationship between expressive and perceptive abilities in the vocal mode. There has been no previous investigation in which the vocal and facial modes of emotional communication have been examined together. As its primary purpose, this study undertook to assess the relationship between vocal and facial emotional expressive abilities. In addition, the study examined the comparative communicative efficiency of the vocal, facial, and combined vocal-facial modes.

Sound motion picture recordings were made of 50 Ss' portrayals of six emotions through both their voices and facial expressions. Judges, taken from the same population, were randomly divided into three groups. These were designated the vocal, facial, and vocal-facial groups. An analysis of sample judgments by all the judges in all three modes indicated that they were of comparable judging ability. Reliability coefficients ranging between .67 and .82 demonstrated that judging ability in the three modes under examination were statistically reliable. Additional data were obtained in the form of estimates of intelligence as measured by a vocabulary test and a test of abstract ability.

A significant correlation was found between vocal and facial emotional expressive abilities. A comparison of the comparative accuracy of communication through the three modes showed that emotional meanings were more effectively communicated facially than vocally. Vocal-facial communication, while superior to vocal communication, was not more effective than facial communication alone. No significant sex differences were found in expressive abilities. While verbal intelligence was positively correlated with vocal-facial expressive ability, no significant relationship was found between verbal intelligence or abstract ability and either the vocal or facial modes of expression.

The results were discussed in terms of the assumption that a general factor underlies different behaviors involved in emotional communication. Possibilities were advanced regarding the description of such a hypothesized general factor; namely, symbolic, physiological, or attitudinal in nature. Since the experimental data showed that only a small part of the variance in emotional communication could be accounted for by a general factor, it was postulated that there are also specific factors involved in specific aspects or modes of communication.

8

Auditory correlates of vocal expressions of emotional meanings

Joel R. Davitz

The research presented in this chapter investigated some of the auditory cues associated with/vocal expressions of emotional meaning. To investigate this problem, two sets of variables were selected, one set concerned with dimensions of emotional meaning, and a second concerned with auditory characteristics of speech. The variables of emotional meaning were based on Osgood, Suci, and Tannenbaum's (1957) research, which suggested three aspects of emotional meaning: (1) valence, (2) strength, and (3) activity. Selection of speech variables was based on the characteristics of sound commonly considered in psychophysical studies of audition: (1) loudness, (2) pitch, (3) timbre, and (4) rate of speech. The research considered the relation between each of the three variables of emotional meaning, valence, strength, and activity, and each of the four speech variables of loudness, pitch, timbre, and rate.

METHOD

Four female and three male speakers each expressed 14 different feelings by content-standard speech, using a method originated by Ortleb (1937) and utilized by Fairbanks and Pronevost (1939). To standardize content of the expression, the same two sentences, in terms of content, were embedded in 14 different paragraphs, each paragraph designed to express one of the 14 feelings. The speakers read aloud each paragraph, trying to express the particular feeling with which the paragraph was concerned. In addition, the speakers also read one paragraph containing the standard sentences in a nonemotional "normal conversation" context. These readings were tape recorded, and then the readings of the two sentences identical in content for all paragraphs were taken out of context and spliced so as to provide a recording of different emotional expressions with standard content.

The 14 feelings expressed were: (1) admiration, (2) affection, (3) amusement, (4) anger, (5) boredom, (6) cheerfulness, (7) despair, (8) disgust, (9) dislike, (10) fear, (11) impatience, (12) joy, (13) satisfaction, and (14) surprise. Based on data of a previous study (Davitz and Davitz, 1959b), these feelings were selected with the aim of providing as wide a range as possible on each of the three dimensions of emotional meaning, valence, strength, and activity.

The two sentences used to express each of the feelings were: "There is no other answer. You've asked me that question a thousand times and my reply has always been the same." Examples of paragraphs concerned with each of the feelings are:

Boredom. A high school teacher is just beginning his eleventh year teaching the same course, going through the same mechanics, repeating the same phrases. There will be two semesters to look forward to, interrupted by the same vacation days, the same football games, and worst of all, the same faces. He'll say, for the eleventh year in a row, "Shakespeare was a fine dramatist, and Thornton Wilder's works are modern classics," and the students will write the same notes in the same spiral notebooks. Thoroughly bored, he says:

"When I started it was exciting enough. But after ten years there isn't any enthusiasm anymore. The faces begin to look the same, the names begin to sound the same. I thought it wouldn't be so bad this year, the same bland little smiles, the 'Oh you're so intelligent teacher' looks, but when I started class today with the same joke I've been repeating the first day of class for ten years, I knew I'd had it. I know now the real meaning of boredom, plodding along. But I've got to do it. *There is no other answer. You've asked me that question a thousand times and my reply has always been the same.* Over and over again, year in and year out, the boredom of a lifetime."

Joy. This person has just received a check for 20 thousand dollars. He bought a lottery ticket without thinking much about it, and his number was pulled from a drum containing thousands and thousands of numbers. He walked to the stand, listened to the crowds go wild, and was so overjoyed himself that he forgot to go wild. But now, with the check delivered, he's just become aware of the great, overwhelming joy he feels and what the money means to him. He says:

"I won. I never won anything before in my life, not even a plaster piggy bank at a carnival. Twenty thousand dollars on a drawing, and just the perfect time for it. Look at this check. I don't even see the numbers. You know what I see? Europe, a car, no debts, some decent clothes, maybe a house. I'm going to spend and spend. *There is no other answer. You've asked me that question a thousand times and my reply has always been the same.* Spend, spend. Just once in a lifetime maybe, but it's the greatest thing that could happen to me."

Affection. Evening. The playroom is a shambles, but the little boy is immaculate, dressed for bed, hair still damp from his evening bath. Outside it is dark and the street is quiet. It's time to curl up on your son's bed for one hug, two hugs, and a dozen kisses. You feel deeply and warmly affectionate.

"Come on closer. Here, sit right here on my lap. I'll put my arms close around you and tell you a very, very small story with a very, very big meaning. You always ask "Why?" Why is a good word for any question except why I love you. The answer to that is just because I do. *There is no other answer. You've asked me that question a thousand times and my reply has always been the same.* I love you in the morning when you pull the covers off my bed, and I love you in the afternoon and at night just as you are now, sitting very still, with your hands in mine and your head on my shoulder."

The recordings of all seven speakers were judged by 20 persons who were given the list of 14 feelings and asked to identify the feeling expressed by each reading of the standard two sentences after hearing the nonemotional, "normal conversation" reading by each speaker. For each of the 14 feelings, the reading most frequently identified correctly was determined separately for the three male speakers (X, Y, and Z) and the four female speakers (A, B, C, and D). The final tape used for ratings of vocal characteristics consisted of the reading of each feeling identified most frequently for male speakers and for female speakers, plus the nonemotional "normal conversation" reading by each speaker. Thus, the vocal communication of a feeling was defined both by intent of the speaker and judgment of listeners. Although the standard two sentences were undoubtedly more consistent with the discursive context of some of the paragraphs than they were with others, the purpose of the research concerned the feelings expressed within each context. Therefore, the fact that speakers intended to express a given feeling, regardless of contextual effects, and the fact that a plurality of listeners identified the feeling intended without the discursive context, would seem to assure that each of the vocal items did indeed represent a communication of the specifically intended feeling. Table 8-1 presents a summary

Table 8-1. Percentage of Correct Identifications of the Expressions of Each Feeling

Feeling	Male speakers Per cent correct		Female speakers Per cent correct	
	Speaker	Identification	Speaker	Identification
Admiration	Y	25	D	30
Affection	Z	60	D	75
Amusement	Z	90	A	95
Anger	X	80	C	90
Boredom	Y	75	C	95
Cheerfulness	Y	45	D	45
Despair	Y	100	B	100
Disgust	Z	60	A	55
Dislike	Z	50	D	45
Fear	Z	90	D	100
Impatience	X	100	C	75
Joy	Z	55	D	60
Satisfaction	Y	35	B	50
Surprise	Y	60	C	55

of the data for the 28 items selected, indicating for each feeling the male and female speakers whose readings were identified correctly most frequently. The percentage of correct identifications could have occurred by chance once in a thousand times, and although there were differences among speakers in the number of times their readings were contained in the final tape, for both males and females, each speaker was represented at least twice.

Vocal Characteristics. The final tape was played to a second set of 20 judges who were asked to rate each expression on four seven-point scales dealing with: (1) loudness (loud to soft); (2) pitch (high to low); (3) timbre (blaring to resonant); and (4) rate of speech (fast to slow). A speaker's expression of a given feeling was played twice, each time followed by a recording of that speaker's nonemotional, "normal conversation," which served as the base line against which the emotional expression was rated.

For example, the timbre of a speaker's expression of anger was judged on the following scale: (1) much more blaring than base speech; (2) more blaring than base speech; (3) a bit more blaring than base speech; (4) about the same as base speech; (5) a bit more resonant than base speech; (6) more resonant than base speech; (7) much more resonant than base speech. Similar scales were used to rate loudness, pitch, and timbre. In every instance, all expressions were rated on one variable; then, the entire tape was replayed, and the expressions rated on a second variable, etc. Of the 20 judges, however, four sets of five judges each rated the vocal characteristics of the expressions in a different order. For example, one set of judges first rated pitch, then rate, loudness, and finally timbre. Reliability of the judgments was estimated by comparing the sum of ratings of 10 judges, randomly selected, on each dimension with the sum of ratings of the other 10 judges. For the four vocal characteristics, the product moment correlations were: (1) loudness, r was .93; (2) pitch, r was .91; (3) timbre, r was .86; (4) rate, r was .91.

Dimensions of Emotional Meaning. The paragraphs dealing with the 14 different feelings were rated on nine scales of the Semantic Differential by a third set of 20 judges. Each of the three dimensions defined by Osgood, et al. (1957) was represented by three scales: valence, by (1) good-bad, (2) pleasant-unpleasant, (3) beautiful-ugly; strength, by (1) strong-weak, (2) large-small, (3) heavy-light; activity, by (1) fast-slow, (2) active-passive, and (3) sharp-dull. The mean ratings of the 20 judges for each feeling on the three scales representing each dimension were summed, and these scores operationally defined the three aspects of meaning. Reliability of the judgments was estimated by comparing the sum of ratings of 10 judges on each dimension with the sum of ratings of the other 10 judges. For each of the three dimensions, the product moment correlations were: (1) valence, r was .94; (2) strength, r was .85; (3) activity, r was .90.

For valence, the rank order of feelings, from most positive to most negative was: joy, affection, cheerfulness, admiration, satisfaction, amusement, surprise, boredom, impatience, dislike, disgust, despair, fear, anger. For strength, the rank order of feelings, from strongest to weakest was: despair, anger, joy, fear, affection, disgust, dislike, cheerfulness, satisfaction, admiration, boredom, impatience, amusement, surprise. For activity, the rank order from most active to most passive was: fear, anger, joy, dislike, disgust, cheerfulness, surprise, impatience, amusement, admiration, satisfaction, affection, boredom, despair.

RESULTS

The data were analyzed by correlating each of the dimensions of emotional meaning, valence, strength, and activity, with each of the vocal characteristics of speech, loudness, rate, pitch, and timbre. Inspection of the scatter plots revealed that activity was positively and linearly related to the speech variables, but both valence and strength appeared to be related curvilinearly, if at all, to the speech variables. Therefore, product moment correlations were computed for the activity dimension, and correlation ratios were computed for the valence and strength dimensions.

The correlation of activity with each speech variable was statistically significant: (1) Activity $\times$ loudness, $r = .84$, $p < .01$; (2) Activity $\times$ pitch, $r = .59$, $p < .01$; (3) Activity $\times$ timbre, $r = .76$, $p < .01$; (4) Activity $\times$ rate, $r = .88$, $p < .01$.

The correlation ratios between valence and each of the speech variables did not attain statistical significance; (1) Valence $\times$ loudness, $\eta = .39$, $p > .05$; (2) Valence $\times$ pitch, $\eta = .59$, $p > .05$; (3) Valence $\times$ timbre, $\eta = .53$, $p > .05$; (4) Valence $\times$ rate, $\eta = .61$, $p > .05$. Similarly, the correlation ratios between strength and the speech variables did not attain statistical significance: (1) Strength $\times$ loudness, $\eta = .29$, $p > .05$; (2) Strength $\times$ pitch, $\eta = .46$; $p > .05$. (3) Strength $\times$ timbre, $\eta = .38$, $p > .05$. (4) Strength $\times$ rate, $\eta = .34$, $p > .05$. Although the correlation ratios obtained indicate curvilinear relations between valence and strength and the four speech variables, the magnitudes of the ratios do not permit generalization beyond the present data.

The pattern of vocal characteristics of the emotional expressions was essentially the same for male and female speakers. This is shown by the correlations between ratings of male and female expressions on each of the speech variables over the 14 different feelings: (1) loudness, $r = .85$, $p < .01$; (2) pitch, $r = .76$, $p < .01$; (3) timbre, $r = .81$, $p < .01$; (4) rate, $r = .74$, $p < .01$. These results, of course, do not mean that the pitch of female speech, for example, is the same as that of male speech, but rather that the relative pitch, and other speech characteristics, varied over the 14 emotional expressions in about the same way for males as for females.

As indicated in Table 8-1, there were individual differences among the feelings in the number of times they were communicated accurately. It was possible, therefore, that these differences in accuracy might have influenced the results obtained in relating vocal characteristics to dimensions of emotional meaning. Therefore, the relationship between accuracy of communication, as indicated by the per cent of correct identification in Table 8-1, and each dimension of emotional meaning, and each of the speech variables, was investigated by computing product moment correlations. None of these correlations differed significantly from zero, which is consistent with a previously reported study in this area (Davitz & Davitz, 1959b). Therefore, differences in accuracy of communication cannot account for the results obtained in relating dimensions of emotional meaning to vocal characteristics of speech.

AN ANALYSIS OF ERRORS IN IDENTIFICATION OF EMOTIONAL EXPRESSIONS

In previous research, errors in identification seemed to follow a consistent pattern in that incorrect judgments about the expression of a given feeling usually clustered in terms of relatively few other feelings. For example, despair was mistakenly identified as affection or boredom much more often than as anger or joy. Similarly, fear was mistakenly identified as joy or anger much more often than as admiration or despair.

Although little is known about errors in emotional communication, the results of one study which investigated the patterning of such errors (Davitz & Davitz, 1959b) demonstrate that subjective similarity of two feelings, as rated by judges, is positively related to the frequency with which the feelings are mistaken for each other. However, "subjective similarity" is a vague, ill-defined variable, and the results of the initial study reported in this paper suggest a possible refinement of this variable in terms of a particular dimension of emotional meaning. Specifically, the results of the first study indicate that major vocal characteristics of emotional expression are a function primarily of the subjectively rated activity level of the feeling communicated. This suggests that errors in identification are a function of subjective similarity of rated activity level of the feelings concerned rather than similarity of either valence or strength. Thus, despair is mistaken more often for affection than for anger as a consequence of the greater similarity in rated activity levels of despair and affection in comparison to despair and anger.

These considerations led to the hypothesis that erroneous judgments of vocal expressions of feeling are more similar to the feeling intended in terms of activity than in terms of either valence or strength.

METHOD

The tape recording of emotional expression described in the first study, consisting of 28 items, the expression of 14 different feelings by male speakers and the same 14 feelings expressed by female speakers, was played to 16 listeners who were provided with the list of feelings and asked to identify each expression.

Ratings of the 14 feelings on the three dimensions of emotional meaning, valence, strength, and activity, were transformed into standard scores. Listeners' errors in identification were determined. For each error, and for each dimension of emotional meaning, difference scores were computed between the feeling intended by the speaker and the listener's erroneous judgment. For example, the standard scores for despair were: (1) valence, 62.1; (2) strength, 32.1; (3) activity, 70.2. For satisfaction, the scores were: (1) valence, 44.2; (2) strength, 57.1; (3) activity, 55.1. Thus, if the speaker intended despair and a listener erroneously judged the expression as satisfaction, the difference scores for that item were: (1) valence, 17.9; (2) strength, 25.0; (3) activity, 15.1. According to the hypothesis, the difference scores for activity are less than the difference scores for either valence or strength.

RESULTS

Mean difference scores for the 16 listeners for all errors over the 28 items and for each dimension of emotional meaning were computed. The mean difference score for valence was 306.7, SD = 54.8; for strength, $\overline{X}$ = 295.5, SD = 52.1; for activity, $\overline{X}$ = 228.5, SD = 50.3. The difference between means for valence and strength was not statistically significant, t = .65, p > .05. However, the difference between means for valence and activity, in the direction hypothesized, was statistically significant, t = 4.2, p < .01; and the difference between means for strength and activity, also in the direction predicted, was statistically significant, t = 3.8, p < .01. Thus, the hypothesis was supported by the data.

DISCUSSION

The results of this research support the following generalization: *In the vocal communication of emotional meanings, auditory cues of loudness, pitch, timbre, and rate are a function of the subjectively rated activity level of the feeling communicated.* This generalization summarizes the results of the first research reported, and accounts, at least in part, for the pattern of errors found in identification of the emotional meanings of vocal expressions.

Failure to obtain statistically significant relationships between valence and strength and each of the auditory variables cannot be accounted for by unreliability of measurement, for the internal consistency of each set of ratings used was sufficiently high for the purposes of this study. Moreover, differences in accuracy cannot account for the results. It would seem, therefore, that the activity aspect of emotional meaning is carried by the relatively simpler elements of the vocal symbol, such as pitch and loudness, while both valence and strength are probably communicated by subtler, and perhaps more complex, vocal patterns of inflection, rhythm, etc.

Obviously there is some semantic overlap between the scales used to define emotional meaning and the scales used to define vocal characteristics. The clearest instance concerns one of the scales in the Semantic Differential which defined activity, i.e., fast-slow, and the scale used to describe rate of speech, which also ranged from fast to slow. This overlap, however, cannot account for the results obtained. In the first place, judges who rated the speech variables were independent of those who rated the feelings, and knew nothing about that aspect of the research concerned with dimensions of emotional meaning. They were merely told to listen to each recitation and describe the speech in terms of one of the vocal characteristics. But more important than this precaution is the fact that semantic overlap between the two sets of rating scales does not account for the null results obtained or for the positive results other than the relation between activity and rate of speech. That is, ratings of loudness, for example, were obtained on a scale ranging from *loud* to *soft*. Osgood, et al. (1957) report that the factor loading on the loud-soft scale is heaviest in terms of the strength dimension. Therefore, if semantic overlap could account for the results, one would expect loudness to correlate primarily with strength of the feeling expressed, and not necessarily with the activity level. A similar argument holds for the high-low scale of pitch and the blaring-resonant scale for timbre. Thus, semantic overlap of scales cannot account for the results obtained; in fact, the results clearly contradict this possibility.

The results of this research emphasize the significance of activity level as an important dimension of emotional meaning, perhaps in contrast to more usual considerations of feeling in terms of valence and strength. Feelings are frequently characterized as pleasant or unpleasant, strong or weak, but less often described as active or passive. But it is the activity dimension of emotional meaning which is consistently related to major auditory cues of vocal expression, and also accounts for a large part of the variance in errors of communication.

Notwithstanding the importance of the activity dimension of emotional meaning, as Schlosberg (1954) and Osgood, et al. (1957) suggest, valence and strength also contribute to the definition of a particular emotional message. Unfortunately, the present study did not discover the specific auditory cues associated with these dimensions of meaning, though repeated hearings of the vocal recordings did suggest to the experimenter some possible leads for further study. For example, the rhythm of speech, a fairly subtle but nevertheless distinguishable auditory cue, seemed more or less consistently related to valence. In so far as the experimenter's informal judgment was concerned, positive feelings tended to be expressed with somewhat more regular rhythms than were negative feelings. Moreover, expressions of positive feelings, in comparison to negative feelings, seemed to be more often characterized by relatively regular, rather than irregular, inflections or changes in pitch. However, these are merely informal observations and serve only as leads for further research.

Although this research has defined some of the characteristics associated with vocal expressions of particular kinds of emotional meaning, it is obvious that these data cannot serve as a general dictionary of vocal, emotional communication. The most apparent limitations in this regard concern the small number of speakers and the relatively simple vocal characteristics considered. But perhaps even more important is the specificity of the categories of emotion. That is, the vocal expressions of affection, joy, anger, etc., were appropriate to the particular situations in which the emotions presumably were expressed. The emotional labels of anger, joy, etc., cover a range of concrete situations, and while the situations chosen to define each emotion were designed to be as obvious as possible, and thus facilitate communication, it is reasonable to expect that there are more or less subtle changes in expression of a given emotion as a function of different situations. A clear-cut illustration of these differences involves the expression of anger. In the situation defining anger for this study (an explosive argument), the description indicated that the anger in this case would be expressed freely. Thus, the loud, blaring speech of anger. But in another situation in which there might be some prohibition in directly expressing anger, anger might well be expressed by characteristics diametrically opposed to those found in the present study. In the latter case, anger could be conveyed by the extremely slow, sharply measured tones of a voice—in a sense, a kind of reaction formation to expression of anger in a free situation.

Undoubtedly, there are other kinds of emotional expressions one might cite to illustrate this reservation about establishing a dictionary of emotional expressions that would have widespread validity. Suffice to say that it is unlikely that such a dictionary could be established on the basis of relatively simple correlational studies. There is little question that the vocal expressions studied in this research did indeed communicate broad categories of emotional meaning but there is also little doubt that the full range of either emotions or expressions has been but partially sampled.

Despite these limitations, the findings in support of the significance of activity in determining emotional expression provide some basis for possibly useful speculation about the unlearned, innately determined aspects of emotional expression. In this study, active feelings were communicated by loud, blaring, high pitched, fast vocalizations. There is an interesting parallel here with the vocalizations emitted by infants. Consider the hungry infant just before feeding. Presumably, he is in a highly active state (at least in so far as one can infer reasonably from overt behavior), and his cries are likely to be loud, blaring, and high pitched —in these respects, not unlike the vocalizations of adults expressing active feelings. In contrast, after feeding and probably in a more passive state, if the infant emits any vocalizations, they generally tend to be relatively softer, more resonant, and lower pitched—once again, vocal characteristics paralleling those of adults expressing passive feelings. Certainly one must recognize the tentativeness of such speculations, but they do suggest that characteristics of emotional expressions directly associated with the activity dimension of emotional meaning are present in the infant and are probably unlearned, while the more subtle cues of inflection and intonation which carry emotional meaning in terms of valence and strength are likely to reflect culturally determined patterns of learning.[1]

SUMMARY

This research investigated the relation between each of three variables of emotional meaning, valence, strength, and activity, and each of four auditory vocal cues, loudness, pitch, timbre, and rate. Using content-standard speech and Semantic Differential ratings of 14 different feelings, the correlation between each dimension of emotional meaning and each of the auditory variables was obtained. The correlation of activity with each auditory variable was statistically significant. Because of the apparent curvilinear relation between valence and strength and the auditory variables, correlation ratios were computed; however, none of these ratios attained statistical significance.

Results of the first study led to the hypothesis that erroneous judgments of vocal expressions of feeling are more similar to the feeling intended in terms of activity than in terms of either valence or strength.

[1] Shortly after finishing the research reported in this chapter, the writer made one of his frequent visits to the local zoo. He was in the Lion House just before feeding time, and the animals, hungry and highly activated, were emitting vocalizations which could properly be called loud and blaring. After feeding, when the animals were in a clearly more passive state, the sounds gradually became softer and more resonant, obviously communicating satisfaction in much the same way as do highly civilized, human, adult speakers.

Transforming the Semantic Differential ratings into standard scores, listeners' errors in identification of content-standard expressions of feeling were determined. For each error, difference scores were computed between the feeling intended by the speaker and the listener's erroneous judgment for each dimension of emotional meaning. The results supported the hypothesis.

The data support the generalization that the loudness, pitch, timbre, and rate of speech are a function of the subjectively rated activity level of the feeling communicated. Presumably, valence and strength are communicated by other, perhaps more subtle and complex, auditory cues.

9

An ear for an eye: sensory compensation and judgments of affect by the blind

Sidney Blau

The idea that the blind have somehow been granted the gift of a "see-ing" ear has a long history (French, 1952). Literature and folklore are rich with references to the blind man who could perform unusual feats of hearing. The implication invariably is that a transposition of sensory modes has taken place, and that by some unknown but more merciful process, the law of talion has been amended. Instead of an eye for an eye, an ear has been made to *serve* for an eye.

The ancient Greeks believed that victims of blindness were bene-ficiaries of a "divine compensation." The gods blessed the blind with prophecy and poetry. Homer's blind minstrel is "the muse's beloved" to whom both evil and good had been granted.

Usually accompanying a belief in sensory compensation is the notion that the blind can see into the human heart and read the feelings of men with greater sensitivity than the sighted. Blind persons themselves fre-quently feel they understand people better because of their blindness (Voorhees, 1949). The blind poet, Milton, believed: "God took away outward sight to give inward vision" (Hanford, 1949).

Not until the turn of the century was any serious attempt made to establish the scientific validity of sensory compensation. In general, researchers have found no superiority among the blind, as a group, in any sensory modality (Axelrod, 1959; Hayes, 1941). Nor were blind subjects better able than the sighted to make global judgments of character, such as age, profession, or aggressiveness, when these judgments were based only on voice (Cantril & Allport, 1938). But if the notion of sensory acuity in the blind has been rejected, some authorities have nonetheless suggested the possibility that blindness may result in a greater sensitivity in making judgments of vocal affect. The weight of this opinion tends toward the view that facial expressions and body gestures are under greater individual and social control than is the voice, and that sighted persons fail to note cues of feeling communicated in the voice. By contrast, these authorities believe a great many blind persons develop in their responses to the voice a keen awareness of subjective moods and feelings, and of traits such as sincerity and hostility.

On the other hand, opposing views have been offered regarding the consequences of sensory deprivation. These authors contend that the loss of either sight or hearing results in the impairment rather than the enhancement of the remaining senses. For this reason, presumably, the blind should be inferior judges of what they hear (Myklebust, 1953).

The purpose of the present study was to investigate the long-standing and controversial belief that the blind are better able than the sighted to judge feelings communicated by the voice. It seemed evident that such a study must employ a measure which avoided the communication of verbal cues. In addition, any attempt to measure the ability of blind persons to identify feelings must also take into consideration the abundant anecdotal evidence suggesting that the blind have a remarkable ability to identify a wide variety of sounds (Hayes, 1941). For example, a respected French scholar once suggested using the presumably supersensitive blind on boats, in foggy weather, as a kind of human sonar system to detect passing vessels (Hayes). Thus, the ability to judge feelings correctly might be only a specific aspect of a general capacity to identify sounds. With these considerations in mind, the following hypothesis was formulated: Controlling for the ability to make correct judgments about everyday sounds, blind persons differ from the sighted in their ability to identify feelings communicated by means of nonverbal vocal cues.

A second hypothesis was suggested by the work of psychologist Vita S. Sommers (1944) who found that blind females were less emotionally disturbed than blind males. The hypothesis reads as follows: Blind female subjects are superior to blind male subjects in their ability to make correct judgments of feelings communicated by means of nonverbal vocal cues.

In the course of a pilot study, several variables other than those explicitly suggested by previous writers were encountered. While examining data derived from a test of ability to identify everyday sounds, it was noted that congenitally blind adolescents, as compared to the sighted, seemed to display a greater tendency to find affect in sounds which contained no explicit affectual connotation. For example, blind *S*s more often described a barking dog as, "a dog when he's been hurt," "a friendly dog," etc. A measure was developed to study this tendency toward *affect-attention* in spoken dialogue.

It was also observed that blind *S*s seemed to be distinguishable from the sighted in their proclivity to be more specific, more detailed, and analytic in their identifications of various sounds. Regardless of accuracy, blind *S*s manifested greater effort to interpret a sound actively and to place it more specifically in the world of sound. For example, a blind *S* described the sound of coffee percolating as the sound of "a liquid being sucked through a straw."

Another consequence of the pilot study was the decision to pursue further the role of a variable best described as "confidence." Beldoch (Chapter 3) had noted a significant relationship between the ability to judge emotions and the ability to estimate one's performance on a test of vocally-expressed emotions. Because of the vital role of experience and the possible influence of test attitude in two such divergent groups, it was decided to follow Beldoch's technique on both the accuracy-of-feelings measure and the sound-accuracy measure.

Thus, in addition to the experimental hypothesis, this study investigated the following variables: (1) tendency to attend to affect in spoken dialogue; (2) specificity in reporting content of sounds; (3) confidence in judgment of feelings; (4) confidence in judgment of sounds.

METHOD

Subjects

Subjects (*S*s) were 57 congenitally blind adolescents (28 males; 29 females) and 66 sighted adolescents (38 males; 28 females). None of the blind children had vision better than light perception. They had never seen a human face express an emotion. The mean age of blind children was 16.0 years, standard deviation, 2.11.

In order to qualify for the study, *S*s had to be within normal intelligence range, free from a history of emotional disturbance or organicity, and free from hearing deficiency and fluent in English. The *S*s were initially screened by administrators of the cooperating schools. The Institute of Psychological Research Vocabulary Test-GT (Form 1) was used as a screening test of intelligence and a general measure of mental age (Thorndike, 1942). Vocabulary scores were converted into MA equivalents for the Otis Self-Administering Tests of Mental Ability. An MA of 12 or a minimum IQ of 90 on a standardized intelligence test was required for an S to be included in the study.

Measures

Six measures were used. Derived from three tape recordings, the instruments were:

1. *Sound Accuracy Test.* The test consisted of 28 items, 25 of which had proved by means of item analysis to be among the most successful in discriminating high from low-scoring Ss in the pilot study. Three items were included because of their rapport value or their potential for drawing specific responses. Sounds from rural and urban life and indoor and outdoor activities were represented.

Sighted Ss were given printed instructions. Blind Ss were given Braille transcriptions of this and all other printed instructions used in the study. Ss were asked to identify the sounds as precisely as they could. Scoring was based on an item-by-item manual which used a four-point scale. An S earned credit to the degree that he identified a sound with greater accuracy. The scoring paralleled a progression from the general to the particular. An interjudge reliability study of scoring procedures yielded 95 per cent agreement.

2. *Confidence in Identifying Sounds.* After the final sound on the accuracy measure was played, Ss were asked to guess the total they had identified correctly. This estimate was S's Sound-Confidence score.

3. *Accuracy-of-Feelings Test.* A tape recording developed by Beldoch (1961) was used. It consisted of 37 readings by five actors of a content-standard speech: "I'm going out now. I won't be back all afternoon. If anyone calls, just tell them I'm not here." Ten emotional states were represented: admiration, amusement, anger, boredom, despair, disgust, fear, impatience, joy, and love.

Ss were given printed instructions, and the correct answer was selected from a list of 10 emotions provided with the instructions. Each speaker's reading of emotions was preceded by one delivered in his normal conversational tone. An answer received one point if S's judgment agreed with the speaker's intention.

4. *Confidence in Judging Feelings.* At the end of every speaker's group of readings, Ss were asked to guess the number they identified correctly. The sum of the five estimates constituted S's Feelings-Confidence score.

5. *Affect-Attention Test.* In order to obtain a measure of Ss' tendency to note affect in spoken dialogue without explicit instructions, the Affect-Attention Test was devised. It consisted of 20 brief exchanges

between a male and a female speaker. The material was relatively neutral in content. No dialogue was included unless its content could also have been read in a contradictory affect state, i.e., an angry reading might also have been delivered lovingly. Thus a discussion of food is read with boredom, a list of numbers with alternating joy and despair— joy when the numbers go down, despair when they go up.

Instructions for all Ss were: "These are your instructions. Listen carefully. I cannot repeat them. I am going to play a tape recording. What do you hear? Please write your answer in no more than 25 words."

Each response was given one point if S noted affect or emotional atmosphere, zero if S restricted his answer to the content of the dialogue. An interjudge reliability study of the scoring procedures yielded 98 per cent agreement.

6. *Specificity.* The specificity measure was derived from answers to the Sound Accuracy Test. This measure studied the effort made by Ss to account for texture, atmosphere, precise numbers, and complexes of sound. One point was given to each answer specifying the components of a sound or interpreting components above and beyond mere labeling. For example, an S who responded, "Someone pouring into a jar some water, ice in the jar," earned credit. The S who merely noted, "Something being poured into a container," did not. Correctness was not a prerequisite for earning specificity credit, although a reasonable relationship to the sound had to exist. Notations of affect were not included in the specificity scores in order to avoid overlap between the affect-attention and specificity measures. An interjudge reliability study of the scoring procedures yielded 93 per cent agreement.

Administration

Tests were administered to groups, and there were no time limits. No explanation of the study was made except to identify the experimenter. The sequence of tests was: (1) Affect-Attention; (2) Accuracy of Feelings; (3) Sound Accuracy; (4) Vocabulary. The multiple-choice vocabulary test was given in printed form to the sighted, orally to the blind.

RESULTS

Equivalence of the Groups

The two groups did not differ significantly with respect to CA ($t = 1.11$, $p > .05$). The blind group achieved an MA of 15.86 as compared to the sighted group's MA of 15.18, but the difference is not significant ($t = 1.75$, $p > .05$).

The subjects had been asked to estimate the average number of hours spent listening to the radio and watching television each week, since the sound-accuracy measure was derived from the sound library of the National Broadcasting Company. The sighted group spent twice as much time watching television; $\overline{X} = 12.06$ hours, blind Ss $\overline{X} = 5.99$. Since the variances were significantly different, the Mann-Whitney test was used, and the difference is significant beyond the .01 level ($z = 3.97$).

Blind Ss listened to the radio 22.54 hours per week in contrast to the sighted who devoted 13.26 hours. Employing the Mann-Whitney test, the difference is significant beyond the .05 level ($z = 2.39$).

Tests of Hypotheses

Hypothesis 1. The abilities of blind and sighted Ss to judge emotions accurately, controlling for abilities to identify everyday sounds, was studied by means of analysis of covariance. Table 9-1 lists variances

Table 9-1. Means, Variances, and Standard Deviations of 57 Blind and 66 Sighted Ss on Measures of Sound Accuracy and Judgment of Feelings

Measure and statistic	Blind	Sighted	F
Sound accuracy			
Mean	45.07	41.59	
Variance	122.03	66.40	1.84*
SD	11.05	8.15	
Accuracy of feelings			
Mean	19.02	21.62	
Variance	24.55	16.61	1.48
SD	4.96	4.08	

* $p < .05$.

and standard deviations of the two groups. Comparing blind and sighted Ss on their ability to identify sounds correctly, an analysis of variance (Table 9-2) found the blind Ss to be more accurate ($F = 4.02$;

Table 9-2. Analysis of Variance of Scores, Blind and Sighted Ss, on Accuracy of Judging Sounds

Source of variation	Sum of squares	df	Mean square	F ratio
Between groups	370.24	1	370.24	4.02*
Within groups	11149.68	121	92.15	
Total	11519.92	122		

* $p < .05$.

$p < .05$). With respect to ability to judge feelings, controlling for ability to identify sounds (Table 9-3), sighted Ss were significantly more correct in their judgments ($F = 15.36, p < .01$).

Table 9-3. Analysis of Covariance Comparing Blind and Sighted Ss' Abilities to Judge Feelings, Controlling for Abilities to Judge Sounds

Source of variation	Sum of squares of errors of estimate	df	Mean square	F ratio
Total	2551.31	121		
Within groups	2261.77	120	18.85	
Adjusted means	289.54	1	289.54	15.36*

* $p < .01$.

It was decided to control, routinely, for the difference in MA between the groups on those measures in which the blind achieved higher mean scores than the sighted. Analysis of covariance of the sound accuracy scores, controlling for MA, yielded $F = 2.59$ ($p > .05$). The difference could thus be accounted for in terms of the difference in MA.

Hypothesis 2. On the accuracy-of-feelings test, blind males achieved a mean of 20.04 (SD = 4.29) in contrast to a mean of 18.03 for blind females (SD = 5.41). The difference between the means is not significant ($t = 1.56$) at the .05 level. Consequently the hypothesis is not supported.

Tendency toward Affect-attention

On the Affect-Attention Test blind Ss achieved a mean of 4.26 (SD = 3.70), whereas sighted Ss achieved a mean of 2.64 (SD = 3.17). The resulting t statistic of 2.61 is significant beyond the .01 level. Controlling for differences in MA, analysis of covariance failed to change the direction of the results ($F = 5.38, p < .05$).

Tendency toward Specificity

Blind Ss achieved a mean score of 2.90 (SD = 2.02), while sighted Ss' mean score was 1.50 (SD = 2.22). Significantly different variances necessitated use of the Mann-Whitney test, and the resulting z-statistic, 3.49, is significant beyond the .01 level. Controlling for differences in MA, the F ratio (17.49) is significant beyond the .01 level. Thus the blind Ss emerge as the more specific reporters of sounds.

Confidence

The two groups showed no significant difference in confidence when identifying sounds. The mean score of the blind Ss was 18.11 (SD =

5.05). Sighted Ss achieved a mean of 18.14 (SD = 5.15). The difference is not significant ($t = .03, p > .05$).

Similarly, no difference was found in confidence when judging feelings. Blind Ss obtained a mean score of 25.44 (SD = 4.88). Sighted Ss obtained a mean of 26.58 (SD = 5.29). The resulting t statistic of .72 is not significant at the .05 level.

In both groups, a significant correlation was found ($p < .05$) between confidence scores and the ability to judge feelings correctly. Blind Ss showed an r of .30, the sighted, .25. Among sighted Ss a significant relationship ($r = .30, p < .05$) was found between abilities to identify sounds accurately and confidence scores. While the 28 blind Ss who reported sound confidence scores showed a higher r, .33, it did not achieve significance.[1]

Relationships among the Variables

Relationships among the variables and such subject characteristics as MA and CA are summarized in Table 9-4. While all the correlation

Table 9-4. Interrelationships among 57 Blind and 66 Sighted Ss on Measures of Six Variables

Variable and group	Feelings	Sound accuracy	Affect-attention	Specificity
Age				
Blind	.38**	.32*	.16	.50**
Sighted	.21	.36**	.38**	.33**
MA				
Blind	.34**	.26*	.09	.05
Sighted	.16	.24	.26*	.24
Feelings				
Blind		.33*	.52**	.22
Sighted		.30*	.08†	.03
Sounds				
Blind			.20	.29*
Sighted			.30*	.18
Affect-attention				
Blind				.21
Sighted				.40**

* $p < .05$
** $p < .01$
† Difference between blind and sighted groups is significant, $p. < .05$.

[1] Because of an oversight in administration, sound-confidence estimates were not obtained from 24 blind Ss. Another five blind Ss failed to make the necessary estimates. Consequently, sound-confidence data for the blind is based on $N = 28$. One sighted S also omitted his confidence guess, thus sighted $N = 65$.

coefficients are positive and most are significant, only in the relationship between affect-attention and accuracy in judging feelings does the blind group differ significantly ($p < .05$) from the sighted.

The relation of sex to performance on the various measures was further studied. Only one significant difference in mean scores was observed: Blind males were found to be better judges of sounds ($\overline{X} = 50.57$) than blind females ($\overline{X} = 39.76$), $t = 4.24$. This difference is significant beyond the .0005 level.

DISCUSSION AND CONCLUSIONS

The general aim of this research was to study a cluster of phenomena regarding the blind which have been observed by mankind for over 2,500 years. The study represents an attempt to find order and structure in several age-old, common-sense observations of human experience. And the results would seem to support a view that the behavior or "sensitivity" commonly associated with the ability of the blind to judge sounds and emotions falls into a pattern which is meaningfully interrelated. Glancing back over the ages, this study of mankind's traditional belief in the substitution of an ear for an eye would seem to suggest a view both more complicated and less satisfying than the poetic justice of sensory compensation. At the same time, the research would suggest that, as usual, there is also some fact buried in the cracker barrel of folklore.

Does sensory compensation exist? The answer suggested by the performance of Ss participating in this research would appear to be yes and no. To be sure, no aspect of the data can be interpreted as evidence of any "sharpening" of hearing as a result of physiological change among blind Ss. However, blind Ss as compared to the sighted showed themselves to be more attentive to the affective underpinnings of dialogue. In addition, blind Ss were more attentive to specific details and more active in interpreting everyday sounds.

However, a negative reply would seem to be justified by the remaining test results: Blind Ss were inferior to the sighted as accurate judges of emotions. After controlling for differences in mental age, the data showed the blind Ss to be no more accurate than the sighted as judges of everyday sounds.

The Measures and the Results

The apparent contradictions in the results may perhaps be resolved by discussing further the nature of the measures and the degree to which they lend themselves to learning. For it would appear that despite the handicap with which the congenitally blind *S* began life, he was able to keep abreast of his sighted counterpart in learning to identify sounds. Yet this is not true of his ability to identify emotions.

Consider first some a priori contrasts between everyday sounds and vocal expressions of emotions. The noises of life are, by their very nature, easier to learn. In terms of major characteristics influencing identification, everyday noises are more obvious, both in their structure and their differences, than vocal expressions of emotions. Distinctions—hence identifications—are easier to make. In addition to being simpler to discriminate and identify, noises are more stable; the cry of cats and the bubbling of a percolator vary little compared to man's expressions of admiration or despair. Excluding the verbal content, one man's expressions of love may sound like another's cry of despair, and even these may differ from time to time in the same person. This difficulty in discrimination assumes an inablity to use vision to make the necessary judgments.

Opportunity may also be a contributing factor. The congenitally blind person has fewer opportunities to acquire as rich a repertoire of emotional expressions as the sighted because he has less occasion to meet people and to observe them in the stress of life. The range of the blind person's emotional experience may also be restricted by the fewer people around him as a consequence of his reduced mobility. Moreover, the sighted person's response to blindness undoubtedly modifies the range of emotions he will display in dealing with a blind man. Indeed, one of the persistent public relations problems of workers with the blind is educating the sighted person to talk to a blind man as he would any other human being.

A fourth factor which probably contributes to more effective learning of everyday sounds is the relative ease with which people, blind or sighted, can check on the nature of sounds. It would not be remarkable if a blind person asked a sighted companion about the sound of a barking dog or an approaching car. It is quite another thing to get consensual validation, using Sullivan's term, regarding a vocally expressed emotion. For instance, no interpersonal strain is caused when a blind person inquires whether a quacking sound is a duck. But a veritable army of conventional inhibitions stands arrayed against attempts to find out if a man is feeling anger, disgust, or joy. The sighted, of course, have the advantage of vision to check nonverbally on an auditory emotional experience and to gain a more accurate sense of the range and variety of vocally expressed feelings.

Thus the lower scores of blind *S*s as judges of emotions in this study, the lack of difference between blind and sighted *S*s as judges of everyday noises, may be explained, in part, by reference to the nature of the auditory experiences and the social context in which they are encountered; that is, their contrast in simplicity, stability, opportunity, and susceptibility to consensual validation.

Turning to the affect-attention and specificity measures, it is interesting to note at the outset that the behavior most likely to result in score credit on these two measures constitutes the closest auditory analogue to vision demanded in the study. Lacking sight, the blind person must rely on hearing for information about the world beyond the reach of his fingertips. His survival may depend on whether he can determine if love or anger lies behind the words being expressed to him. The significantly higher scores of blind Ss in affect-attention would suggest a meaningful difference between the two groups in their reaction to complex verbal messages. This result supports those writers who contend that the sighted make less use of auditory channels than the blind to receive cues from the environment.

Affect-attention·may be related to Cameron's concept of reaction-sensitivity. Cameron (1947) defines the term as, "A selective readiness-to-react to certain components of a stimulating situation and not to others, which is the result of one's having acquired a system of related attitudes and responses." Quite aside from the issue of accuracy, blind Ss seem to show a readiness to note affect, and it is interesting to speculate that something akin to this phenomenon may have led to the popular notion of "sensitivity" in the blind. The sighted S, because he can "tell by looking," has less need to develop the habits of listening which the blind S apparently manifests. Some support for this view can be found in the observation of Licklider and Miller (1951) that: "Speech contains many more discriminative cues than the listener really needs." Clearly this is less true of the blind.

The results concerned with specificity of identification may be viewed in similar fashion. Taken as a measure reflecting relative effort to extract information from hearing, interpreted as an attempt to comprehend the environment, the significant difference between the blind and sighted Ss may reflect the blind S's need to overcome the loss of a teleceptive sense.

In general, the blind group achieved significantly higher scores on those measures where attention, motivated by need, could be most effective. They were inferior to sighted Ss on the one measure, accuracy of emotional identification, where performance would seem to be most dependent on experience and consensual validation and where the relatively obscure nature of the stimuli make learning conditions most difficult. No difference between the two groups was found on the measure (sound accuracy) whose contents would appear to lend themselves most readily to casual learning. In this connection, it seems worth recalling, at least in so far as a sound inventory may be acquired through radio listening, that blind Ss spent twice as much time as the sighted at this activity. The possible roles of learning and opportunity in these results carry interesting implications for educators of the blind and, indeed, of the sighted.

Education and the Auditory Environment

Taken in the broadest possible terms, the results of this study support the view of writers such as Abel (1958) who stress the need of the blind child for an environment which is focused on what he *has* rather than what he has *not*. The "lag" of blind children when compared to the sighted, a frequent concern of educators, would seem not to exist among the blind Ss, at least in so far as they are accurate judges of noises. Given the opportunity—radio listening may serve as some slight measure of opportunity—no significant difference can be found between blind and sighted Ss.

The potential fruitfulness of an enriched auditory experience and education is also suggested by the results of the specificity measure. Specificity scores may be taken as an index of a tendency toward the analysis and interpretation of everyday sounds. Licklider and Miller have observed: "There appears to be no better way to teach listeners than to motivate them and have them listen." In the case of the congenitally blind, there seems little reason to doubt that the need for additional auditory information—and hence their motivation—is in part established by their sensory deficit. Certainly an additional readiness to listen to the sounds of life would already seem to exist among the blind Ss in this study.

The results concerning the judgment of emotions suggest a need for more active teaching even in this less defined area of experience. The significant superiority of blind Ss in affect-attention argues in support of those writers who have noted the tendency of the blind to listen for feeling, attitude, and emotion in speech. The existence of such readiness should in itself justify added effort among teachers to encourage this useful means of gaining further mastery over the environment. Paradoxically, the *failure* of blind Ss to match the performance of sighted Ss as accurate judges of feeling adds force to the position. The assumption of some teachers of the blind regarding the sensitivity and accuracy of their charges in ascertaining the feelings of those around them would not seem to be justified. The judgment of vocally expressed feelings is one of considerable subtlety, and the intervention and guidance of his more sophisticated teacher would thus seem to be a valuable experience for a congenitally blind child. By taking a self-conscious teaching approach to interpersonal communications, educators would also contribute to the prevention or correction of a possible distortion in the blind child's dealings with others.

Lowenfeld (1955, p. 227) writes:

. . . it often happens that blind individuals rely too much upon the voice as an indicator of a person's character and either accept or reject the person on that ground alone. In this respect, they are no different from seeing persons who form impressions on the basis of pleasant or unpleasant appearances.

Effective teaching of blind Ss would stress not only the advantages of active listening but also appropriate cautiousness.

Since no effort was made to study the motivation of the individual S, no evidence is available regarding the personality characteristics which may distinguish high- from low-scoring Ss on the affect-attention and specificity measures. However, it would be interesting to explore the extent to which attempts to compensate, defensively, for the loss of sight influence the readiness of blind Ss to extract information from auditory channels (it will be recalled that accuracy was not a criterion for credit on the two measures). Compensation, here, refers to "the overemphasis of a type of behavior which serves to reduce tensions resulting from frustration or conflict" (Shaffer & Shoben, 1956). Because compensatory behavior may be either integrative or maladjustive, the educator's shaping role gains added importance in a situation where compensation may be a factor.

In the context of this discussion of education for the blind in a world of sound, it seems particularly interesting to consider the correlation observed between affect-attention and the ability to judge emotions. The sighted Ss showed virtually no correlation (.08). However, the more audio-dependent blind demonstrated a significantly higher correlation (.52). In order to tend to the world's work, the sighted, superior in judging emotions, equipped with vision for appropriate teleceptive functions, have relatively little need of faculties such as affect-attention. Obviously, the blind person who can successfully combine the two functions is in a far better position to exert control over his environment than the blind man who cannot. And this conclusion would seem to carry its own argument regarding the role of the educator.

Sight and Sound

The tradition of sensory compensation usually attributes recondite auditory powers to the blind as compared to the sighted. Of course, nothing in this study lends credence to such a view. On the contrary, the evidence tends toward the conclusion that there is no substitute for sight, only a greater need for sound.

Nevertheless, educators of the sighted may find pause for thought in the evidence that many of their charges are probably failing to maximize the information available in their auditory environment. The results of this study give added weight to the view of such writers as Norris, et al. who write: "He (the blind child) is forced to turn to senses other than sight to explore his world. Such avenues are equally open to people with normal vision, although they are less used or understood because of the sighted person's preoccupation with visual stimuli" (Norris et al., 1957, p. 75). It is interesting to speculate whether the vision-centered teaching approach which has been criticized for being "frustrating" to the blind child and the sighted teacher (Norris, et al.) also deprives the sighted child, to some extent, of training in the full use of his hearing.

Other Variables

The low but significant correlations obtained between the ability to estimate test performance and accuracy in judging feelings support Turner's observation on the role of confidence as a variable in performance. The positive correlation observed between confidence and the identification of sounds in both blind and sighted groups also lends support to Turner's suggestion. However, the failure of the correlation coefficient of the blind group to achieve significance leaves the question regarding the identification of sounds and confidence somewhat in doubt. Perhaps of greater importance to this study is that the differences in the results cannot be attributed to differences in the degree of confidence with which blind and sighted Ss approached their tasks.

Sex appeared to play no major role in the results of this research. But for one variable, sound accuracy, no significant difference was found between male and female Ss, blind or sighted. In sound accuracy, however, blind males were significantly better judges. While the hypothesis regarding the performance of blind males and females in the judgment of emotions derived from a study of the adjustment of the two groups, no conclusion concerning the emotional adjustment of Ss is warranted on the basis of this investigation.

Problems for Future Research

The results of this study suggest several avenues for further research. The need for a cross-validation study of the various unhypothesized results seems self-evident. A comparison of the performance of congenital and late-blind Ss on the reported measures would be of interest to those studying the effect time of onset has on the functioning of the blind. For students of both the blind and sighted adolescent, it should be of interest to see what influence differences in rearing and familial relationships have upon the ability to judge emotions accurately and tendencies toward affect-attention. The problem of rearing, in the case of the blind, may also be linked to the difference between males and females in the judgment of sounds. None of the variables studied in this research account satisfactorily for the difference, and it seems plausible to look to differences in rearing to explain the discrepancy. For example: Are blind females reared under more restrictive regulation than blind males? Are their object relationships in any sense narrower than those of blind males?

Another area of potentially fruitful research lies in the development of appropriate teaching devices aimed at enriching the sound environment of the blind. Other research has already demonstrated that learning to use sound cues can be greatly facilitated for the blind person by the application of imaginative teaching methods (Chevigny & Braverman, 1950). Finally, the approach taken in this research would appear applicable to the deaf where the problem of sensory compensation is frequently discussed. The consequences of deafness to the judgment of gestures and facial expression raise questions of interest to students of both sensory deficit and nonverbal communication.

10

Schizophrenics as judges of vocal expressions of emotional meaning

John le B. Turner

The ability to identify accurately and sensitively the emotions expressed in speech sounds probably helps people to understand one another and to make satisfactory mutual adjustments. Distorted or insensitive perception of the cues that reveal emotion might well interfere with interpersonal functioning. Conversely, any disturbance in a person's interpersonal functioning might affect or be reflected in his ability to identify emotions in speech sounds. In short, it seems reasonable to expect some correlation between accurate auditory perception of emotions and adequate interpersonal adjustment, whether adjustment affects perception, perception affects adjustment, or both.

Such was the conceptual point of departure for the study to be reported in the present chapter. The strategy was to determine the status in ability to judge emotions expressed in speech sounds of a group characterized by particularly inadequate interpersonal functioning—namely, schizophrenic patients—as compared with a suitably matched control group. The comparison is of particular interest because various clinical and theoretical descriptions of schizophrenia give divergent pictures of the schizophrenic as a perceiver of persons with correspondingly divergent implications for the present problem. For example, it has been suggested that schizophrenics should be exceptionally insensitive, that they should be exceptionally sensitive but likely to distort, and that they should not differ from psychiatrically normal persons except in so far as cognitive confusion interferes with their performance on the measuring instruments. A fourth possibility, derived from the belief that "schizophrenia" is more than one thing, is that a group of persons so labeled should show greater variability than a normal group.

A conceptual distinction can be made between two sources of inaccuracy in judging emotions. *Insensitivity* would be a high absolute or differential threshold for recognition of emotion; *distortion* would be a tendency to misreport, perhaps even to oneself, originally sensitive perception. The distinction is extremely hard to implement experimentally, but when the study was planned it seemed possible that something might be learned about it if the patterning of errors were studied as well as sheer frequency of "correct" responses, and if paranoids, most often described as sensitive but likely to distort, were separated from other schizophrenics.

The following specific hypotheses were tested:

I. Schizophrenics identify emotions from the sound of speech less accurately than do nonschizophrenics.

II. Among schizophrenics, paranoids make more accurate judgments of emotions from speech sounds than do others.

III. Paranoids' judgments of emotions from speech sounds, as compared with those of normal persons and of other schizophrenics, show more projection of hostility—i.e., they more often erroneously attribute anger.

The statement of the first two hypotheses is somewhat arbitrary. Differences opposite to those predicted are conceivable and would be of considerable theoretical interest if found. In other words, these are not really "one-tailed" hypotheses.

METHODOLOGICAL CONSIDERATIONS

Several methodological problems were encountered. One of them arises whenever schizophrenics are compared with other persons by means of a test requiring the subjects' attention and cooperation. Cognitive or motivational interference with the schizophrenics' performance on the measuring task may produce differences in scores which would be quite irrelevant to the hypotheses being investigated. Means must be found of assessing and correcting for such irrelevant differences. An appropriate method in such cases is to administer a control measurement task to both groups. The ideal control task would be identical with the principal measurement task in formal structure and would make the same demands on the subject's attention and require of him the same type of formal response. It should not be sensitive to variations in the attribute which the principal task is designed to measure, but it should be sensitive to any irrelevant sources of variation in scores on the principal task. However, it should not also accidentally measure something else which the principal task does not measure. If it does, the outcome may be hard to interpret, particularly if there is any doubt as to the identity of the "something else" measured by the control task, or any likelihood that it might be an attribute on which the groups do in fact differ.

The control task used in the present study successfully met several of the above criteria. It was closely similar to the principal instrument in formal structure, and probably made very much the same demands on the subject's attention and cooperation. Thus it was presumably sensitive to several possible sources of low scores on the principal instrument. It was not intended to be sensitive to anything else, for the auditory discriminations it required were rather gross, namely, between the voices of a little girl, an adolescent boy, a mature young man and woman, and a faltering male and female octogenarian. Low scores, it was anticipated, could be due only to difficulties with the formal requirements common to both instruments such as might be caused by impaired attention, motivation, or cognitive clarity. The instrument turned out, unfortunately, to have difficulties of its own for many subjects, so that it was evidently measuring some as yet unidentified human attribute or attributes.

Construction of the principal measuring instrument gave rise to several interesting methodological considerations. The most challenging problem was to obtain suitable recorded samples of speech to constitute the items. Each sample should be such that the "correct" response could be clearly specified—that is, one must have confidence that a particular emotion "really is" expressed. Yet identification of the emotions expressed must not always be easy. Ideally the items should vary over a wide range of difficulty. The ultimate solution may be to collect a large number of extended samples of the natural speech of persons in various situations, so that their emotional states are already known or can be confidently judged from the larger context. From such material one could select sentences or phrases whose wording gives no clue as to the speaker's emotion. These would constitute items for which the questions of "correct response" and "genuineness of expression" would already be settled without recourse to expert judgments or item analyses of subjects' responses. Level of difficulty would then be determined empirically, and ultimately a set of items would be assembled having the desirable range of difficulty of identification in a variety of expressed emotions. Until somebody performs this very considerable task, we must be content with feigned emotional expressions, analogous to the posed photographs used in the early studies of facial expressions—and, we must caution ourselves, with an analogous risk that what we are now studying may have more to do with theatrical conventions than with actual emotional expression.

If the items had to be recorded by actors, a relatively minor problem was to choose material for them to read or speak. The sentences used in the present study had the structure of English, but all nouns, verbs, and adjectives were nonsensical. Such material was chosen to give the actors more scope than totally meaningless sounds while avoiding possible emotional meanings of supposedly "neutral" English sentences. The schizophrenics might be disturbed by the nonsense, but it was argued that any consequent effect on their scores would also be picked up by the control task along with other irrelevant sources of variation, since both instruments used the same nonsense sentences. Still, the risk remains that the nonsense may have affected schizophrenics' identification of emotions more than their performance of the control task. With hindsight, the use of nonsense that sounds like English seems unnecessary in general and distinctly risky in the case of schizophrenics. In defense of the procedure used it can be added that the only clear instance of a patient basing his response on the nonsense instead of on the sound of the voice occurred on the control task. "Borple," according to one patient, meant "portal," so the voice had to be that of the young boy "standing at the portal."

A more difficult and important problem was to select items for which the "correct" response could be coded unambiguously, but to do so without eliminating all but the easiest and most obvious items. One might simply assume that if a competent professional actor records an "angry" sentence and then listens to it and is satisfied, it *is* an angry sentence. A long instrument composed of such items could later be purified by item analysis. Since some check on the actors' success and genuineness seemed essential and since a fairly brief instrument was important in working with schizophrenics, the present investigation resorted to a panel of judges consisting of experienced psychotherapists and psychodiagnosticians, persons accustomed to listening to human speech in a context where the speaker's emotional state is of great concern. It was not assumed that their judgments could be used in any absolute sense, but only that their status in the ability to be measured should be toward the upper end of its distribution. A satisfactory item, it was argued, would be one which a majority of such a panel would identify in agreement with the actor's intention while the rest of the panel would either guess, producing a scattering of responses, or judge the item "neutral." The actual criterion of acceptance was that six or more members of a jury of 10 must judge an item in accordance with the actor's intention, while not more than two might agree on any alternative response other than "neutral." Whenever more than one attempt at an item met the criterion, the apparently less easy one was selected, but the majority of the items finally included produced greater agreement among the judges than the criterion required. The resulting instrument, as it turned out, contained rather too much dead wood in the form of items which very few subjects failed to identify correctly, but it is not clear that a less stringent criterion would have improved matters.

PROCEDURE

Subjects. Three groups of subjects were used, each consisting of 30 white male veterans between the ages of twenty and fifty-three. The schizophrenic nonparanoid and schizophrenic paranoid groups consisted of men who were in hospital with an official diagnosis of schizophrenic reaction, and who were judged by their ward administrators to be currently schizophrenic. Patients in the former group were without any history of active paranoid attitudes or delusional ideas. Those in the latter group currently manifested such symptoms. The control group consisted of convalescing medical and surgical patients, all expected to recover fully, and none suffering from diseases of suspected psychogenic etiology. Distributions of age and educational level were closely similar in the three groups. Subjects in the control group had generally spent much less time in hospital than those in the other two groups.

Instruments and Procedure. Task A, the principal measuring instrument, consisted of a tape-recorded series of 36 nonsense sentences read "emotionally" by professional actors, each sentence preceded by an identifying number and followed by 10 seconds of silence in which the subject could respond by pointing to one of six cards bearing the words "sad," "happy," "angry," "surprised," "frightened," and "neutral." Six nonsense sentences were used, each of them being spoken once neutrally and once as if in each of the five emotions. The items finally used were selected from a much larger pool after pretesting on a group of 10 sophisticated judges to eliminate misleading or ambiguous items.

Task B was the comparison task, designed to assess the extent to which schizophrenics' scores might be lowered by characteristics irrelevant to the hypotheses being tested. It was identical to task A in formal structure, consisting of the same 36 sentences with the same timing, and requiring the same response of pointing to one of six cards. But this time the sentences were read unemotionally by one of six persons, a girl of seven, a boy of fourteen, a young man, a young woman, an old man, and an old woman. The cards were marked accordingly.

Thus task B required a simple identification of one of six distinctly different voices instead of a judgment of the speaker's emotion.

Both tasks were administered to each subject individually in a single session lasting less than half an hour including instructions. The experimenter recorded the responses as the subject listened and pointed. In each case the subject's score was the number of correct responses out of a possible 36.

RESULTS

Table 10-1 summarizes the performance of the three groups on the two tasks and gives intercorrelations and reliability coefficients (split

Table 10-1. Performance of Schizophrenic and Control Groups on Tasks A and B

	Group 1 Schizophrenic nonparanoid (N = 30)	Group 2 Schizophrenic paranoid (N = 30)	Group 3 Control (N = 30)	Total (N = 90)
Task A				
Range	12–32	11–33	18–34	11–34
Mean	22.57	20.10	26.90	23.19
SD	4.98	5.79	3.89	5.65
Reliability	.64	.75	.68	.75
Task B				
Range	22–36	22–36	23–36	22–36
Mean	29.53	29.47	31.23	30.08
SD	4.29	4.05	4.04	4.16
Reliability	.89	.77	.91	.86
Correlation				
A × B	.42*	.24	.11	.32*

* $p < .01$.

half with Spearman-Brown correction). Task A yields a fairly symmetrical distribution, and has sufficient reliability for group comparison. Task B is a remarkably reliable instrument considering its small range. Its distribution is somewhat skewed, with a concentration of very high scores. But considering the purpose for which it was intended, one may question why task B's distribution is not far more skewed than it is, particularly in the control group. When one-third of a group of cooperative, psychiatrically normal subjects made six or more errors on Task B, something must have been measured besides mere willingness or ability to handle the formal requirements of the test.

Test of Hypothesis I. Confirmation of the first hypothesis requires that the 60 schizophrenics differ from the control group in task A to an extent not attributable to any difference there may be in task B. Table 10-2 gives the relevant comparisons.

Table 10-2. Tasks A and B: Comparison of Schizophrenics with Non-schizophrenics

	Schizophrenics ($N = 60$)	Controls ($N = 30$)	
Mean A score	21.33	26.90	Difference = 5.57, $t = 5.55$ ($p < .01$)
Variance	30.19	15.13	$F = 1.996$ ($p < .05$)
Mean B score	29.50	31.23	Difference = 1.73 $t = 1.89$ ($.10 > p > .05$)
Variance	17.10	16.32	

Schizophrenics vary more widely than nonschizophrenics in their task A performance, and their average score is significantly lower. Does this represent a real difference in ability to identify emotions, or might it be accounted for by irrelevant factors affecting schizophrenics' performance, such as should be measured by task B? Since the two tasks are correlated in the schizophrenics, and since the groups may differ in the same direction on both of them (the task B difference is significant only at the .10 level), the question had to be investigated. An analysis of covariance by the method of matched regression estimates was performed to determine the effect on the task A difference of holding task B constant. The difference varies considerably depending on the *value at which* task B scores are held constant (see Figure 10-1). The two instruments are somewhat correlated in the schizophrenic group but scarcely at all in the control group, and those schizophrenics who do extremely well on task B (exceptionally well even for nonschizophrenics) tend to do as well on task A as do nonschizophrenics similarly selected. Table 10-3 gives the limits of B scores within which the groups differ

Table 10-3. Schizophrenics and Nonschizophrenics: Limits of B Scores within Which Differences of $\tilde{A}$ Are Significant

Level of significance	Lower limit of B	Upper limit of B
.01	22.00	29.97
.05	22.00	33.74

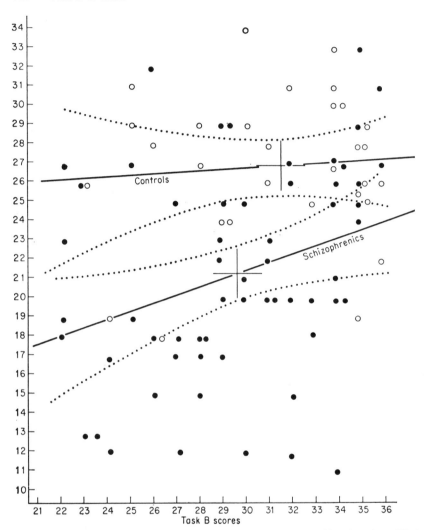

Fig. 10-1. Scatter plot of task A and task B scores for schizophrenics (filled circles) and controls (open circles). Regression lines (estimates of A) for the two groups are also shown, and group means on the two tasks are indicated by crosses on the respective regression lines. Dotted lines indicate interval estimates MA.B with Confidence .95.

significantly in regression estimates of A scores. As shown in Table 10-3, the schizophrenic Ss differ significantly from control Ss on the emotional identification task when considering only those Ss whose scores on task B ranged from 22.00 to 33.74. This included 53 Ss in the schizophrenic sample and 21 Ss in the control group. Therefore, for these Ss, controlling for scores on task B, the first hypothesis clearly is supported. But among the seven schizophrenic and nine control Ss whose scores on task B were 34 and above, the difference in performance on the emotional identification task is not significant. Therefore, even if we accept the .05 level of significance, we must somehow qualify any statement we make about the confirmation of the first hypothesis as to exclude from it subjects with B scores of 34 and above. Framing such a statement in general terms becomes a somewhat speculative undertaking in the absence of any certainty as to just what task B measures, especially at these upper levels of its distribution. The problem was alluded to in the above discussion of methodological questions, and will be taken up again in the summary and discussion of conclusions.

Test of Hypotheses II. The second hypothesis, concerning the expected difference between paranoids and other schizophrenics, was tested and not confirmed, as can be seen from Table 10-4. The sample

Table 10-4. Tasks A and B: Comparisons of Paranoid and Nonparanoid Schizophrenics

	Group 1 Schizophrenic nonparanoid	Group 2 Schizophrenic paranoid	
Mean A score	22.57	20.10	Difference = 2.47 $t = 1.77$ ($p > .05$)
Variance	24.81	33.47	$F = 1.35$ ($p > .05$)
Mean B score	29.53	29.47	
Variance	18.40	16.40	

means differed in the opposite direction to that hypothesized, but not significantly.

Test of Hypothesis III. The third hypothesis, which predicted that paranoid Ss would more often erroneously attribute anger, was tested by comparing the three groups as to proportion of subjects making one or more such errors. As Table 10-5 shows, the paranoid group had the

Table 10-5. Numbers of Subjects with and without "Angry" Errors

	Group 1 Schizophrenic nonparanoid	Group 2 Schizophrenic paranoid	Group 3 Control	Total
1 or more "angry" errors	13	18	12	42
No "angry" errors	17	12	18	47

Chi square = 2.76, $n = 2$ ($p > .05$).

largest proportion of such subjects, but the difference could well be due to chance.

Hypothesis III may have been too specific. It was intended as a special case of the general expectation that distortion, rather than insensitivity, would account for a larger proportion of the paranoids' errors than for those of the other subjects. An effort was made to test the more general hypothesis. "Errors due to insensitivity" were operationally defined as those where the subject either failed to respond or erroneously identified an item as "neutral," whereas all errors where the subject erroneously attributed *any* emotion were called "errors due to distortion." The groups did not differ significantly in the relative proportions of the two types of errors. There is a serious flaw in the definitions of insensitivity and distortion on which the test of the more general hypothesis rests: an erroneous identification of an item as "neutral" did not always reflect insensitivity. One paranoid subject listened to the blatantly angry shout of the first item, then pointed to the "neutral" card, eyed the experimenter cautiously, and said, "I'll take a neutral stand on that." Another paranoid responded to a "frightened" item by saying, "He sounds frightened, but I don't think he *is* frightened, so I'll say 'neutral.' " Both of these errors had to be classified as "due to insensitivity"; but the first was certainly a distortion, and the second was at least *not* due to insensitivity and could be defended as showing excellent sensitivity to the fact that the speaker was only an actor. The latter response might be compared to those of another subject, blatantly paranoid but cooperative and highly intelligent, who conscientiously went through the entire test saying, "simulated anger," "simulated fear," etc., and obtained one of the three highest scores in the entire sample of 90 subjects. The only possible conclusions regarding the third hypothesis are that the hypothesis as stated was not confirmed and that no satisfactory method was devised for testing the more general conception from which it was derived.

Other Correlates. A number of relationships were investigated between the two instruments and such variables as duration of hospitalization, age, education, and degree of illness as crudely measured by comparing "privileged" patients with those on locked wards. None of these variables had an appreciable effect on task B, so that their relationships with task A can be interpreted as genuinely due to differences in ability to judge emotions in speech.

Duration of hospitalization correlated significantly with task A only in the schizophrenic nonparanoid group, and the relationship was positive $(r = .44)$. This somewhat puzzling correlation might represent a difference between recently admitted acute schizophrenics and better stabilized or chronic patients who have been in the hospital for several years. At least the finding strengthens our confidence in the conclusion to be drawn from the test of hypothesis I, for it argues against the possibility that the lower scores of the schizophrenics are due to the fact that they have spent more time than the normal subjects in the hospital, isolated from the community at large.

Ability to identify emotions appears to decrease with age and to increase with amount of schooling, at least among normal persons. In the control group task A correlated negatively with age ($r = -.45$) and positively with last school grade completed ($r = .55$). These are suggestive findings, but they must be interpreted with caution pending replication with better controls. For one thing, age and education are not independent of each other in such a group as this; the older men tend to have had less schooling. Again, it is likely that older men who choose to be treated in a veteran's hospital differ from younger men making the same choice in more respects than age, for different selective factors probably operate. Age, intelligence, and general sophistication should certainly be included in any comprehensive study of the correlates of the perceptual ability under investigation.

Since schizophrenics identify emotions less accurately than psychiatrically normal persons, one may well ask whether there is corresponding variation *among* schizophrenics as a function of severity of illness. A crude but useful criterion of severity of illness is an administrative decision made about each patient; he is either well enough to be granted a privilege card and permitted to move freely around the hospital, or so disturbed that he must be confined to a locked ward. Of our sample of 60 schizophrenics, 23 had privilege cards, 37 were on locked wards. Between the two groups there was a difference in mean task A score in favor of the privileged patients, significant at the .05 level. It is tempting to conclude that severity of illness has a direct effect on ability to identify emotions in speech. A closer scrutiny of the difference in the paranoid and nonparanoid groups separately casts serious doubt on such a conclusion. The difference between privileged and nonprivileged patients was entirely because of a large difference in the paranoid group. The average task A score of nonparanoid patients on locked wards was precisely the same as that of nonparanoids with privilege cards. And yet the decision whether to grant privilege cards is probably at least as closely related to severity of illness in the nonparanoid as in the paranoid group, in which the decision is often influenced by considerations not directly related to severity of illness, such as conformity to hospital routines or likelihood of elopement or of mailing complaining letters to persons in high places. It seems safest, therefore, to attribute the difference between privileged and nonprivileged patients to the exceptional cooperativeness of the privileged paranoids as against the resistance and suspiciousness of those on locked wards, such as were manifested by the patient referred to above who identified a whole block of items as "neutral," apparently to avoid committing himself.

CONCLUSIONS AND DISCUSSION

Schizophrenics vary in ability to identify emotions in speech sounds more widely than psychiatrically normal persons. Their average ability is lower because their distribution extends considerably lower than that of normal persons, though it also extends just as high. No evidence of exceptional sensitivity of schizophrenics was found, but it is not clear that the present measuring instrument has a high enough "ceiling" to assess such exceptional sensitivity if it exists. It is certainly possible for a seriously ill schizophrenic, and especially for a deluded but cooperative paranoid, to identify emotions in speech more accurately than the majority of normal persons. Four possible views of the schizophrenic as a perceiver of persons were mentioned in the introductory paragraphs. One of these gains some support from the present investigation, namely, the view that "schizophrenia" is more than one thing. Two of the views can hardly be reconciled with the present findings. Schizophrenics *do* differ from normal persons, even when allowance is made for irrelevant differences in motivation and cognitive clarity. They are *not* necessarily insensitive. The possibility that they are sensitive but likely to distort is still left open; but this formulation, though attractive in its clinical sophistication, has limited scientific value because it could hardly be ruled out by any empirical finding whatever, though it could be supported by appropriate evidence if it is correct, or correct for certain classes of schizophrenics.

More than one reference has been made to difficulties in interpretation raised by the fact that the control instrument unintentionally measured something it was not designed to measure. The point needs further discussion. To begin with, the conclusions in the above paragraph are not seriously called in question by the difficulties referred to. Task B did its job well enough to give a negative answer to the question of whether the observed differences on task A could be attributed entirely to difficulties with its formal requirements. The problem is, rather, that if only one knew what task B measured, one would be able to say at least something about what distinguishes the schizophrenics who can identify emotions in speech sounds as well as normal persons from those who cannot. The higher the score on task B, the less do schizophrenics differ from normal subjects on task A. One seemingly plausible interpretation is that an important portion of task B variance for the schizophrenic group, but not for the control group, was contributed by just those cognitive and motivational variables which the test was supposed to measure. That would account for the fact that the two tasks are correlated in the schizophrenic group but not in the control group, and would permit an interpretation of the covariance analysis. But the interpretation cannot be reconciled with the fact that task B scores do not differ at all between privileged and nonprivileged patients; in fact, among nonparanoids the patients on locked wards did slightly better on the average (not significantly) than those with privilege cards. All we can say at present about those schizophrenics who show little or no impairment in ability to identify emotions is that they tend to be cooperative and without serious cognitive confusion, and also to possess in marked degree some other person-perceiving or auditory-person-perceiving skill in which normal persons also vary. The statement adds very little to what was said in the first two sentences of the above paragraph.

As for the comparison of paranoids with other schizophrenics, the results are inconclusive. No differences were found in absolute accuracy, nor in the patterning of errors. There is good reason for believing, from informal observations in the present study as well as on other grounds, that paranoids distort their perceptions of other persons' emotions more than other schizophrenics or normal persons, but satisfactory techniques for measuring distortion or distinguishing it from insensitivity were not devised. The only difference found between paranoids and other schizophrenics was that it was only among the paranoids that privileged patients identified emotions more accurately than those on locked wards. The finding was interpreted as reflecting something more like distortion than insensitivity, but cannot be taken as clear evidence of distortion by paranoids.

Among schizophrenics task A performance may be influenced by such factors as general attentiveness (or perhaps more specific attentiveness to persons' voices), cognitive clarity, and tendencies to give distorted or overly guarded reports. Among nonschizophrenics, where the above factors are not important sources of variation, correlations with age and education emerge. It is not surprising if intelligence or sophistication makes a difference, though it would be a sorry comment on task A's validity if it correlated *too* highly with intellectual or socioeconomic variables or with such things as exposure to television and motion pictures.

The negative relationship with age might disappear upon replication with careful control of such variables as education, social status, and level of occupational ambition. On the other hand, variations in auditory acuity or general alertness may account for the relationship, or it may be due to factors of cultural change: the actors who made task A are all young men.

SUMMARY

A test of ability to identify speakers' emotions in speech sounds apart from sense or content was constructed and administered to 30 nonparanoid schizophrenics, 30 paranoid schizophrenics, and 30 psychiatrically normal control subjects. A parallel control test was administered to every subject to correct for possible irrelevant sources of low scores obtained by schizophrenics on the first instrument. The performances of the three groups were studied both as to accuracy of performance on the two instruments and as to patterning of errors on the emotion-judging test. Analyses were also made of differences between patients with and without hospital privileges, and of correlations of both instruments with duration of hospitalization, age, and amount of education.

The principal findings were as follows:

1. Schizophrenics vary more than nonschizophrenics in ability to identify emotions in speech sounds, and on the average they are inferior. The higher average ability of normal persons is due to a more compact distribution which does not extend as low but which also does not extend appreciably higher than that of the schizophrenics.

2. Paranoid schizophrenics do not, on the average, differ significantly from nonschizophrenics in the ability in question, so far as it is measured by the instrument developed.

3. No evidence of projection of hostility by paranoids nor of other kinds of distorted perception could be found in the patterning of their errors as compared with those of other subjects.

4. Patients with hospital privileges identify emotions in speech sounds more accurately than those on locked wards, but the difference is found only within the paranoid group.

5. Among nonschizophrenic persons ability to recognize emotions in speech sounds correlates positively with education and negatively with age; but these relationships, especially the latter, should be taken with caution pending replication.

11

Minor studies and
some hypotheses

Joel R. Davitz

During the course of our research, many small-scale studies were conducted. Some were specifically designed as pilot studies for larger researches; others simply were informal exploratory investigations of what seemed to be interesting questions. For various reasons, these researches must be relegated to "minor" status. In some cases, the samples studied were too small to warrant firm conclusions; in one case, there was an unresolved statistical problem, which could not be resolved to complete satisfaction with the data at hand, but suggested new ways of collecting further data on an important issue; in another study, interesting post hoc findings occurred, but could hardly serve as a legitimate basis for generalization beyond the sample. Nevertheless, several of these studies suggest interesting new lines of investigation and thus deserve at least brief report. As a matter of fact, these studies represent an important aspect of our whole research effort, for it is largely on the basis of minor studies like those reported in this chapter that our research has progressed beyond the obvious.

THE STABILITY OF ERRORS IN
VOCAL COMMUNICATION

As part of standardizing the content-standard tape of vocal expressions described in Chapter 5, the vocal test was administered on two occasions, a week apart, to 38 subjects. The main purpose, of course, was to obtain an estimate of test-retest reliability, which proved to be 82.

This estimate was based on the number of correct responses made by each respondent, and the correlation obtained indicated fairly high consistency of performance over the two trials. But the data provided an opportunity to investigate another aspect of reliability, namely, the kinds of errors made and the stability of these erroneous responses.

The test consisted of 45 items, five expressions of eight different emotional meanings and five neutral or nonemotional expressions. Subjects (Ss) were instructed to identify each expression by choosing a response from the following list: affection, anger, boredom, cheerfulness, impatience, joy, sadness, satisfaction, and neutral or nonemotional.

The number of identical errors made on both trials was computed and transformed to per cent of total errors on both trials. An identical error was defined as the same erroneous response to the same item on both trials. The range of identical errors was from 52 to 95 per cent, with a mean of 74.9 per cent and standard deviation of 10.5. Thus, Ss, on the average, were remarkably stable in the specificity of their erroneous responses, though there were large individual differences in degree of stability.

A second way of analyzing erroneous responses is in terms of Osgood's three dimensions of connotative meaning: valence, activity, and strength (Osgood, et al., 1957). On the basis of previously obtained ratings, the eight emotional meanings were divided along each dimension as follows: (1) Valence: affection, cheerfulness, joy, and satisfaction were defined as positive; anger, boredom, impatience, and sadness as negative; (2) Activity: anger, cheerfulness, impatience, and joy were defined as active; affection, boredom, sadness, and satisfaction as passive; (3) Strength: affection, anger, joy, and sadness were defined as strong; boredom, cheerfulness, impatience, and satisfaction as weak.

Each S was assigned nine scores to describe the types of errors made. A *positive* error was scored when an S erroneously identified the expression of a negative valence emotion as a neutral or positive feeling; the erroneous response was closer to the positive end of the valence scale than was the meaning intended. For example, mistaking anger for joy was considered a positive type error. A *negative* error, on the other hand, was scored when an S erroneously identified the expression of a positive valence emotion as a neutral or negative feeling; the erroneous response was closer to the negative end of the valence scale than was the meaning intended. For example, mistaking affection for sadness was considered a negative type error. Similar scoring procedures were followed for each of the other two dimensions of meaning, activity and strength, and thus nine scores were computed for each S for each administration of the test: (1) total valence errors, (2) positive errors, (3) negative errors, (4) total activity errors, (5) active errors, (6) passive errors, (7) total strength errors, (8) strong errors, (9) weak errors.

Correlations between scores for the two administrations were computed, and the data are summarized in Table 11-1 under the column labeled "raw scores." All of the correlations are significantly different from zero at or beyond the .05 level. However, the test-retest correlation of total number of errors (or the inverse, total correct) was .82; therefore, simply the total number of errors could well have influenced the correlations obtained for each type of error. To obviate this effect,

Table 11-1. Test-Retest Reliabilities of Types of Errors Made on a Content-standard Test of Vocal Communication of Emotional Meanings

Type of error	Test-Retest raw scores	Correlation per cent of total errors
Total valence	.74**	.60**
Positive	.68**	.45**
Negative	.54**	.34*
Total activity	.59**	.47**
Active	.36*	.34*
Passive	.58**	.35*
Total strength	.65**	.48**
Strong	.55**	.47**
Weak	.35*	.00

* Significant at .05.
** Significant at .01.

each error score was transformed to per cent of total errors made on both administrations. For example, a total valence score of 50 per cent on test 1 means that the number of errors involving mistakes of valence on the first administration was 50 per cent of the total number of errors. The results of this analysis are summarized under the column labeled "per cent of total errors" in Table 11-1. All but one of these correlations are significantly different from zero, though in every case correction for total errors results in a reduction of the test-retest correlation.

The results demonstrate moderate test-retest stability of errors scored in terms of the three dimensions of connotative meaning. Thus, if a person makes a large number of valence errors on one occasion (mistaking positive for negative feelings, and vice versa), it is likely that he will make many valence errors on a second testing. This is also true for the activity and strength dimensions, though the correlations for these dimensions are somewhat smaller than that for total valence errors. Within each dimension, there is some stability, particularly within the valence and activity dimensions, though the correlation for weak type errors, when corrected for total errors, is zero.

In general, the results show considerable stability of specific erroneous responses. On the average, nearly 75 per cent of the erroneous responses on two occasions were identical; thus, since people tend to be consistent in the errors they make, one might ask, what kinds of people make what kinds of errors? Who is relatively consistent; who is inconsistent? Can we account for stable kinds of errors on the basis of motivational variables? Personality characteristics? Cognitive styles? Perceptual sets? Obviously, there are many possible leads for research, and certainly, this aspect of communication behavior is worth further investigation.

A COMPARISON OF ERRORS MADE BY PSYCHOTIC AND NONPSYCHOTIC PERSONS

Following a lead suggested by the previous study of errors, Naomi Rosenberg compared the kinds of errors made by three groups: (1) 15 paranoid psychotic males; (2) 15 nonparanoid psychotic males (comprised of patients diagnosed as schizophrenic, but without paranoid symptoms); and (3) 30 nonpsychotic males. The three groups were equated for age, verbal intelligence, socioeconomic class, and education. The 45-item content-standard tape of vocal expressions was administered and the erroneous responses were analyzed in terms of specific kinds of emotional meanings.

The erroneous responses made by each group are summarized in Table 11-2. Statistical analysis of this data was complicated by lack of

Table 11-2. Number of Erroneous Responses Made by Paranoid and Nonparanoid Psychotic Patients and a Nonpsychotic Sample

Group	N	Affec-tion	Anger	Bore-dom	Cheer	Impa-tience	Joy	Sad-ness	Satis.	Neutral
Normal	30	66	71	112	69	113	23	100	107	260
Nonparanoid psychotic	15	31	33	72	58	70	21	50	73	72
Paranoid psychotic	15	39	42	57	29	54	12	22	63	154

homogeneity of variance among the three groups in error scores for each category of emotional meaning, thus precluding an analysis of variance. In general, the paranoid group was consistently more variable than either of the other two groups. Therefore, the difference among the three groups for the total matrix was tested by chi square. The significance levels estimated by this analysis must be interpreted with caution because each S may have contributed more than once to any cell entry for his group; the total matrix thus does not satisfy the chi-square assumption of independence of observations. For exploratory purposes however, the chi-square analysis seemed most appropriate for evaluating the reliability of differences among the three groups.

The chi-square analyses, summarized in Table 11-3, show that the three groups in the present sample were clearly different from each

Table 11-3. Comparisons among Paranoid and Nonparanoid Psychotic Patients and a Nonpsychotic Sample in Terms of Erroneous Responses

Comparison	X^2	df	P
Nonpsychotic vs. paranoid vs. nonparanoid psychotic	73.2	16	< .001
Paranoid vs. nonparanoid psychotic	57.3	8	< .001
Nonparanoid psychotic vs. nonpsychotic	51.6	8	< .001
Paranoid psychotic vs. nonpsychotic	17.3	8	< .05
Psychotic vs. nonpsychotic	13.7	8	< .10 > .05

other in the kinds of erroneous responses emitted. Considered singly, each psychotic group differed significantly from the nonpsychotic sample; however, comparing the total psychotic group (paranoid and nonparanoid) with the nonpsychotic Ss, the difference does not achieve significance at the .05 level. Apparently the differential errors made by the paranoid and nonparanoid Ss mitigated the overall psychotic–nonpsychotic differences, an interpretation indirectly supported by the significant difference between the two psychotic samples. This difference in the pattern of errors made by the two psychotic subgroups also lends credence to the differential diagnosis of paranoid and nonparanoid psychosis.

Inspection of Table 11-2 reveals some of the obvious differences among the three groups. The nonparanoid psychotic Ss, in comparison to the other two groups, more frequently emitted responses of boredom, cheerfulness, impatience, and satisfaction (all relatively weak emotions); while the paranoid Ss much more frequently made erroneous responses in the neutral category. For the so-called strong emotions (affection, anger, joy, and sadness), there seemed to be comparatively few large differences among the groups, though the paranoid Ss made more frequent erroneous responses of both affection and anger. In the main, however, differences seem greatest for the relatively weaker emotional meanings (boredom, cheerfulness, impatience, satisfaction, and neutral). These categories tend to have the highest response frequencies, perhaps reflecting some sort of defensiveness, or at least some unwillingness among all Ss to respond in terms of the stronger emotional meanings.

None of these findings are conclusive, and certainly the specific differences found in this sample cannot be generalized. Nevertheless, the results offer some support for the potential value of investigating erroneous responses to emotional expressions. Though these data tell us little about the nature of schizophrenia, further research along this line may clarify the meaning of schizophrenic behavior in terms of disordered emotional communication.

CROSS-CULTURAL COMMUNICATION

A preliminary study of cross-cultural communication was conducted by Rina Kretsch, who investigated three questions: (1) Can speakers from one language culture communicate emotional meanings nonverbally to listeners from another culture? (2) Is nonverbal communication more accurate within cultures than across cultures? That is, do speakers communicate emotional meanings more effectively to listeners within their own language culture than they do to listeners from another cultural group? (3) Are there differences among cultures in the kinds of emotional meanings communicated most accurately?

To investigate these questions, Kretsch recorded three American, three Israeli, and three Japanese speakers, who expressed six emotional meanings by reciting the alphabet in their native languages. The six categories of emotional meaning were: (1) anger; (2) jealousy; (3) love; (4) nervousness; (5) pride; (6) sadness. These recordings were then played to 18 American, 15 Israeli, and 17 Japanese listeners, who were asked to identify the emotional meanings intended by each speaker. Accuracy of communication was defined as agreement between a listener's judgment and intent of the speaker.

All of the Ss in this study, both listeners and speakers, were students, and the Japanese and Israeli Ss had been in the United States for periods ranging from 6 to 18 months. Of course, this limits the generality of cross-cultural conclusions one can make on the basis of the data, since it is reasonable to expect that some learning of American vocal patterns occurs during a foreign student's residence in the United States. However, two factors probably minimized the effect of this learning on the present data: (1) speaking the alphabet in his native language probably enhanced each speaker's use of vocal cues characteristic of his own language; (2) the Israeli and Japanese Ss had had no direct experience with each other's language, and thus were not directly contaminated (for the purposes of this research) by common experience with American English. The results nevertheless must be interpreted within the limits imposed by the fact that all Ss were students with at least some common knowledge of American English.

The results are summarized in Table 11-4. Each listener tried to identify 18 expressions in each language. Thus, Table 11-4 shows that, on

Table 11-4. Means and Standard Deviations of Scores on Accuracy of Identification by Each Group of Listeners for Each Group of Speakers

Subjects		Japanese	Speakers Israelis	Americans
Japanese	$\bar{X}$	7.89*	7.64	6.94
	SD	1.96	1.66	1.82
Israelis	$\bar{X}$	7.26	9.00	7.73
	SD	2.63	2.92	2.02
Americans	$\bar{X}$	6.66	9.50	8.72
	SD	2.00	3.11	2.32

* A total of 18 items were expressed in each language.

the average, listeners correctly identified over one-third of the expressions both for speakers in their own language group and for speakers in other language groups. By chance, with six categories of emotional meaning, one would expect one-sixth correct identifications; the results obtained are significantly different from chance at or beyond the .01 level. Therefore, for the present sample at least, emotional meanings are indeed communicated with considerable accuracy across language cultures.

The second question Kretsch addressed herself to concerned differences in accuracy of communication within and between cultures. Combining scores for all groups of listeners, the mean accuracy score for "own language" speakers was 8.48 with a standard deviation of 2.41; for "other lanugage" speakers, the mean accuracy score obtained was 7.64 with a standard deviation of 2.61. The difference between these means is not statistically significant. In fact, within the present sample, the Israeli speakers communicated most accurately to American listeners. Moreover, considering only the Japanese and Israeli Ss, accuracy for "own language" speakers was not significantly higher than accuracy for "other language" speakers. Thus, the data not only suggest that emotional meanings are communicated accurately across cultures, but also, cross-cultural nonverbal communication is about as effective as nonverbal communication between speakers and listeners within the same language group.

Finally, the rank order of accuracy with which the various emotional meanings were communicated within each culture was examined. The results show a striking homogeneity among cultures. For both the American and Japanese groups, the emotional meanings were communicated in the following rank order of accuracy: anger, sadness, pride, love, nervousness, and jealousy. The Israeli data followed the same rank order except that sadness preceded anger by a slight difference.

Cross-cultural similarities, rather than differences, characterize the findings of this research. Of course, only small samples of speakers and listeners were studied; all of them were "contaminated" by some experience with American English; and all of them were students, certainly not representative of native speakers in each language. Despite these restrictions, the fact that the data consistently fail to show stable differences between language groups as different as American, Israeli, and Japanese certainly calls for further, more rigorous research in this intriguing area.

SENSITIVITY TO THE COMMUNICATION OF EMOTIONAL MEANINGS AND INTERPERSONAL COMPATIBILITY

It is usually assumed that mutual understanding is an important basis for successful interpersonal relationships, that people must be able to communicate with each other if they are to relate to each other in any positive way. Beginning with this assumption, Marion Hornstein investigated the relationship between compatibility among college roommates and their ability to understand each other's expressions of emotional meaning.

Among a large sample of freshman students living in the dormitory of an undergraduate college for women, Hornstein identified high and low compatible pairs of Ss. Low compatible pairs were defined as former roommates who had requested a change of roommates after living together for one semester, and whose combined preferences for each other on three sociometric devices was below the median of the total sample. High compatible pairs were defined as roommates who had lived together for at least one semester without requesting any change, and whose combined preferences for each other on the sociometric devices was above the median of the total sample. On this basis, two clearly different groups were selected; nine high compatible and seven low compatible pairs.

Following a content-standard procedure, each member of a pair tried to communicate to the other member of the pair eight emotional meanings plus one nonemotional or neutral category of meaning. The specific categories were: affection, anger, boredom, cheerfulness, impatience, joy, sadness, satisfaction, and neutral. The recitations were repeated twice in random order, so that each member of a pair attempted to identify 18 items expressed by the other person. In addition, general sensitivity to vocal expression was measured by responses to the 45-item tape described in Chapter 5.

The results for both groups are summarized in Table 11-5. Neither the difference in scores for the general tape nor the difference in scores

Table 11-5. Comparisons of High and Low Compatible Pairs on General Sensitivity and on Ability to Understand Roommate's Expressions of Emotional Meanings

	Low compatible (N = 14)	High compatible (N = 18)	t	p
General tape				
$\bar{X}$	22.14	21.22	.31	> .05
SD	3.94	3.39		
Roommate expression				
$\bar{X}$	8.93	9.39	.38	> .05
SD	2.94	1.84		

for identifying roommate's expressions is statistically significant. However, inspection of the distribution of scores for understanding roommate's expressions revealed that Ss in the low compatible pairs appeared either at the top or at the bottom of the distribution, while Ss in high compatible pairs were consistently in the middle of the distribution. The total sample of 32 Ss was divided into quartiles 1 and 4 (the extremes) versus quartiles 2 and 3 (the middle of the distribution); the distribution of high and low compatible Ss was compared, and the significance of the differences evaluated by chi square with 1 degree of freedom. The chi square obtained was 4.6, significant beyond the .05

level, thus supporting the observations that high and low compatible Ss were distributed differently over the range of sensitivity.

The results suggest a curvilinear relationship between interpersonal compatibility and sensitivity to each other's expressions of emotional meaning. Both very high and very low sensitivity were associated with low compatibility in Hornstein's sample, while the high compatible pairs were neither too sensitive nor too insensitive to each other. Perhaps interpersonal compatibility requires some minimal level of sensitivity to each other; without this minimal level, it seems likely that conflicts would occur simply as a result of ignorance of each other. On the other hand, too great a sensitivity to each other may interfere with interpersonal functioning; perhaps some "blindness" or "interpersonal repression" of information is necessary for getting along together in daily living. Or, it is also possible that the experiences which led to high and low compatibility may have led to differential sharpening or dulling of sensitivity to expressions of the other person. At any rate, notwithstanding the limitations of the present study, the results suggest that the relation between emotional sensitivity and interpersonal compatibility is a profitable line for future research. Moreover, the assumption of a simple linear relationship between sensitivity and compatibility hardly is tenable in light of the present results. Certainly this research needs to be replicated, for if it is reasonable to assume that emotional sensitivity plays an important role in interpersonal relations, it is also obvious that that role is not clearly understood.

INCREASING SENSITIVITY TO EMOTIONAL EXPRESSIONS

The research thus far reported has not been concerned directly with practical or applied problems, but one conceivably useful outcome of research in this area is the development of techniques for increasing a person's emotional sensitivity. Steven Mattis addressed himself to this problem in a study comparing the performance of Ss who were given experience expressing and identifying emotional expressions with the performance of a control group who received no special training.

The Ss were 44 undergraduate college students. The control group consisted of 21 Ss who first tried to identify the emotional expressions on the tape developed by Beldoch (Chapter 3), were then given a 15-minute "coffee break," and then repeated the procedure with the Beldoch tape.

The pre- and posttesting procedure for the 23 experimental Ss was the same as that for the control group; however, between the pre- and posttests, the experimental Ss received a variety of experiences. They were divided into subgroups of three or four Ss each. They first listened to a practice tape in which speakers recited the alphabet trying to express each of the emotional meanings contained in the Beldoch test. Ss tried to identify the emotional meanings expressed on the practice tape; then the practice tape was replayed, and before each item, Ss were told which emotional meaning the speaker was trying to express. Then, each S attempted to express each emotional meaning contained in the Beldoch test, and these expressions were discussed by the other members of each S's subgroup. These training sessions lasted approximately 15 minutes, and after training, the Ss once again took the Beldoch test.

The results are summarized in Table 11-6. Both groups showed an increment of scores on the second trial. For the experimental group,

Table 11-6. The Mean Number of Correct Identifications of Vocal Expressions of Emotion

Group	N	Test Mean	SD	Retest Mean	SD	Difference between means
Experimental	23	22.58	2.32	24.92	3.13	2.34
Control	21	20.52	3.48	21.86	3.33	1.34

the correlation between initial score and increment was —.49; for the control group, —.57. Both correlations are significantly different from zero beyond the .01 level, indicating that most of the increment for both groups occurred with those Ss whose initial scores were relatively low. Comparing the increment of scores in the two groups by analysis of covariance, controlling for initial scores, an F of 7.7 was obtained, which is significant beyond the .01 level. Thus, the results support the hypothesis that training increased accuracy of identification.

The training procedures used in this study were too gross to permit specific designation of the degree to which each aspect of the training influenced final performance. But this was not the purpose of the study. Mattis's aim was to determine whether or not *any* kind of short-term training effected a stable difference in test performance, and his findings demonstrate that the particular procedures he used indeed had such an effect. Therefore, while the methods used in this study may or may not be the most effective ones to follow, the results clearly indicate that sensitivity to emotional expressions can be increased by training. Further research can thus be aimed at the more precise goal of defining those experiences which are most fruitful in increasing sensitivity.

SUMMARY AND DISCUSSION

Although the studies reported in this chapter may not provide enough rigorously collected data to establish a basis for confident generalizations, each of the studies suggest a variety of interesting problems for further investigation.

Consider, for example, the finding that people tend to be rather stable in the kinds of errors they make when reacting to vocal expressions of emotional meaning. Most of the research in this area has used a gross estimate of sensitivity based on total correct identifications, but obviously, this represents only one aspect of the overall communication process. People undoubtedly make errors in communication not only in a laboratory situation but also in everyday life. And if these errors are consistent, as they appear to be, one might infer that something about the person determines the particular kinds of errors he makes. If his channels of communication are consistently distorted in one way or another, we can expect his behavior to be similarly distorted. Thus, the investigation of stable patterns of error in communication offers a potentially useful way of investigating various intrapsychic as well as interpersonal phenomena.

From the personality theorist's point of view one might ask, what kinds of persons make what kinds of errors? Rosenberg's study of paranoid and nonparanoid psychotic patients represents a beginning in this direction, but certainly many other problems relevant to personality theory present themselves as one considers the general question of why different people consistently make different kinds of errors. Within the normal range of psychological adjustment, the previous study of possible personality correlates of emotional sensitivity, based on a measure of total correct identifications, Chapter 5, clearly indicated a blind alley for research in this direction. However, with more precise measures of communication behavior, specifying, perhaps, the *pattern* of both right and wrong responses, a more profitable and more meaningful avenue of research is open. In my opinion, the initial stage of research in this area is represented by studies using gross measures of communication behavior, such as an overall estimate of sensitivity based on a count of total correct responses. We know that the behaviors we've studied in this way are fairly stable, and are related to certain other variables. But I suspect that a next stage of research, at least in part, will involve more specific measures of communication behavior, illustrated by our preliminary studies of errors in identification.

Kretsch's study of cross-cultural communication provides an exciting hint of the knowledge to be gained in this area of investigation, knowledge which may have not only important theoretical, but also potentially significant, applied implications. The results of this small study, with all its limitations, are indeed encouraging for international, cross-cultural understanding. Perhaps the verbal aspects of communication create more noise, in this case, than the nonverbal, and it is intriguing to imagine, for a moment, the meetings of a nonverbal United Nations. At any rate, the problems in this area have only tentatively been touched by Kretsch's study, and a host of questions remain to be investigated. The fact that nonverbal, cross-cultural communication occurs with considerable accuracy does not preclude differences among cultures in expressing certain emotional meanings. But Kretsch's results suggest that among the three cultures compared in her study, the Israeli, Japanese, and American, there are more similarities than differences in communication. It seems likely that the differences involve subtle cues of intonation and inflection which communicate shades of meaning that were not measured in this preliminary study. Also, of course, before making a generalization with reasonable confidence, we will have to study communication between persons who have had no appreciable experience with each other's language.

In an indirect way, further cross-cultural investigation is likely to shed some light on determining those aspects of emotional communication which are independent of learning. Language learning obviously differs from culture to culture, and presumably this learning influences the way in which emotional meanings are communicated. But if Kretsch's findings are indeed stable and can legitimately be generalized to other cultures, the overlay of differential learning may have less effect on nonverbal communication than one might expect on the basis of obvious verbal differences. For the most part, writers have emphasized differences between cultures in manner of communication, though most of the evidence in this area is remarkably casual. The point, of course, is not to argue about similarities or differences, but rather to turn to the task of discovering who communicates what to whom, with an empirical account of the means and results of cross-cultural communication.

The possibility of teaching people to be more sensitive to emotional communication is encouraged by Mattis's results. In the schools, of course, and in most informal education situations in our culture, discursive communication, primarily in the verbal mode, is emphasized. Ability to understand nonverbal expressions of emotional meaning develops largely without formal tuition, and in light of the complexity of this kind of communication, it is somewhat surprising that people perform as well as they do in understanding the messages expressed. Nevertheless, Mattis's results offer some hope that directed, planned experiences in nonverbal communication can influence a person's sensitivity in this area. For those involved in the training of clinical psychologists, psychiatrists, social workers, and other professionals concerned with emotional communication, fostering emotional sensitivity through some sort of educational experience is an exciting possibility. However, before such a possibility can even remotely be realized, we need to specify in considerable detail the kinds of experiential factors which are likely to increase sensitivity. On the basis of Mattis's study little can be said about what sort of training will be most effective for modifying general sensitivity. It is possible, for example, that the usefulness of procedures followed in this study is restricted to the kind of response required by his test instrument. That is, he may have taught his experimental Ss merely to be test-wise in regards to the specific test he used. But at least we know that emotional sensitivity, whether or not it is specific to one kind of response or one kind of instrument, can be altered by training. The problem for further research, therefore, is to discover those kinds of experiences which influence a more generalized ability to understand emotional communications.

The interesting results obtained by Hornstein suggest at least one way of identifying some factors which influence interpersonal compatibility. If Hornstein's results are replicable, we would need to revise a common assumption that sensitivity to another person is always a positive determinant of compatibility. Too great an awareness of another person's emotional expressions may be as detrimental as too little awareness. Perhaps different kinds of interpersonal relations require different kinds and degrees of sensitivity; a marital relationship may have communication requirements different from those of an everyday work relationship. And perhaps different kinds of incompatibility result from various patterns of mutual sensitivity or insensitivity. High mutual sensitivity may result in recurrent irritation, while mutual ignorance may lead to a different brand of confusion, misunderstanding, and incompatibility. None of these questions is answered by Hornstein's results, but her study clearly indicates an important area for research and a valuable technique of investigation.

12

The communication of emotional meaning by metaphor

Joel R. Davitz and Steven Mattis

Although most of the studies reported in this book are concerned with nonverbal modes of communication, emotional meanings obviously are communicated by verbal, as well as nonverbal, means. The present study, therefore, focuses on a verbal technique of expressing emotional meanings, namely, the use of metaphorical statements.

The research had three major purposes: (1) to define the characteristics of metaphors which communicate each of several different emotional meanings; (2) to develop a reliable test of ability to identify metaphorical expressions of emotional meaning; and (3) to investigate the relation between ability to identify emotional meaning expressed metaphorically and ability to identify emotional meaning expressed in other modes of communication.

CHARACTERISTICS OF METAPHORS

To identify the characteristics of metaphors which communicate various emotional meanings, a sample of metaphors was obtained, judges identified those metaphors which communicated particular emotional meanings, and these statements were then examined for cues which characterized the metaphors in each class of emotional meaning. These cues were then cross-validated with a second sample of metaphors.

157

Procedure

Webster's *New Collegiate Dictionary* defines metaphor as: "A figure of speech in which a word or phrase literally denoting one kind of object or idea is used in place of another by way of suggesting a likeness or analogy between them." In a sense, the Rorschach procedure is designed to elicit metaphors, words or phrases "literally denoting one kind of object or idea" in describing or responding to an inkblot. Therefore, a modification of standard Rorschach procedure seemed highly appropriate as a means of obtaining samples of metaphors. The first sample was obtained by presenting cards 2, 4, 6, 8, and 10 of the Rorschach to 16 *S*s, and asking each *S* to report what the blot reminded him of or what the blot looked like. In each case, however, the *S* was asked to report a percept which expressed one of five emotional meanings: anger, anxiety, joy, love, or sadness. The emotional meanings associated with each card were rotated so that different *S*s were asked to express different meanings for each card. Thus, for example, one *S* was instructed to express anger in response to card 2, anxiety to card 4, joy to card 6, love to card 8, and sadness to card 10, while for a second *S*, sadness was paired with card 2, love with card 4, anger with 6, anxiety with 8, and joy with 10.

Following this procedure, 72 statements were collected. These statements, of course, were metaphors in that the responses, such as, "A bear was just shot," were obviously not literally applicable to the ink blot stimulus, but rather, they were based on some sort of perceived resemblance. In some instances, similes were obtained, such as, "It looks like a monster coming after me," but for the purpose of this study, the distinction between similes and metaphors seems irrelevant, and the total sample of statements might reasonably be considered within a general class of metaphors.

The 72 metaphors were then presented to 26 judges who were asked to identify which of the five emotional meanings was being expressed. A metaphor was said to express a given emotional meaning if it satisfied two criteria: (1) a plurality of judges agreed with the intent of the *S* who made the statement; and (2) the number of judges who agreed with the intended meaning exceeded the number expected by chance at the .01 level. Of the total sample, 51 metaphors satisfied these two criteria.

Results

The 51 metaphors which communicated the intended emotional meaning are listed in Table 12-1. Grouping the metaphors in categories

Table 12-1. First Sample of Metaphors Which Communicated Emotional Meanings

Anger
1. Looks like a bull charging.
2. It looks like a cat that's hissing at something.
3. They look like reindeer. There's a bridge and this side is at war with that side.
4. Two little dogs stamping on each other.
5. A kind of insect which annoys me.

Anxiety
6. It looks like a class that's hoping for high marks.
7. Fragmentation.
8. It looks like unstableness, instability. Looks ike emotion, confusion. The person doesn't know what to do. He wants to put these things together but doesn't know how.
9. It looks like confusion.
10. Two animals having a foot in a trap. He doesn't have sufficient footing.
11. The backside of a gorilla, arms extended menacingly looking. Has a long tail.
12. It looks like a monster coming after me.
13. Two pink figures on the right are two wild birds and rat combinations treading upon grey part to devour it.
14. A fox. His hair is standing up because he might be shot by a hunter. He's going to be shot.
15. Some kind of bird who flew up there because someone is after him.
16. Two animals searching for food or something. Looking.

Joy
17. An infant lying on its back, hands extended in the air.
18. Two people. Looks like they're at a party and having fun.
19. All sorts of crazy animated animals having a party.
20. A whole group of people getting together and expressing different ideas and having agreement.
21. It looks like a face with a smile, like someone laughing.
22. The colors seem to be free and not set in a pattern. Relaxed and bright.
23. A person sitting on chair, laughing, sitting back and saying, "Yay."
24. It looks like a birthday coloring. The kind of colors used for decorating for a party.
25. A huge giant laughing uproariously. Seems to be throwing his head back and laughing.
26. Two people dancing, clapping hands.
27. A dancing mote, fleck of dust, in the sun. Bubbles of champagne.
28. A skin or pelt. A fine fur coat.
29. It expresses brightness. It looks adventurous.
30. Two men with beards extending their hands in greeting.

Love
31. Looks like two animals trying to get together.
32. A male and female. There's equality in it.

Table 12-1. First Sample of Metaphors Which Communicated Emotional Meanings. (*Continued*)

33. Two animals climbing up a mountain to get to each other. They're mates on opposite sides of a mountain.
34. The blending of the colors are serene and peaceful. Reminds me of a sunset.
35. Two puppies that are very close. Could be siblings.
36. A symbol of unity. Reminds me of an eagle. Some sort of bird.
37. A merging or union of two separate bodies.
38. Two bears hugging each other.
39. Two creatures talking, having an animated conversation, interested in each other. Two snakes together meaning nearness. All these express two of a kind.
40. Seems like everything there is looking to get together. Two crabs, two animals. The color is like springtime.

Sadness
41. It looks like death and someone is crying. Like it's all smeared.
42. A bear was just shot.
43. Looks like a face with a dropped mouth.
44. Two bears caught in a trap, bleeding all over. Look like mates.
45. It looks like somebody or something that's lying there.
46. The colors are going from light to dismal, birth, life, then death.
47. A placenta. Loss of an unborn child.
48. A person lying prostrate with no urge to do anything.
49. Looks like dirty tears.
50. It just reminds me of the sun going down with the colors in the sky. The reds, oranges, blues, and then the grey descending on all of it. It's nightfall.
51. Because of the shades it looks empty and hollow.

of emotional meaning, they were studied with the aim of discovering cues which charactized the statements in each category. As indicated by the statements in Table 12-1, there is a good deal of obvious commonality among the metaphors in each category, but the goal of the research was to define, with as much specificity as possible, the nature of these commonalities.

There appeared to be three kinds of cues contained in the statements: (1) those describing a situation; (2) those referring to what might best be called "symptoms," or expressive behaviors; and (3) words with apparently connotive or subjective referents. For example, the metaphors which communicated anxiety contained one or more of the following characteristics: (1) a threatening situation; (2) an expressive behavior or symptom like "hair standing up"; or (3) words such as "fragmentation, instability, confusion."

The tripart scheme of classification seemed more or less appropriate for all five classes of emotional meaning, and thus, a tentative table of characteristics was compiled in terms of these three categories. The results of this tentative classification are summarized in Table 12-2.

Although the characteristics noted in Table 12-2 were comprehensive enough to account for the first sample of metaphors, our aim was to develop a dictionary with some generality beyond that of our initial sample of metaphors. Therefore, the study was replicated for the purpose of cross-validating the code or dictionary of characteristics defined in the first part of the study.

Table 12-2. Characteristics of Metaphors in First Sample

Emotional meaning	Situation	Characteristic expressive behavior	Words with subjective referent
Anxiety	Threat, danger	Hair standing up	Fragmentation, instability, confusion
Anger	Active hostility	Hissing	
Sadness	Loss, death	Drooped mouth crying, lying prostrate	Empty, hollow
Love	Two coming together	Hugging	Serene, peaceful
Joy	Pleasure, enjoyment on going	Smiling, laughing	Animated, brightness

Cross-validation

For this part of the study, cards 1, 3, 5, 7, and 9 of the Rorschach were presented to 15 Ss with the same instructions given in the initial collection of data. A total of 73 statements were collected, and these were submitted to 27 judges who were asked to identify which of the five emotional meanings was expressed by each statement. Using the same criteria defined in the first part of this study, 62 metaphors were found to communicate the intended emotional meaning.

The 62 metaphors collected in the cross-validation procedure are listed in Table 12-3, and inspection of these statements in relation to those contained in Table 12-1 reveals marked similarities between the two sets of data.

To estimate the applicability of the tentative dictionary of characteristics developed on the basis of the first sample of metaphors (Table 12-2), three judges were asked to classify the 62 metaphors in the second sample using the characteristics noted in Table 12-2. The judges were given a copy of Table 12-2, except that *group 1* was substituted for "anxiety," *group 2* for "anger," etc.; they were instructed to place a statement in a particular group if it contained any of the characteristics cited for that group. Thus, if the tentative dictionary was also valid for the second set of metaphors, and if the judges made no judgmental

Table 12-3. Second Sample of Metaphors Which Communicated Emotional Meanings

Anger

1. Face of a cat, eyes slanted down, mouth open hissing. Pffft.
2. I see two men, tribal men, kicking, a ritualistic way of expressing their feelings about some act committed against their tribe. Red is a symbol for the feeling of the group and of them. There has been a great transgression and something must be done to compensate for this according to the custom of the tribe. Red is the symbol for the bloodshed that will come. The tiger is a symbol of their method of dealing with transgression.
3. Two old ladies hissing at each other. They were having a fight and started to walk away from each other. Then it occurred to each simultaneously that the other might be watching her and so they both turned around simultaneously and are saying something vituperative. Maybe they both said at the same time, "You old witch."
4. I'm impressed with the rock-like hardness of these figures who seem diametrically opposed to each other across an insurmountable chasm.
5. I see a cat's mask glaring. The kind of mask one buys for Halloween.
6. Some sort of funny man, furrow in his brow, menacing look in his eyes. Some sort of helmet on his head, a war bonnet. A mustache looks like something worn at the turn of the century. A big superbly adorned face with a menacing look.
7. This appears to be some ferocious person, a glint in his eyes, smoke springing from his mouth, probably from a cigarette. His wife probably did something he didn't like. Maybe she slapped him.
8. A large bird with outspread wings preparing to attack another bird in rivalry.
9. Two opposing forces in opposition. Two things that are conflicting against each other.
10. Two women facing each other. This looks as if they're about to haul off and hit each other. You can tell they're about to hit each other because their faces are close together. One is saying "Yeah" and the other is saying "Yeah."
11. This is a bat with holes shot in its face and it's coming toward the person who shot it with its teeth bared.

Anxiety

12. A being that's kind of deformed symbolizes the inner state of an individual. Aloneness. A kind of reaching out but not getting any place. Big wings trying to grasp but not really making it.
13. Two people. Two horrible things are emerging from their heads. From their minds. A kind of ectoplasm emerging from their brain pads. Two orange things, horrible nightmarish creatures. The green people seem to be frowning and the orange things smiling maliciously as if they know the harm they were doing to their owners. And the harm is pressing down.
14. Two distrustful forces staring at each other not being able to do too much.
15. This figure seems to be disintegrating, falling apart from within. The white separation makes it look like the side is departing from the center of the figure. The two figures here are a feeble attempt to solidify it.
16. A huge sort of monster with two legs, arms, a mouth with arms to scoop something up. An octopus or some sort of crustacean. Some sort of headpiece or crown on top.

Table 12-3. Second Sample of Metaphors Which Communicated Emotional Meanings. (*Continued*)

17. Here is a plane that's about to crash. It's in flames. There's nothing that can be done. It's completely out of control.
18. A crocodile rearing its head out of the water. A very gloomy figure. A symbol of some impending fated danger.
19. A grimacing, evil, black cat staring at me.
20. This is two girls with their feet in buckets resting on a crest in the ground. The buckets are rocking and they are about to fall backwards.
21. Two things attached at the bottom and trying to come together at the top in the same way. A reaching out to come together, in a sense to complete the figure.
22. It appears that this bat is flying and there's someone, who can't be seen in the picture, trying to hide from it, probably crouching behind a rock.
23. A bat, a big black bat circling over my head coming closer and closer darting at my head.
24. Finding oneself surrounded by strange creatures sort of poised ready to spring.
25. I see a chasm. There are Arabs and one is holding on to the arm of another who is going to fall into a chasm. He is in a very precarious situation.

Joy
26. A bird soaring high in the sky.
27. This looks like a little creature such as you might see in a Walt Disney picture. Reminds me of "Fantasia." It's flying upward. It's soaring as if the sky is the limit, just bursting with vitality and exuberance.
28. It's spring. Birds singing. Little bug-like things dancing. A groundhog came up.
29. Two girls, pixie-like, talking to each other, chatting with each other and giggling.
30. These people are dancing around doing some sort of a fancy type step.
31. Colorful, light-hearted. A lot of little figures scurrying around. An air of lightness and brightness.
32. Two gazelle-like birds, alive, gazelle-like birds, alive, gracefully expressing their feeling. They might be figures used in a Mike Todd production, used to publicize a ballet. There's a light airy quality to them, gracefulness of neck and movement of wings carry off lightness.
33. This is two women at a wild party after winning a reward for designing the best bow-tie in the United States. They're bouncing a large replica of it on a blanket between them.
34. Bright colors. Dancing figures. A great deal of movement.
35. I see dancers and they are in the middle of a fantastic leap. They are Russian dancers, two men and a woman in the middle. The men have their arms linked with the woman's arms which are extended to the side. Her head is thrown back revealing her high stiff collar. The men are wearing peaked fur caps and their legs are drawn up indicating that they have made a tremendous leap. The music is fast and wild and you really get a sense of movement.
36. A butterfly soaring into the air, looping and curving.
37. Two lambs. They're looking at each other. They're playfully on hind legs, their paws in the air, rather graceful. There appears to be a smile on their mouths.
38. A flower garden that gives many people pleasure as they pass by on a cheerful sunny morning.

Table 12-3. Second Sample of Metaphors Which Communicated Emotional Meanings. (*Continued*)

Love

39. Two people flirting with each other, lips puckered, standing on opposite sides of a table. It must be Spring because there is a pretty red butterfly.
40. Two people looking at each other.
41. It's warm and soft. The masses of blot at the sides I associate it with something furry. Someone lying down wrapped in a blanket or something furry. Probably two people although they are ill-defined.
42. Harmony, balance of right and left-hand side. In both shape and color bilateral harmony. A combination of elements coming together. Togetherness. Even elements apart are harmonious.
43. Two symmetrical sides seem to be coming together in a sort of unity.
44. Two people meeting on a street who have bumped into each other accidentally and are picking up their packages. They see each other and smile at each other.
45. Two individuals finding each other, shy of each other, not sure if they should approach each other.
46. Two little girls sitting across from each other with their knees touching, talking very friendly in a best-friend manner.
47. This looks like two arms coming out as if they were going to embrace you or envelop you. It gives me a feeling of warmth. If I were to be enveloped by these arms, I would feel wanted.
48. There is a man and a woman. They are taking their baby for a stroll. They are bending over the child each looking at it.

Sadness

49. One animal looking at another in a mirror. They died and went to heaven. They want to go back down for a day but can't.
50. A moth whose wings are worn out, about to die. He's about had it.
51. I see two figures looking kind of mournfully at each other. Their feeling is there but it's being expressed in a somewhat stylized form, eye movement and gesture of face. This is a way of both expressing and containing the feeling.
52. Two native women beating a drum softly. Sort of a mourning background music.
53. Native mourners around a ceremonial drum. They're dancing around the drum. A sort of dirge. Someone's death symbolized by red blood.
54. This is a moth who is living the last moments of his life. His wings are tattered and torn and he is crawling along the ground toward death.
55. Faded costumes, lying around. Probably belonged to a great dancer at the height of her career, but now she's old and so are they. They're of no use because they've gone out of style. They're only reminders of something that's past.
56. The colors are gray, dark, and somber.
57. These people are leaving their loved ones behind. They are waving goodbye.
58. Two little babies that have been abandoned on someone's doorstep.
59. A little dog moving along pushing some kind of cotton candy in a kind of mournful way. As though his master has gone away on a trip and he's on his own. He's not very well compensating for this feeling by relating to his inanimate object which doesn't substitute for the warmth and protection of his master.

Table 12-3. Second Sample of Metaphors Which Communicated Emotional Meanings. (*Continued*)

---

60. A skeleton of a poor animal that was trapped and that just died and rotted there.
61. The wings droop down. It's not moving. It's incapacitated.
62. This looks like pallbearers carrying a coffin, dressed in black and the coffin in black. It looks as if they're just lowering it into the grave.

---

errors, one would expect 100 per cent correct classification; at the other extreme, if the judges operated at chance level, one would expect 20 per cent correct classification.

Judge 1 correctly classified 84 per cent of the statements; judge 2, 75 per cent; and judge 3, 82 per cent. Obviously, these results suggest a fairly high degree of generality for the tentative dictionary, but such an interpretation is somewhat mitigated by the judges' probable awareness that each group of statements had a similar emotional meaning; therefore, classifying the statements according to the stated criteria was undoubtedly influenced by the judges' guesses about what emotional meanings were involved. The results nevertheless lend credence to the generality of the initial system of classification.

Despite the fairly high accuracy of the judgments, indicating that the majority of metaphors within each category of emotional meaning had the same characteristics as those in the first sample, the success of any one judge was far from perfect. Errors in classification might have at least two sources: (1) they might arise as a function of the invalidity or limitations of the guide for judgment; or (2) they might be a function of the judges inability to correctly classify a statement even though the guide for classification was valid. Errors stemming from the judges themselves or the judgmental process are not our concern; however, if errors arising from a faulty dictionary or guide for judgment (Table 12-2) could be identified, we would have some basis for correcting the faults of our tentative scheme of classification.

There is no sure way of identifying such errors, but an examination of the data obtained from the three judges provided a possible basis for making such an identification. It was reasoned that an erroneous classification of an item by only one judge probably was a function of the judge, while if all three judges erred in classifying an item, it was more likely to be a function of an invalid scheme of classification. If two of the three judges erred in classifying an item, the appropriate inference about the source of error is more difficult, though a somewhat stronger case might be made for assigning the error to an invalid dictionary if the two judges who erred in classifying an item placed it in the same incorrect category. On the basis of this reasoning, the following, admittedly arbitrary, criterion was used in identifying items which reflected a defect in the scheme of characteristics presented in Table 12-2: The item was incorrectly classified (i.e., placed in a category of emotional meaning other than that intended) by at least two of the judges, and at least two judges placed the item in the same erroneous category.

Six such items were identified. Following the numbering scheme of items listed in Table 12-3, these were numbers 6 and 8, both of which communicated anxiety, but were classified by the judges in the anger group; number 21, which also communicated anxiety but was grouped with the love items; and number 44, which was intended to express love but was classified in the group meant to express joy.

These specific items were examined in greater detail to search for some lead in modifying the characteristics for each emotional meaning. Three of the six items involved the confusion of anger and anxiety. Neither item 6 (the man with the war bonnet) nor item 8 (the bird preparing to attack) actually satisfy the criterion of active, ongoing hostility specified for metaphors of anger in Table 12-2, and thus the judges appropriately did not classify them in the anger group. Yet these items did indeed communicate anger to a large plurality of Ss. In item 6, the word "war" might have carried the active meaning of anger; in item 8, the act of hostility seems momentarily imminent. At any rate, both items suggest some revision of the table of characteristics.

Item 13 (horrible creatures emerging from two heads) was classified in the anger group, but actually communicated anxiety. A relatively long statement, in comparison to the other metaphors obtained, the first part seems to fit well with the characteristics of anxiety. The last two phrases, however, do not clearly fit the criteria for anxiety: (1) the next to last phrase is, "they know the harm they *were* doing to their owners," which seems more appropriate, according to the tentative guide, for sadness, and (2) the last phrase is, "The harm is pressing down," which clearly fits the active hostility criterion for anger. All three judges apparently focused on this last phrase and classified the item in the anger group.

This item illustrates a problem not successfully dealt with in the initial outline of characteristics. Any single metaphor may well contain characteristics of several emotional meanings. Item 13 has characteristics of both anxiety and anger, and perhaps even sadness; the problem, of course, is to specify some criterion for deciding which of these is the primary meaning, though it must also be recognized that in everyday communication, verbal statements probably simultaneously express more than one emotional meaning. Limiting the identification of meaning for each statement to one category, while perhaps experimentally useful, may thus serve to distort the results in terms of their relation to everyday communication.

Item 12 (a deformed being) presents the same problem. Although it communicated anxiety, the judges indicated that this item had the characteristics of sadness. In this instance, the word "aloneness" probably was the major influence on the judges' decisions. In another instance, item 21, which communicated anxiety, seemed to contain the characteristics of metaphors of love (two becoming one), though in this item, the tension expressed by the phrase "trying to come together" does not quite fit the "successful coming together" implied in the outline of characteristics associated with the communication of love.

The final item clearly indicating a defect in Table 12-2 was number 44, intended to express love, and indeed containing a major characteristic of this category of meaning (two people coming together), but also containing a bit of expressive behavior, a "smile," usually associated with joy. Joy and love, of course, are presumably closely allied emotional states, and perhaps the more remarkable aspect of the data is that so few of the love metaphors contained characteristics of joy.

The results of the cross-validation tend to support the generality of the tentative outline of metaphor characteristics which communicate each of the five emotional meanings; however, an examination of the second sample of metaphors, and in particular, those metaphors which clearly did not fit into the original scheme, led to further modification and expansion of the dictionary of characteristics associated with the various categories of emotion. This revised outline is presented in Table 12-4. Though not intended as a universally applicable dictionary of metaphorical meaning, the encouraging results of the cross-validation, plus the fact that the revised outline is based on a fairly large number of statements (113) which reliably communicate a particular emotional meaning lends some support to the hypothesis that the characteristics listed in Table 12-4 have validity beyond the scope of this immediate study. At any rate, Table 12-4 represents a beginning in the direction of empirically defining the characteristics of one kind of verbal statement which communicates emotional meaning.

THE METAPHOR TEST

The next step in this research was to develop a test which measured the ability to identify emotional meanings expressed metaphorically. Starting with the pool of metaphors that successfully communicated each of the emotional meanings (i.e., the items contained in Tables 12-1 and

Table 12-4. Revised Characteristics of Metaphors Which Communicate Emotional Meanings

Emotional meaning	Situation	Expressive behavior	Words with subjective referent
Anxiety	Threat; impending hostility or danger; fearful object	Grimacing, staring, hair standing up	Fragmentation, instability, confusion, tension
Anger	Hostility ongoing or momentarily imminent; warlike figure	Hissing, teeth bared, smoke springing from mouth	Harsh
Sadness	Loss; death or dying; hostility already occurred	Drooped mouth; crying; lying prostrate	Empty, hollow, dismal, dark, grey, somber
Love	Two animals or persons coming together; objects in harmony or unity	Hugging, kissing	Serene, peaceful, warm, soft
Joy	Ongoing active pleasure	Smiling, laughing	Animated, pleasant, brightness, lightness

12-3), and proceeding by a series of item analyses, the metaphor test, presented in Table 12-5, was developed. It is comprised of the 63 most discriminating items from the total pool of 113 metaphors collected in the first part of the study. On the basis of data obtained from 62 Ss, a test-retest reliability coefficient of .85 was obtained.

Some Intercorrelations

Having developed a reliable test of the ability to identify emotional meanings expressed in a verbal mode, our attention shifted to the relation between emotional sensitivity in the verbal mode and sensitivity to emotional expressions in nonverbal modes. This problem, of course, is related to the investigation reported by Beldoch (Chapter 3), who found that abilities in various nonverbal modes of communication were positively interrelated. The question we were concerned with, then, was whether or not emotional sensitivity in a verbal mode was positively related to sensitivity to nonverbal expressions of emotional meaning.

To investigate this problem, the metaphor test, the test of vocal communications described in Chapter 5, and a test of ability to recognize the emotional meaning of facial expressions were administered to 45 Ss who were graduate students enrolled in a summer session at Columbia University. All Ss were native speakers of English.

Table 12-5. The Metaphor Test

Listed below are a number of statements. In each case, the person who made the statement was trying to express one of five different emotional meanings: anger, anxiety, joy, love, or sadness. Please read each statement and decide which emotional meaning is being expressed. Write the name of the emotion on the line at the left of each statement.

Anger
Anxiety
Joy
Love
Sadness

Key   Remember, write the name of the one emotional meaning you think is expressed by each statement. Work rapidly and do not omit any items.

Anxiety   1. Here is a plane that's about to crash. It's in flames. There's nothing that can be done. It's completely out of control.

Love   2. It's warm and soft. The masses of blot at the sides I associate with something furry. Someone lying down wrapped in a blanket or something. Probably two people although they are ill-defined.

Sadness   3. A bear was just shot.

Anger   4. Two old ladies hissing at each other. They were having a fight and started to walk away from each other. Then it occurred to each simultaneously that the other might be watching her and so they both turned around simultaneously and are saying something vituperative. Maybe they both said at the same time, "You old witch."

Sadness   5. Faded costumes, lying around. Probably belonging to a great dancer at the height of her career, but now she's old and so are they. They're of no use because they've gone out of style. They're only reminders of something that's past.

Sadness   6. It looks like death and someone is crying. Like it's all smeared.

Anxiety   7. A fox. His hair is standing up because he might be shot by a hunter. He's going to be shot.

Love   8. Two animals climbing up a mountain to get to each other. They're mates on opposite sides of a mountain.

Anger   9. Two little dogs stamping on each other.

Anxiety   10. Fragmentation.

Love   11. Harmony, balance of right and left-hand side. In both shape and color bilateral harmony. A combination of elements coming together. Togetherness. Even elements apart are harmonious.

Anger   12. This is a bat with holes shot in its face and it's coming toward the person who shot it with its teeth bared.

Anxiety   13. It looks like unstableness, instability. Looks like emotion, confusion. The person doesn't know what to do. He wants to put these things together but doesn't know how.

Table 12-5. The Metaphor Test. (*Continued*)

Joy	14. This is two women at a wild party after winning a reward for designing the best bow tie in the United States. They're bouncing a large replica of it on a blanket between them.
Joy	15. It expresses brightness. It looks adventurous.
Joy	16. A dancing mote, fleck of dust, in the sun. Bubbles of champagne.
Sadness	17. A person lying prostrate with no urge to do anything.
Love	18. A merging or union of two separate bodies.
Joy	19. Two people. Looks like they're at a party and having fun.
Sadness	20. It looks like somebody or something that's lying there.
Anxiety	21. It looks like a monster coming after me.
Sadness	22. The colors are going from light to dismal, birth, life, then death.
Anxiety	23. A bat, a big black bat circling over my head coming closer and closer darting at my head.
Sadness	24. A skeleton of a poor animal that was trapped and that just died and rotted there.
Anger	25. A large bird with outspread wings preparing to attack another bird in rivalry.
Love	26. A male and female. There's equality in it.
Joy	27. It looks like a birthday coloring. The kind of colors used for decorating for a party.
Love	28. Two people flirting with each other, lips puckered. Standing on opposite sides of a table. It must be Spring because there is a pretty red butterfly.
Joy	29. A skin or pelt. A fine fur coat.
Sadness	30. Two bears caught in a trap, bleeding all over. Look like mates.
Joy	31. A huge giant laughing uproariously. Seems to be throwing his head back and laughing.
Anger	32. Face of a cat, eyes slanted down, mouth open hissing. Phffft.
Love	33. Looks like two animals trying to get together.
Sadness	34. Because of the shades it looks empty and hollow.
Anxiety	35. A grimacing, evil, black cat staring at me.
Joy	36. A person sitting on a chair, laughing, sitting back, and saying, "Yay."
Sadness	37. A moth whose wings are worn out, about to die. He's about had it.
Anxiety	38. It looks like a class that's hoping for high marks.
Love	39. Two creatures talking, having an animated conversation, interested in each other. Two snakes together meaning nearness. All these express two of a kind.
Joy	40. Colorful, light hearted. A lot of little figures scurrying around. An air of lightness and brightness.
Joy	41. Bright colors. Dancing figures. A great deal of movement.

Table 12-5. The Metaphor Test. (*Continued*)

Sadness	42. These people are leaving their loved ones behind. They are waving goodbye.
Love	43. Two puppies that are very close. Could be siblings.
Anger	44. Some sort of funny man, furrow in his brow, menacing look in his eyes. Some sort of helmet on his head, a war bonnet. A mustache looks like something worn at the turn of the century. A big superbly adorned face with a menacing look.
Joy	45. I see dancers and they are in the middle of a fantastic leap. They are Russian dancers. Two men and a woman in the middle. The men have their arms linked with the woman's arms which are extended to the side. Her head is thrown back revealing her high stiff collar. The men are wearing peaked fur caps and their legs are drawn up indicating that they have made a tremendous leap. The music is fast and wild and you really get a sense of movement.
Anxiety	46. Some kind of bird who flew up there because someone is after him.
Anger	47. They look like reindeer. There's a bridge and this side is at war with that side.
Joy	48. These people are dancing around doing some sort of a fancy step.
Joy	49. The colors seem to be free and not set in a pattern. Relaxed and bright.
Anxiety	50. Two green people. Two horrible things are emerging from their heads, from their minds. A kind of ectoplasm emerging from their brain pads. Two orange things, horrible nightmarish creatures. The green people seem to be frowning and the orange things smiling maliciously as if they know the harm they were doing to their owners. And the harm is pressing down.
Anger	51. I see a cat's mask glaring. The kind of mask one buys for Halloween.
Sadness	52. Looks like dirty tears.
Love	53. Two bears hugging each other.
Love	54. Two little girls sitting across from each other with their knees touching, talking very friendly in a best-friend manner.
Anxiety	55. It looks like confusion.
Anger	56. A kind of insect which annoys me.
Anger	57. Two women facing each other. This looks as if they're about to haul off and hit each other. You can tell they're about to hit each other because their faces are close together. One is saying "Yeah."
Sadness	58. A placenta. Loss of an unborn child.
Anxiety	59. A being that's kind of deformed symbolizes the inner state of an individual. Aloneness. A kind of reaching out but not getting any place. Big wings trying to grasp but not really making it.
Love	60. Two symmetrical sides seem to be coming together in a sort of unity.
Anger	61. I'm impressed with the rock-like hardness of these figures who seem diametrically opposed to each other across an insurmountable chasm.
Sadness	62. The colors are gray, dark, and somber.
Joy	63. All sorts of crazy animals having a party.

The facial expressions test was developed from the data obtained by Levitt (Chapter 7). Levitt had asked 50 Ss to express facially six emotional meanings: anger, contempt, disgust, fear, joy, and surprise. These expressions were recorded on motion picture film, thus providing an initial pool of 300 facial expressions. From this pool, and by a series of item analyses paralleling those reported for the development of other tests described thus far, the 67 most discriminating items were selected for the facial expressions test. This film was then shown twice to 45 Ss, and a test-retest reliability coefficient of .80 was obtained.

Because the metaphor test involved a verbal mode of communication, the relation between results on the metaphor test and a measure of verbal intelligence would obviously be important for interpreting results obtained with the metaphor test. Therefore, a 40-item vocabulary test developed by Thorndike (1942) was administered in addition to the three measures of emotional sensitivity.

The results are summarized in Table 12-6, and as indicated in the table, ability to identify emotional meanings expressed metaphorically

Table 12-6. Intercorrelations among Various Measures of Emotional Sensitivity and Verbal Intelligence

Metaphor	Vocal	Facial	Vocabulary
Metaphor	48**	.12	.57**
Vocal		.66**	.29*
Facial			.09

* Significant at .05 level.
** Significant at .01 level.

is indeed positively related to verbal intelligence. Its relation to sensitivity as measured by the two nonverbal tests is not entirely consistent: the metaphor test is positively related to the vocal test but independent of the facial expressions test.

An incidental finding lending further credence to Beldoch's hypothesis of a general factor of emotional sensitivity to nonverbal modes of expression is the high positive correlation between the vocal and facial tests; people who are sensitive to vocal expressions also tend to be sensitive to facial expressions. However, there is no clear-cut verbal-nonverbal division, for while the correlation between sensitivity to facial and sensitivity to metaphorical expressions is not significantly different from zero, sensitivity to vocal and sensitivity to metaphorical expressions are substantially correlated with each other beyond the .01 level. Partialling verbal intelligence from the correlation between the vocal and metaphor tests somewhat reduces the correlation, from .48 to .40, but this partial correlation is significant at the .01 level.

DISCUSSION

The first major aspect of this study was the development of a dictionary of metaphors, defining metaphorical statements classified on the basis of emotional meaning in terms of specific characteristics. The task of inductively delineating the characteristics of each class of metaphors proved feasible, and the resulting "dictionary" (Table 12-2), appeared to be applicable to most of the metaphors collected in the second sample, thus supporting the generality of our initial table of characteristics.

The tripart scheme of classification presented in Tables 12-2 and 12-4 seems to offer a useful method of classification. At least it provides some reasonable way of ordering the data and clarifying the obvious commonalities among metaphors in each class of emotional meaning. Inspection of the criteria for each emotional meaning suggests no marked deviation from many characteristics conventionally associated with various emotional states. Indeed, the expressive behavior cues of sorrowful crying, anxious trembling, joyful laughing, etc. seem obvious, and probably provide a major basis for conventions of metaphorical communication in everyday life.

The situational characteristics, however, appear to be somewhat more subtle than the expressive behaviors. Although the situational characteristics outlined in Tables 12-2 and 12-4 are presented as mutually exclusive in the several categories of emotional meaning, some overlap clearly is apparent in some of the metaphors of the second sample which caused difficulties in classification. In some instances, for example, judges were required to make exceedingly fine discriminations, such as differentiating between hostility which is momentarily imminent and hostility impending some time in the future. Our table of characteristics also does not account for metaphors which include cues associated with two or more classes of emotional meaning. Conceivably, a metaphor might contain the anticipation of hostility (anxiety), the actual occurrence of hostility (anger), and the past occurrence of hostility (sadness), without clear-cut indication of what aspect of the statement is "figure" and what is "ground." Similar difficulties in identifying emotional meaning as a function of situational cues were encountered by Hunt et al. (1958) in their study of situational cues of anger, fear, and sorrow. The criteria developed by Hunt and his associates were indeed similar to the situational cues identified in the present study. For example, the concept of "loss," which played an important part in Hunt's data concerning sorrow, is also applicable to our own sample of metaphors which communicate sadness. Thus, while Hunt's data plus the results of our own study provide a fairly substantial basis for identifying situational cues associated with simple, so-called "pure" emotional meanings, the problem of defining the emotional meanings of relatively complex verbal statements remains to be solved. Perhaps in addition to simple, isolated cues, we must also develop some objective scheme for identifying figure and ground within the organization of a particular verbal statement.

Perhaps the most interesting and challenging aspect of our table of characteristics is the category of subjective or connotative referents. Metaphors which apparently contained these kinds of referents were elicited with relatively less frequency than those with either situational or behavioral cues. Phrases such as "fragmentation and instability" (anxiety), "hollow and dark" (sadness), "bright and light" (joy) occurred much less often than statements with clear-cut situational cues. Yet these are the kinds of metaphors encountered in certain types of poetry and literary prose. The relative infrequency of metaphors with these kinds of subjective referents probably is a function of the population sampled in obtaining the metaphors (for the most part, Ss were graduate students in various fields of study), and a very different kind of metaphor may very well have been obtained if we had sampled writers, poets, or others actively engaged in any of the arts concerned with the use of language. Our dictionary of meanings, therefore, may not be very useful in interpreting the metaphors contained, for example, in modern poetry. This of course suggests further study of a sample of writers and poets who might provide data for developing a more comprehensive scheme of defining the emotional meanings of verbal statements.

Despite the obvious limitations of our current work, we are encouraged by this initial attempt in the direction of developing an objective basis for analyzing the emotional meaning of metaphors. On the basis of our first rough approximation of a dictionary of metaphorical meaning (Table 12-2), judges showed between 75 and 85 per cent agreement in classifying the second sample of metaphors; presumably, the modifications and refinements presented in Table 12-4 provide an even more accurate set of definitions which could be used to analyze the emotional meaning of verbal communications. One possible application of such a dictionary concerns the interpretation of verbal responses to projective techniques. Indeed, the basis of our particular method of data collection was the observation that the Rorschach technique elicited verbal statements that might reasonably be identified as metaphors, and perhaps our delineation of the emotional meanings of metaphors will prove useful in interpreting Rorschach responses in a clinical setting. Our current data obviously provide no empirical support for the clinical usefulness of this basis for interpretation, but the results of this study certainly suggest an exciting possibility with potential clinical value.

The test-retest correlation coefficient of .85 indicates that the ability measured by the metaphor test is fairly stable. This reliability coefficient is consonant with those obtained for the nonverbal measures of sensitivity (vocal, .82; facial, .80). Validity of the test, however, presents a more complex problem. The procedure followed in developing the test provides some support for face and content validity; however, construct validity of the test is more difficult to estimate primarily because of the lack of suitable instruments and criteria with which to compare and contrast the metaphor test.

The correlation matrix involving the metaphor, vocal, facial, and vocabulary tests is too small for a meaningful factor analysis; therefore, conclusions based on the matrix must depend on inspection of the individual correlations and the clusters of intercorrelations. The correlation between the metaphor test and the vocabulary test is a perfectly reasonable finding; both obviously involve some kind of verbal ability, though one calls for a knowledge of the emotional meaning of words while the other calls for a knowledge of nonemotional meanings. However, there is some apparent inconsistency in the intercorrelations among the metaphor, vocal, and facial tests. If the facial and vocal tests were positively related to each other, but both were independent of the metaphor test, one could hypothesize a verbal factor and an independent nonverbal factor operating within the general area of emotional sensitivity. However, the fact that the metaphor test is positively correlated with one of the nonverbal measures (vocal) and independent of the other nonverbal measures (facial) complicates the possible interpretations of the data. At least two alternative suggestions present themselves. Either the metaphor test contains a nonverbal factor which manifests itself in the positive correlation between the metaphor and vocal tests, or one of the nonverbal tests (vocal) contains a verbal factor. The former hypothesis is mitigated by failure of the metaphor test to correlate significantly with the facial test. If the metaphor test contained a nonverbal factor, one would expect the clearly nonverbal facial test (facial:vocabulary, r .09) to be related to the metaphor test at least in so far as a nonverbal factor accounted for mutual variance in the two performances. Thus, the statistically insignificant correlation of .12 between the metaphor and facial tests does not support the assumption of a nonverbal factor accounting for much of the variance in the metaphor test. Therefore, the effect of a verbal factor operating in the vocal test seems more likely to account for the correlation between the vocal and metaphor tests. Perhaps the emphasis of some part of the verbal statement contained in the vocal test enhances the communication of certain emotional meanings. The standard verbal statement made by each speaker in the vocal test was, "I'm going out now. I won't be back all afternoon. If anyone calls, tell them I won't be back all afternoon." Thus, for example, emphasizing the phrase, "I'm going out now," in an "angry" tone might underscore the supposition that the speaker is so angry that he must "leave the field." The nonverbal emphasis within the verbal statement may contribute, in part, to the effectiveness with which particular items on the vocal test are communicated. Therefore, performance on the vocal test may involve some interaction between verbal and nonverbal factors.

SUMMARY

This study investigated the communication of emotional meanings in a verbal mode. Metaphors were obtained by means of a modified Rorschach technique, and the characteristics of metaphors which communicated each of five different emotional meanings were identified. A reliable test of ability to recognize emotional meanings expressed metaphorically was developed, and results of this test were studied in relation to abilities measured by vocal, facial, and vocabulary tests. These data were discussed in terms of verbal and nonverbal factors operating in the several tests of emotional sensitivity.

13

Summary and speculations

Joel R. Davitz

Our primary emphasis in this research has been on specific questions that could be answered within the scope of a single study. Many of the studies were interrelated, of course, but for the most part, each researcher began with questions he was interested in, without concern for an overall, theoretical framework. In each case, our immediate aim was to test specific hypotheses and to learn something concrete about emotional communication. Nevertheless, as the number of consistent findings increased, and as the interrelationships among our findings became apparent, we began to speculate not only about our data, but also about the relation between emotional communication and other problems of psychological theory and research. These speculations were not systematic in the sense of leading to a neatly articulated theory of emotional communication; but the ideas that have occurred to us suggest ways of integrating our own research with other investigations in related areas of psychology.

Before presenting these speculations, however, it might be useful to review our major findings and to comment on some methodological decisions that inevitably influenced the results we obtained.

SUMMARY OF FINDINGS

Emotional meanings can be communicated accurately in a variety of nonverbal media. This is the basic proposition upon which our research rests, and it is supported by all our work. Vocal communication has been the principal focus of our attention; but we have also studied facial, musical, and graphic modes of expression. In each instance, the accuracy with which emotional meanings were communicated far exceeded chance expectation. Individuals indeed differ in their ability to communicate, but notwithstanding these individual differences, our results demonstrate incontrovertibly that nonverbal, emotional communication is a stable, measurable phenomenon.

Although most of our research has been concerned with nonverbal media, we also have investigated metaphorical statements as an indirect, verbal means of emotional expression. Metaphors convey emotional meanings more accurately than any nonverbal mode we have thus far studied, but in many respects, the results obtained in our study of metaphors parallel those obtained with nonverbal techniques. Thus, our conclusions are based principally on investigations of nonverbal expressions, with at least tentative evidence that these conclusions might be generalized to some forms of verbal communication.

Having established the fact that emotional communication occurs both in verbal and nonverbal media, we explored individual differences in various aspects of the communication process. Much of our research was designed to account for individual differences in ability to receive and understand emotional messages; this ability was thought of in terms of emotional sensitivity. Problems in transmitting emotional messages were studied separately in terms of expressiveness, although we recognized that transmitting and receiving messages in any communication process are inextricably interrelated. Finally, we focused some of our research on perceived characteristics of the message in relation to the meanings conveyed. Our findings will therefore be reviewed under three broad headings: (1) Problems of Sensitivity; (2) The Message and its Emotional Meaning; and (3) Problems of Expressiveness.

Problems of Sensitivity

A large part of our research focused on problems of emotional sensitivity. We have found marked individual differences in ability to understand emotional messages expressed in vocal, facial, musical, graphic, and metaphorical modes of communication. The range of individual differences does not seem to be greater in any particular mode of communication, nor does the stability of behavior differ markedly from one mode to another. In all media, people differ in ability to identify the meanings expressed, individuals varying from performances at about chance level of expectation to nearly perfect accuracy. But regardless of the individual's level of performance, behavior on any given test of sensitivity tends to be internally consistent and remarkably stable over time.

In most of our research, emotional sensitivity was defined operationally by the total number of items correctly identified on any given instrument. This scoring procedure, similar to that followed in most intelligence tests, was based on the assumption that emotional sensitivity, like intelligence, can best be measured by responses to a variety of items encompassing various emotional meanings expressed by several different persons. For example, our measure of sensitivity to vocal expression was based on an overall estimate of accuracy of response to eight emotional meanings expressed by a number of different speakers.

In addition to an overall estimate of accuracy, we also investigated the kinds of items correctly identified and the kinds of errors made in identification. Both variables were found to be stable characteristics of an individual's response to emotional stimuli. A person who correctly identifies an emotional expression on one occasion is likely to identify that expression correctly on a second occasion. Similarly, a person who makes one kind of error when first confronted with an emotional expression tends to make the identical error when he again encounters that emotional expression. Thus, people who mistake joy for anger, or anger for joy, are consistent over time in the nature of their erroneous responses.

Another aspect of the general response to emotional stimuli deserves brief mention; that is, the tendency to selectively attend, or inattend, to emotional meanings. Blau called this variable "affect attention," and found, in his sample of blind and sighted adolescents, a wide range of differences along this dimension of behavior (Chapter 9). For some people, and perhaps in some situations, the emotional meaning of a message is of primary importance; whereas other people consciously recognize emotional meanings only when instructed to do so. Despite these differences in awareness, it seems reasonable to assume that emotional meanings influence the total response to any communication regardless of whether or not the respondent is aware of the emotional meanings conveyed. The tendency to attend to affective meanings, however, is not necessarily related to emotional sensitivity. Blau found that among blind subjects there was indeed a rather high relationship between his measures of affect attention and emotional sensitivity ($r = .52$, $p < .01$); but among his sighted subjects these two variables were found to be independent. The relation between affect attention and emotional sensitivity, therefore, is a function of other variables, one of which appears to be blindness. On the basis of present evidence, we cannot generalize about the effect of handicap in other sensory modalities, but the results obtained thus far clearly call for further exploration of affect attention as an important dimension of behavior in the communication of emotional meanings.

In summary, then, stable individual differences have been found in the following aspects of receiving emotional messages: (1) overall sensitivity to emotional expressions, measured in terms of accuracy of identification; (2) the kinds of emotional expressions correctly identified; (3) the specific nature of erroneous responses; and (4) the degree to which individuals attend to the emotional meanings of a total communication.

Measures of sensitivity in the several nonverbal modes we've studied are positively interrelated. Beldoch, for example, found statistically significant intercorrelations among abilities measured by vocal, graphic, and musical tests of communication; Davitz and Mattis found a similar relation between abilities measured in vocal and facial modes of expression. Thus, a person who is accurate in identifying the emotional meaning of vocal expressions also tends to be accurate in identifying facial, graphic, and musical expressions. Emotional sensitivity to nonverbal stimuli, therefore, seems to be a function of some general factor that accounts for the common variance among a variety of manifestly different measures.

The intercorrelations among measures in various nonverbal modes, however, tend to be low, though statistically significant. For any two modes of communication, our data show that approximately 10 to 35 per cent of the common variance can be accounted for by some general factor of sensitivity. Thus, while abilities in the several nonverbal modes are undoubtedly related to each other, individuals also show special sensitivities to specific modes of expression. Although as a group, persons who are accurate in one nonverbal mode are generally more accurate in another mode, some persons within the group may be particularly sensitive to vocal expressions, for example, and relatively insensitive to facial expressions.

The argument for a general factor of sensitivity, therefore, is somewhat mitigated by the relatively low intercorrelations we have obtained. However, we have also obtained evidence that sensitivity is related to other aspects of the total communication process. Levy found that sensitivity, expressiveness, and self-understanding are positively interrelated. That is, people who are accurate in identifying the emotional expressions of others are more effective in expressing emotional meanings to others. They are also more accurate in identifying the meanings of their own expressions. These interrelations were investigated only in the vocal mode of communication, but for this mode at least, the positive relation between transmitting and receiving emotional messages is unequivocal.

In conjunction with our findings about the positive interrelations among sensitivities in various nonverbal modes of communication, the positive relation between expressiveness and sensitivity lends further credence to the assumption that a general factor partially accounts for the variance in a variety of manifestly different behaviors. In a subsequent section, we shall offer one possible interpretation of this general factor.

Sensitivity to verbal expressions, as measured by the accuracy of identifying the meaning of metaphorical expressions, is positively related to performance on the vocal test of emotional expression, but independent of sensitivity to facial expression. Thus, a person who accurately identifies the meaning of metaphors also tends to be accurate in identifying the meaning of vocal expressions, but he may be relatively insensitive to the meaning of facial expressions. Verbal intelligence is correlated with ability on both the metaphorical and vocal tests, but even when verbal intelligence is controlled, the correlation between scores on these two tests of sensitivity remains statistically significant. In most interpersonal situations, emotional meanings are expressed simultaneously in vocal and verbal modes, and undoubtedly these simultaneous expressions interact in the communication process. We are currently investigating the nature of this interaction, but at the present time can only note that sensitivity to meanings conveyed verbally is positively related to sensitivity in a mode by which verbal content typically is expressed.

Emotional sensitivity develops chronologically, beginning at least as early as age five and continuing to increase progressively with both chronological and mental age. Dimitrovsky (Chapter 6) found chronological increments in sensitivity through age twelve, and Blau's observations (Chapter 9) suggest continued growth throughout early adolescence. Beyond these age limits, our observations are not sufficiently systematic to permit generalization over the life span, but we suspect that some form of emotional sensitivity occurs even earlier than five years old and begins to taper off, probably as a function of losses in perceptual acuity, at about age forty. Many observers have reported that even very young infants show gross differential responses to strong stimuli, but one cannot equate this kind of response with the labeling behavior measured in our research. It is probably more appropriate to consider the infant's gross reactions as a developmental precursor of subsequent emotional sensitivity as we have operationally defined it, since the types of labeling responses required in our tests depend upon acquisition of fairly complex, symbolic skills. With further refinement of our measurement techniques, perhaps we might obtain reliable estimates of sensitivity below age five. Even at age five, however, most children perform beyond chance expectation in recognizing vocal expressions, and there are stable individual differences in sensitivity at all age levels thus far tested. Our evidence also suggests that consistency of performance over time increases with age, five-year-olds being least consistent from time to time, and twelve-year-olds performing at about the same level of consistency as adult samples.

Beginning at about age six, girls develop more rapidly than boys do, at least in so far as our measure of sensitivity to vocal expression is concerned. This sex difference in sensitivity was not found in our adult samples; presumably, therefore, the factors that influence differential development of boys and girls during childhood are mitigated by subsequent learning or maturation during adolescence. The question of sex differences nevertheless remains unresolved. Many of our adult samples were obtained from a college population and as other research suggests, similarities between male and female college students in a variable like emotional sensitivity may not be representative of the general population. Moreover, the children studied by Dimitrovsky differed in socioeconomic status from the samples of adults studied in most of our other research; therefore, Dimitrovsky's finding of sex differences in children remains to be explored more fully with adults from a wider socioeconomic and educational range than we have thus far sampled.

We have found no consistent evidence of personality correlates of emotional sensitivity, operationally defining these personality variables in terms of paper and pencil measures obtained from psychologically normal adults. These measures include a description of self-concept based on Gough's 300-item Adjective Check List, the Guilford-Zimmerman Temperament Survey, the Allport-Vernon-Lindzey Study of Values, the Edwards Personal Preference Schedule, the Psychaesthenia and Hysteria scales of the MMPI, and the Dogmatism and Opinionation scales developed by Rokeach. Although certainly not conclusive, our preliminary evidence using projective techniques as a source of personality information is not promising. The data, therefore, compel us to conclude that personality variables, as we have measured them, are independent of overall estimates of emotional sensitivity.

Perhaps our most interesting lead in this area comes from the study of errors in identification, for it seems likely that personality factors, if they operate at all in the communication process, influence the errors made in judgment rather than overall sensitivity. A person with high aggressive needs, for example, generally might be sensitive or insensitive to relatively obvious expressions of various emotional meanings regardless of his aggressive needs; but in instances of more subtle emotional expression, when the discrimination involved is relatively more difficult, and the response less "stimulus-bound," the person's aggressive needs might very well play an important role in determining the nature of his erroneous response. In this sense, one might view some of the more subtle and difficult items of emotional expression as stimuli for projective behavior, focusing primarily on an analysis of errors instead of total accuracy in the investigation of personality correlates. This hypothesis, however, is not supported by any systematic data we've obtained and is suggested only for further exploration.

Outside the normal range, we have found that schizophrenic persons, in comparison to nonschizophrenic control subjects, are less sensitive to emotional communication. This relative insensitivity cannot be accounted for by decreased motivation or attention, as measured by performance on a nonemotional control task, but the basis of the schizophrenic person's deficit is not evident from our research. We have also obtained preliminary evidence that specific psychotic subgroups (paranoid versus nonparanoid) differ from each other in the kinds of errors they make in identifying emotional expressions, and both subgroups, in turn, differ from a normal control group. At this stage of our research, however, we are not sure that these findings contribute to the understanding of schizophrenia or psychosis in general, and we have not been able to account for the schizophrenic's lower performance in terms of the various kinds of deficit usually associated with schizophrenia. We can only report that schizophrenics differ from nonschizophrenics in various aspects of emotional communication.

In contrast to our research concerned with personality variables, we have obtained consistent evidence in support of perceptual and cognitive correlates of emotional sensitivity. Among the variables related to sensitivity as measured by the vocal test are: verbal intelligence; abstract symbolic ability; knowledge of vocal characteristics of emotional expression; ability to discriminate pitch, loudness, time, and timbre of auditory stimuli; and ability to distinguish figure from ground in a visual perception task. The intercorrelations among these variables are low, indicating a relatively independent contribution of each variable to the total response of identifying emotional expressions. Inspection of the scatter plots suggests that a minimal level of ability in each of several perceptual and cognitive dimensions is required for successful performance on the emotional identification task, but high ability in any single dimension does not, in itself, result in greater sensitivity. Thus, emotional sensitivity is multidetermined, requiring a variety of perceptual and cognitive abilities, each contributing a necessary but not sufficient factor to the total sensitivity response. A deaf person obviously cannot be very sensitive to vocal expressions simply because he cannot hear the auditory cues involved, but extremely high auditory acuity does not in itself guarantee emotional sensitivity. Similarly, without sufficient abstract symbolic ability, a person is severely handicapped in performing the rather complex symbolic task involved in identifying emotional meanings. But symbolic ability is only a necessary, and not sufficient, basis for sensitivity. We have undoubtedly failed to identify all the perceptual and cognitive variables which contribute to emotional sensitivity. Perhaps other psychological factors, such as interest and motivation, contribute to the total sensitivity response. Nonetheless, our data strongly support an interpretation of emotional sensitivity primarily in terms of perceptual and cognitive processes.

In order to be sensitive to meanings expressed in a given mode, obviously one must be capable of perceiving stimuli in that mode of communication. A major sensory defect, therefore, precludes emotional sensitivity in the particular mode affected. There is a prevalent folklore belief, however, that sensory deficit in one modality is accompanied by heightened, compensatory acuity in another modality. This belief is the basis for a common assumption that blind persons, for example, are particularly accurate in identifying auditory cues.

Although we have found that auditory acuity is not in itself a sufficient basis for sensitivity to vocal expressions of emotion, it seemed reasonable to assume that increased auditory acuity is positively related to emotional sensitivity tested in the vocal mode of expression. Blau investigated this assumption in his study of blind and sighted adolescents (Chapter 9). Contradicting usual assumptions about the blind, Blau found they were no more accurate than sighted control subjects in identifying everyday sounds. Moreover, while blind adolescents, in comparison to a comparable sample of sighted control subjects, pay more attention to the emotional aspects of vocal communication, they are indeed *less* accurate in identifying the emotional meanings expressed. We cannot as yet account for this lower sensitivity among the blind, but our results clearly demonstrate that compensation in terms of increased emotional sensitivity in nonhandicapped modes is not an inevitable consequence of sensory deficit.

Finally, in the area of receiving or understanding emotional messages, we have obtained some evidence about the effect of training. The evidence is indeed slight, and provides only a global picture of short-term training experience; nevertheless, the results support the hypothesis that training increases sensitivity. We do not know the particular aspects of training which are most effective, and we cannot define the generality of effects produced. But we do know that practice in expressing and receiving emotional communications results in higher scores on a subsequent test of sensitivity. In a sense, this vague, tentative conclusion is an interesting commentary on the course of one's research, reflecting the changes that occur, usually without awareness, as one develops a line of investigation. At the very beginning, our primary interest in emotional communication arose from problems in training, specifically, the problem of training student therapists in the task of recognizing emotional meanings expressed by their clients. However, we have completed only one small study directly concerned with this problem, and can only report that training seems to have a positive effect. Having accumulated other information relevant to the total communication process, perhaps we can return to the original training problem with greater insight and technical skill.

The Message and Its Emotional Meaning

In comparison to the amount of work concerned with problems of sensitivity, proportionately less of our research has been focused on the emotional message itself and the meaning it conveys. For the most part, what we know in this area concerns vocal communication, and systematic knowledge even about this mode of expression is limited.

Perhaps our most fortunate hunch in exploring problems of meaning in relation to characteristics of the vocal message was the choice of Osgood's tridimensional scheme as a basis for describing meaning (Osgood, et al., 1957). Thus, we began with three dimensions of emotional meaning, valence, activity, and strength, and searched for correlates of these dimensions in terms of characteristics of the vocal message perceived as auditory cues. Investigating only the more obvious auditory characteristics of speech, we found that the activity dimension of meaning accounted for much of the variance in rate, volume, pitch, and timbre of vocal expressions. Emotions characterized subjectively as "active" tend to be expressed by a fast rate of speech, high volume or loudness, high pitch, and blaring timbre. In direct contrast, relatively "passive" emotions are expressed by a slower rate of speech, lower volume, lower pitch, and more resonant timbre. These vocal characteristics, of course, are physically related to each other in the production of speech, and in this sense, the correlations between activity and each auditory characteristic are not independent of each other.

The findings in regard to the activity dimension are remarkably consistent, but valence and strength have no such simple correlates in the vocal message. Thus, while the relatively obvious auditory characteristics of a vocal message are accounted for by the activity dimension of emotional meaning, it would seem likely that valence and strength are communicated by more subtle aspects of speech, such as changes in rhythm, inflection, and enunciation.

We cannot confidently generalize these findings to other modes of expression, though informal observations tend to support our findings in the vocal area. For example, in the graphic mode, expressions of a sub-jectively active feeling, such as anger, almost always involve much more movement than expressions of a passive feeling, such as boredom; similarly, in metaphorical expressions, items concerned with active feel-ings such as anger (e.g. stamping) and joy (e.g. dancing) typically involve greater movement than items which express a passive feeling such as sadness (e.g. lying down). Activity, therefore, seems to be a major determinant of the form of emotional expression, regardless of the mode of communication.

These findings are related to the types of errors most frequently made in identification. Erroneous responses, by and large, tend to be similar to the intended meaning in terms of activity level. For example, two active emotions, such as anger and joy, are frequently mistaken for each other in the vocal mode; but expressions of two unpleasant emotions, such as anger and sadness, or two strong emotions, such as love and joy, are rarely confused for one another. Once again, our research evidence is based on vocal communication, but our observations about other modes of communication are consistent with these findings.

We have not developed an extensive dictionary of vocal cues asso-ciated with each kind of emotional meaning, though a limited and pre-liminary form of such a dictionary is presented in Chapter 5. In this respect, our work with metaphors has been most successful. With only five categories of emotional meaning, anger, anxiety, joy, love, and sad-ness, a tripart division of characteristics in terms of situational cues, conventional expressive behaviors, and words with primarily subjective, connotative meanings was comprehensive enough to account for almost all the metaphors obtained. Anxiety, for example, was typically expressed by metaphors describing a situation of threatening hostility, expressive behaviors such as trembling, or by words such as "fragmentation and instability," which presumably refer to subjective experiences associated with anxiety. Metaphors of sadness typically describe situations of loss or hostility that has occurred in the past, expressive behaviors such as crying, or words such as "dark and hollow."

This attempt at objective analysis of one kind of verbal expression represents only a beginning and has several obvious limitations. Many verbal statements in everyday communication contain cues associated with more than one dimension of emotional meaning, and, as yet, we have no objective way of determining the "figure" and "ground" of emo-tional communications. Moreover, our dictionary of metaphors probably would not be effective in objectively translating the emotional mean-ings of subtle, literary metaphors whose referents may be highly personal and primarily subjective. Nevertheless, with these limitations in mind, plus awareness of the fact that we studied only five categories of emotional meaning, the tridimensional categorization of verbal characteristics may serve as something of a model for further research along this line of investigation.

One of the most intriguing, and in some ways, disturbing findings of our research concerns the rate of emitting various kinds of responses in identifying emotional expressions. We generally assumed a chance level of emitting each category of meaning in a given list of emotional categories. Thus, if we presented a list of emotions comprised of anger, joy, love, and sadness, we assumed that by chance each emotional meaning would be emitted a quarter of the time. But Dimitrovsky's findings with children clearly contradict this assumption, for in her sample, anger and sadness responses were emitted far more frequently than either joy or love. This does not affect the validity of our assumption that by chance one would expect a quarter of the items to be identified correctly, but it does suggest, for future research, a more careful investigation of the base line of response for each kind of emotional meaning. It also poses the problem of accounting for children's extraordinarily high rate of emitting unpleasant emotional meanings in response to adult vocal expressions. Although the specific vocal instrument used by Dimitrovsky has not been used in studies of adults, data have been obtained with similar tests, and we have found that normal adults generally do *not* emit a larger proportion of responses with unpleasant, rather than pleasant, emotional meaning. Thus, Dimitrovsky's finding seems to be particularly characteristic of children responding to adult voices. In light of these results, one wonders if anger and sadness indeed characterize the world of emotional meanings in which many children live?

Problems of Expressiveness

Of the several aspects of communication, we have devoted least attention to problems of expressiveness. Levitt's study has been our only major investigation focused directly on the expressive function in the communication process.

Paralleling our findings about sensitivity, Levitt found that abilities to express vocally and facially are positively related. The relationship, however, is not high, accounting for only a small part of the variance in each mode of expression. These results are especially interesting in the light of results obtained in several other studies: (1) Levy's finding that expressing and receiving emotional messages are positively related; (2) Beldoch's finding that sensitivities in three modes of communication are positivey interrelated; and (3) Davitz and Mattis's finding that sensitivities to vocal and facial expressions are positively related. Considered together, these researches form a chain of findings that suggest a general factor underlying a wide range of behaviors involved in various aspects of the total communication process.

In most typical instances of everyday communication, emotional meanings are simultaneously expressed in more than one mode. We assumed that expression in two modes (facial plus vocal) would be more effective than expression in either mode taken singly. However, this assumption was not supported; information from two modes of expression does not necessarily result in more accurate communication. Probably the specific modes involved determine whether or not communication is aided or impeded by dual channels of information operating simultaneously. Our own research has thus far considered only two nonverbal modes of simultaneous expression; a study of verbal plus nonverbal information might very well provide quite different results.

The general problem of determining *who* expresses most effectively to *whom* remains virtually untouched. In contradiction to our expectations, we did *not* find that homogeneity of native language among speakers and listeners was related to accuracy of their nonverbal, vocal communication. In fact, our most important cross-cultural finding is the remarkable accuracy with which speakers and listeners from different cultures communicate with each other in a nonverbal mode. This suggests a fairly high degree of similarity in vocal expression across cultures, regardless of obvious differences in verbal communication. But these results are only suggestive because of the small sample studied to date.

Finally, we have obtained some evidence about the relation of interpersonal compatibility to émotional communication. Once again, these suggestions are based on preliminary findings, but the data clearly contradict the assumption that interpersonal sensitivity is linearly related to compatibility.

METHODOLOGICAL COMMENTS

At this point, it might be useful to describe in some detail a paradigm of our general research method, for our findings and the ideas they suggest are inevitably a function of our method of investigation. Because a great deal of our research involved vocal communication, this paradigm will be described primarily in terms of vocal expression; however, our general procedures were the same for all modes of communication.

We typically began with a list of emotional meanings to be expressed.

Sometimes, as in Levitt's study (Chapter 7), the list of meanings had some previous empirical basis, but in most instances, we merely chose emotional meanings which seemed to be clearly different from each other. These meanings were not the same from study to study, in one sense reflecting a looseness in our method, but in another sense, providing, inadvertently I confess, a basis for generalizing our findings across different categories of emotional meaning.

On some occasions we presented the speaker with a situation related to each emotional meaning to help the speaker simulate the particular emotion to be expressed. At other times, we merely presented the speaker with a list of emotions and asked him to express each one as effectively as he could. Without any formal data, I can only report that the more detailed situational descriptions of each emotional category did not result in consistently superior communication. In fact, there seemed to be almost no difference between the results obtained by the two methods.

At any rate, at the very beginning of our method we departed from the reality of everyday communication, for we relied on experimental instructions rather than on actual emotional states as a basis for inducing emotional expressions. Thus, subjects spoke *as if* they were angry or happy, probably rarely experiencing actual anger or happiness during the research procedure. It was possible, of course, that this artificiality of inducing emotional expression might have mitigated the validity of our generalizations about everyday emotional communication, but the substantial number of consistent findings that make "psychological sense" would seem to provide ample evidence for the validity of our techniques.

Each speaker recited standard verbal content with the intent of expressing a variety of emotional meanings. We chose the content-standard technique as the least undesirable of several methods we tried. Reciting the alphabet or saying nonsense syllables seemed to introduce an extraneous factor that complicated, rather than simplified, our investigations. We have subsequently realized that the verbal content we've used may very well have influenced the communication process; we are therefore currently studying the interaction between verbal and nonverbal variables in emotional expression. But for the most part, I believe it is safe to assume that most of the variance in our vocal test is a function of nonverbal rather than verbal factors.

Each vocal expression was tape recorded, and our next step was to identify those items which communicated each emotional meaning. The term "communicate" has been used in a variety of ways by different writers, but for our purposes we needed an operational definition that would permit us to decide concretely that one item *did* communicate a given emotional meaning and another did not. Of course, such a definition must be reasonable in relation to other usages of the term, but we also recognized that whatever definition we chose, it would in some respects be arbitrary and open to question. In everyday conversation, despite individual differences in understanding the meaning of many words, one usually assumes that he is communicating with another person unless he perceives fairly strong evidence to the contrary; in our research, we could not make such an assumption. Therefore, recognizing the arbitrariness of our decision, we defined communication in terms of two specific criteria; we said that vocal expression communicated a given emotional meaning if (1) a plurality of listeners agreed with the intent of the speaker and (2) the number of "correct" responses in the plurality exceeded chance expectation at the .01 level. With this definition we undoubtedly obscured patterns of communication involving special sensitivities of some listeners in response to particular speakers; that is, I might communicate accurately with another person unusually sensitive to my expressions despite the fact that no one else would agree with that person's interpretation of my intended emotional meaning. But our primary concern was not with these kinds of unusual interpersonal sensitivity, but rather, with more common and conventional patterns of communication.

In defining communication, we also had to define "meaning." The meaning of any sign or symbol can be defined in terms of some behavioral response, and just as there are many aspects of behavior, there are many kinds of meaning. We chose a "labeling," or "naming," response on the assumption that the label a listener applied to a vocal expression realistically defined the meaning that expression had for him. If the listener's response agreed with the speaker's intent, we said that the listener was "sensitive to" or "understood" the speaker. In this respect, our research method paralleled everyday communication in so far as labeling behavior is commonly associated with understanding or meaning. But our technique differed from usual interpersonal communication in that the listener was always given a list of emotional names from which to choose his response, and he was required to limit his choice to one category of meaning contained in the list. This certainly differs from the typical everyday situation in which a listener has no explicit list of labels from which to choose his response. At this point, our problem was similar to the psychometric issue of essay versus objective tests; on the one hand, we wanted some standardization of responses to assure reliability of scoring, but on the other hand, we also wanted to achieve a reasonable degree of verisimilitude in respect to everyday communication. Our choice of an objective form of response assured us of scoring reliability, and we can only argue for the verisimilitude of our tests on the basis of the results obtained.

As we worked along, we encountered other methodological problems that were resolved for practical purposes by day-to-day decisions made with relatively little reflection. These encompass the dozens of minor decisions that have to be made in every research effort, and though no single issue in itself is overwhelming, the combination of successive minor decisions undoubtedly influences the entire line an investigation takes. For example, in developing the metaphor test, we chose only five categories of emotional meaning: anger, anxiety, joy, love, and sadness. We chose these categories because they seemed to represent clinically important emotional phenomena. But would our results have been similar if our choice had been based, for example, on relevant literary criteria? If we had started with the metaphors of John Donne or Dylan Thomas and had worked in the direction of discovering the emotional meanings they conveyed, would our dictionary of metaphorical meaning have been the same as that presented in Chapter 12? As in most areas of psychological research, the techniques we used represented a compromise between practicality and some sort of "ideal" solution. With added experience, the quality of our compromises gradually improved, but many problems remain only partially, and hopefully only temporarily, solved.

SPECULATIONS

From time to time during our research, often when one set of studies had been completed and another study not yet begun, there were interludes of inactivity during which we were free to wonder about the meaningfulness of what we had been doing. Perhaps most researchers engaged in a long-term project experience these doubts; they might merely be a consequence of the manic-depressive rhythm engendered by the alternating activity and reflection of the research process itself. At any rate, regardless of the basis for these doubts, we were led to consider the general significance of our investigations.

The questions we were asking seemed reasonable enough, and certainly they were sufficiently interesting to provoke a good deal of work. But they didn't seem to be either earthshaking or astonishingly original. They were questions that probably any person with some common sense might ask about emotional communication. By and large, we were pleased with the research methods that gradually evolved over the years, and our empirical results were consistently encouraging. But did the results add up to anything beyond answering the specific questions we had posed? Were the questions we asked indeed significant?

In this self-conscious search for *significant* questions, one might ask, "Significant for what?" In response, there seem to be a number of possible answers. First, the significance of a particular point of view might arise simply from the amount of research that it provokes. Some psychologists argue, for example, that regardless of the validity of Hull's theory of learning, it is scientifically useful by virtue of the huge amount of research stimulated, in one way or another, by the theory. In support of this view, they argue that the only reliable way to gain knowledge in a given area is by systematic research, and any point of view that results in a large quantity of research is by definition scientifically significant.

Although this point of view might seem like a rationalization of activity for activity's sake, I believe it has considerable validity. Of course, this view does not support or rationalize mere research activity per se, but rather, *systematic* research, which implies a series of interrelated studies about some central problem, each research bearing some conceptual relationship to other studies in the series. Thus, systematic research concerned with a central problem offers some cohesiveness, some sense of "getting a job done," a kind of cumulative progress that dozens of independent, unrelated studies can never achieve. In this sense, one might evaluate the significance of a research question in terms of its relatedness to other researches.

From this perspective, our questions probably have been significant enough in that the series of researches have provided their own context within which the various studies are interrelated. Moreover, our own work follows, and is related to, a substantial body of previous research. But unlike the research'stemming, for example, from Hullian theory, we had no hypothetico-deductive framework from which our hypotheses stemmed; we merely asked what seemed to be interesting questions. Once we began work, we were never at a loss for "interesting questions." Every time we collected some data, additional problems became obvious, and frequently we started to investigate new problems before completing our work on earlier questions. Thus, in so far as stimulating research is concerned, the questions we asked were productive, provocative, and moderately systematic.

Another kind of significance currently emphasized by some psychological research, and certainly dramatized by the achievements of physicists and chemists, is the practical or applied value of the results obtained. Here, of course, I did not necessarily mean the moneymaking or moneysaving results that might accrue as a consequence of what was done, but rather, the usefulness of what we have asked and what has been learned in dealing with problems of human suffering, of mental health, of education. Practical or applied consequences of research are sometimes overtly disdained by the social scientist, as if concrete social benefits were somehow unworthy of his *pure* efforts; but we, I suspect, who are clinical psychologists as well as psychological researchers, would be pleased to make a practical contribution of social significance. In fact our whole research effort began with a practical problem in training psychotherapists. But like other researches, our initial focus on a practical problem was shifted during the course of our work, and at the present time, all we can offer in terms of eventual significance is the promise that we shall return to this kind of concern. Indeed, we are currently engaged in some work that might have fairly immediate application. For example, we are studying the effectiveness of therapists in relation to various measures of emotional sensitivity; if we find consistent positive relations of sufficient magnitude, our measures of emotional sensitivity might be helpful in selecting clinical psychologists, psychiatrists, social workers, and other professional people whose work requires some degree of emotional sensitivity. In addition, following Mattis's early work on training, we are investigating specific techniques for increasing sensitivity to emotional expression. Increasing sensitivity through training is an exceedingly complex and difficult task, but the solution of this training or educational problem will undoubtedly have some practical consequences. Thus, in so far as practical or applied significance of the questions we have asked, we can only report that our research is "promising," though the promise has yet to be fulfilled.

Still another kind of significance, and perhaps that kind of significance with which most of us have been concerned, involves the relation of our work to other broad conceptual or theoretical problems in psychology. In this case, we are concerned with ideas, probably not the ideas with which we began our work, but with ideas suggested by our results, and with the relation of these ideas to conceptual issues within the broader framework of psychology.

Communication and a Theory of Emotion

Throughout our research we used labels such as sadness, love, joy, and anger to define emotional meaning. For our empirical purposes, these labels seemed appropriate as a way of obtaining behavioral measures of the phenomena in which we were interested. But we assumed, implicitly, that these labels referred to events commonly recognized as "emotional."

It is somewhat surprising that among the hundreds of subjects we studied, none asked us what anger or sadness or joy meant. The only category of emotional meaning that anyone ever asked about was love, but questions even about the meaning of love were fairly rare. Perhaps one might infer that each person had his own definition of words like anger and joy, but no two people might "understand" these two words in the same way. This, of course, is a possibility, though not a likely one in view of the fact that most people seemed to use these words in about the same ways when responding to various expressions. That is, there was a good deal of consensus in using these words to label particular emotional expressions. Therefore, the aspect of meaning with which our research was directly concerned, the association between words like anger and joy and their expressive, behavioral referents, showed sufficient intersubjective agreement to permit reliable communication.

But the emotional labels we used also refer to events other than expressive behaviors, to other phenomena commonly recognized as emotional. It is therefore appropriate to relate our research to a more general theory of emotions, with the eventual aim of integrating studies of emotional communication with research in other areas of emotional behavior.

From my own point of view, the most persuasive theory of emotional behavior has been developed by Schachter, who has emphasized the interaction of cognitive and physiological factors in defining emotional states (Schachter & Singer, 1962; Schachter & Wheeler, 1962). Schachter begins with the general observation that various emotional states seem to differ in terms of the organism's gross level of physiological arousal or activation, a concept developed more fully by Duffy (1962), Malmo (1959), and others. But differences in activation do not account for apparent subjective differences in emotional states. For example, joy and anger might both be accompanied by relatively high levels of activation, so that subjectively different emotional states are associated with similar physiological responses. Schachter then argues that these differences in emotional states are accounted for by the individual's cognitive interpretation of the situation in which he experiences the state of activation. Thus, given the same level of high activation, a person labels his emotional state as "joy" or "anger" as a function of how he sees the precipitating situation.

In defining emotions, therefore, Schachter's view suggests a joint consideration of the individual's state of activation as well as the cognitive variables which determine the specific emotional response. In our research, we have no direct test of Schachter's cognitive and physiological model, but if one considers emotional communication in everyday speech, there is a possible parallel between this theory and the kinds of communication behaviors with which we have been concerned.

Speech obviously conveys information both in the vocal and verbal modes. The meaning of a sample of speech, including its emotional meaning, is a function of *what* is said and *how* it is said, the interaction of verbal and vocal aspects of the total message. Although the evidence certainly is not clear-cut, perhaps the verbal aspect of speech primarily reflects the cognitive determinants of emotional states, while the vocal aspects are a function of the speaker's state of activation.

Some indirect support for this view is provided by the results of our research concerned with vocal correlates of emotional expressions. Briefly, these findings indicate that subjectively *active* feelings tend to be communicated by a loud voice, with relatively high pitch, blaring timbre, and fast rate of speech. In contrast, subjectively *passive* feelings are communicated by a relatively softer voice, with relatively lower pitch, more resonant timbre, and slower rate of speech. Therefore, assuming that subjective *activity* parallels physiological *activation,* the vocal aspects of speech might well reflect the level of activation associated with particular emotional states.

The assumption that subjective *activity* and physiological *activation* are positively related is supported by studies that demonstrate that anger, for example, which is typically described as an active feeling, is also associated with a relatively high state of physiological activation (Ax, 1953; Schachter, 1957). But it would be unreasonable to assume a one-to-one relation between physiological activation and subjective activity or between activation and various expressive behaviors. Undoubtedly suppression and inhibition affect emotional behaviors in almost any social situation, and various social conventions influence patterns of communication. Nevertheless, other things being equal, a person in a highly activated state probably tends to behave in ways which involve a relatively high degree of energy expenditure; that is, to speak in a loud, blaring voice, with a relatively fast rate of speech. A very angry child, for example, is more likely to shout than speak in softly modulated tones; and the speech of a depressed adult, presumably in a state of low activation, is likely to be slow and halting. Thus the activation dimension of emotional states is reflected to some extent in the form of behaviors which communicate emotional meanings.

This formulation, though indeed tentative and incomplete, provides some basis for a potentially meaningful line of investigation. In our previous research, the form and content of emotional expressions have been treated separately. That is, many of our studies have involved vocal expressions with standardized content, controlling for the information conveyed by the verbal aspects of the message. But in normal conversation, meanings are communicated both verbally and vocally, so that an important problem for further research is the interaction of these components of speech in determining meaning.

If our speculations in terms of Schachter's two-factor theory are valid, one would expect the vocal aspects of speech to influence chiefly the *activity* dimension of emotional meaning, while the verbal aspects of speech might reflect to a greater extent the *valence* and *strength* of the meaning communicated. Of course it is unlikely that either vocal or verbal parts of the total message are completely independent of each other, and in fact most normal communication probably involves a certain degree of congruency among the variety of behaviors which make up the total communication. Each aspect of the overall behavior, however, might be particularly important in influencing a specific dimension of meaning.

We have only begun research along this line, and while the data generally support our speculations, these results can be considered only in a most tentative and preliminary fashion. For example, a group of 30 Ss were asked to describe a series of printed sentences using a semantic differential technique. Each sentence was designed to express one of the following categories of emotional meaning: anger, happiness, love, or sadness. These sentences were then read in a tone of voice congruent with the emotional meaning intended by the verbal content, and a second group of 30 Ss was asked to describe the emotional meaning conveyed by the reader, once again using the semantic differential technique. Obviously this minor study requires a considerably larger sample of speakers and more adequate experimental controls, but even in this preliminary form, the data show that the greatest difference in meaning communicated by the two modes of expression (i.e., the printed sentence versus the spoken sentence) is reflected in the active-passive dimension. For example, the intended "angry" sentence was described as much more active when spoken than when presented in printed form, while the intended "sad" sentence was perceived as much more passive when spoken. In contrast, there was almost no difference in ratings of the relative pleasantness or unpleasantness of the sentences when presented in the two different modes.

The results of this research are presented merely to illustrate the potential fruitfulness of investigations stemming from a consideration of a general theory of emotion in relation to problems of emotional communication. One can hardly conclude that this kind of speculation provides a close articulation of our research with a more general theory, but at least our data are consistent with such a theory, and the conceptual framework proposed by Schachter leads to significant questions for further research concerned with problems of communication.

Emotional Sensitivity and Intelligence

A second broad area of psychological theory and research closely related to our work concerns the concept of intelligence, though I confess that we realized the importance of this relationship only after a most devious and indirect route of data collection. Despite our behavioristic pretentions, I believe that most of us engaged. in this work were looking for some mysterious dimension of being that would account for emotional sensitivity. We were searching for a "third ear" that could be investigated empirically. Therefore, our discovery of rather simple, common-sense, perceptual and cognitive correlates of sensitivity came as something of a surprise, though upon further reflection it seems obvious that perceptual and cognitive processes *must* be involved in responding to complex stimuli.

Granted that our investigations of possible personality correlates were not overly imaginative, relying, as we did, on various paper-and-pencil questionnaires, we finally realized that regardless of whether or not personality factors entered into the total response we called sensitivity, certainly perceptual and cognitive factors played an important role in this kind of behavior.

In general, two propositions are suggested by our data: (1) the psychological processes underlying emotional sensitivity involve both perceptual and cognitive variables; (2) there is some general factor which influences a wide variety of behaviors involved in nonverbal, emotional communication; however, the consistently low intercorrelations among our various measures also suggest that there are special factors, or clusters of variables, associated with particular aspects of the communication process.

Evidence for the first proposition is only indirect because of the correlational nature of our data. We have thus far obtained only correlations between perceptual and cognitive abilities and our measures of sensitivity; we have not experimentally manipulated these perceptual and cognitive variables and measured the effect of these manipulations in terms of differential sensitivity. We can only infer from our correlational evidence that variables such as abstract symbolic functioning actually enter into the process of identifying vocal expressions. Nevertheless, this seems to be a reasonable inference.

Evidence for the second proposition about general and specific factors is found throughout our research, supported by the numerous positive, statistically significant, but consistently low correlations among many different measures of sensitivity and expressiveness. Such evidence is contained in the work reported by Beldoch (Chapter 3), Levy (Chapter 4), Levitt (Chapter 7), and Davitz and Mattis (Chapter 12).

Early in our research (Beldoch, Chapter 3), we thought of interpreting emotional sensitivity as a nondiscursive symbolic ability, following Langer's terminology (1942). We proposed that the usual measures of intelligence tapped discursive ability, while our measures of emotional sensitivity tapped a nondiscursive symbolic ability. Langer's distinction between two kinds of symbolic activity was appealing, in part because it reflected the distinction we made between verbal and nonverbal communication, and in part because Langer developed a theory of aesthetics in terms of the communication of emotional meanings by nondiscursive symbols. Yet, after further consideration, we recognized that Langer's concept of nondiscursive symbols did not adequately fit our nonverbal messages. Langer specifies several criteria which characterize nondiscursive symbols; (1) there is no vocabulary in nondiscursive symbolism; (2) there can be no dictionary of meanings associated with nondiscursive symbols; (3) nondiscursive symbols cannot be defined in terms of other nondiscursive symbols; (4) the nondiscursive symbol is the direct presentation of an individual object, and, as such, has no general reference or general meaning. Our nonverbal messages do not satisfy these criteria, for there is indeed a vocabulary of symbols that people use in communicating within any given mode. These symbols, to be sure, are nonverbal, but the specific characteristics of vocal expressions of anger, for example, are as much a part of the vocabulary of speech as many explicitly discursive symbols. Furthermore, a dictionary of meanings associated with nonverbal stimuli, while for the most part implicit, is certainly a realistic, even partially accomplished, goal of research (see Chapters 8 and 12).

Langer's statement that nondiscursive symbols cannot be translated offers a third difficulty in interpreting our nonverbal stimuli as nondiscursive symbols. In fact, my own discomfort with our earlier formulation in terms of nondiscursive symbols began with an amusing little study of translation. I selected six line drawings that expressed various emotional meanings with about 50 per cent accuracy in communication. I then devised a set of arbitrary rules for translating these line drawings into musical notation. For example, I divided a total drawing vertically into eight equal sections, assigning one note on the musical scale to each vertical section; each half-inch of line drawing was assigned a full note value in 4:4 musical time; etc. These musical compositions were then played by a pianist who had no idea of the purpose of the procedure, and subjects were asked to identify the emotional meaning expressed by each item. On the average, the musical items communicated the emotional meanings intended by the line drawings from which they were translated with about 30 per cent accuracy. This was far beyond chance expectation. Thus, while something undoubtedly was lost in translation, apparently some sort of translation from one nonverbal mode to another, even with gross, arbitrary rules, is possible. Despite our earlier suggestions, therefore, we were forced to conclude that while nonverbal communication differs from verbal communication, just as nondiscursive symbols differ from discursive symbols, nonverbal communication is not the same as nondiscursive symbolization.

Nevertheless, I believe the early formulation of emotional sensitivity as an intellectual factor involving, without doubt, nonintellectual variables in the total response, is a useful way of conceptualizing the data we have obtained. Our typical test of sensitivity, such as the vocal test, is different from a standard vocabulary test in certain obvious respects. We do not present a written or spoken word to be defined in terms of other words, and the content of the responses we ask for differs from the content of definitional responses usually required in vocabulary tests. For example, the first item in the Thorndike vocabulary test we used in our research lists the word "pair," and asks the respondent to choose the word that most nearly corresponds to "pair" from the following list: "bag, list, two, yard, party." In contrast, the first item on our vocal tape presents a speaker reciting the standard lines, and asks the respondent to choose the emotional meaning expressed by the speaker from a list including anger, joy, love, etc. Comparing these tests, it is clear that the stems presented to the subject and the kinds of responses called for are substantively different in the two instruments.

Notwithstanding these obvious differences, however, the symbolic processes involved in the two tests are probably quite similar. In both cases, a more or less complex stimulus is presented; the subject attends to this stimulus and is asked to interpret it as a symbol with a particular kind of meaning; finally, he is required to label the symbol using some word or phrase. In one instance, of course, the symbol presented is verbal, and in the other, it is vocal; but both tests present symbols which call for a labeling response.

It is not remarkable, therefore, to find cognitive or intellectual factors, such as abstract symbolic ability and knowledge of vocal characteristics, positively related to our measure of emotional sensitivity. In fact, it seems most reasonable to interpret emotional sensitivity itself as one kind of intelligence related to, but in some respects different from, other measures of verbal and nonverbal intelligence.

If emotional sensitivity is indeed a kind of intellectual ability, we may assume that it shares with other kinds of intellectual functioning a common variance which Spearman interpreted as reflecting a general factor commonly referred to as "*g*." We have flirted with this notion in our earlier work (see Chapter 3), postulating a general factor of emotional sensitivity *like g;* but at this point, on the basis of further evidence, it is more parsimonious and consistent with the data to account for the consistent intercorrelations we've found in terms of *g* itself. There is no need to postulate an independent general factor if we recognize emotional sensitivity as one form of intelligent behavior.

This is not to say that people who obtain high scores on a verbal intelligence test are necessarily sensitive to emotional meanings. Anyone who has trained beginning psychotherapists is cognizant of the fact that the correlation between these two kinds of intelligence is not very high. The student who has never received anything less than an "A" in academic work may turn out to be the dolt of practicum training. But I suspect that these instances of verbal brightness accompanied by nonverbal, emotional stupidity involve problems of inhibition, restricted prior experience, or selective inattention as a consequence of personal, psychological problems. Probably no one can be highly sensitive to emotional meanings without a good deal of general intellectual ability, but certainly a high IQ is no guarantee of emotional sensitivity. Our emphasis, perhaps, should be on different kinds of intelligence, all sharing some common ability to deal with symbolic stimuli.

Subsuming emotional sensitivity under the general rubric of intelligence hardly reduces the importance of sensitivity as a psychological variable, but rather, brings into focus the relation between one kind of symbolic functioning and an enormous field of psychological research and theory. We, of course, have emphasized emotional meanings, whereas most research concerned with intellectual functioning has dealt with nonemotional meanings. However, our definition of emotional meaning obviously involves a verbal response similar to responses required by more common measures of intellectual functions.

Perhaps our major contribution to the investigation of intelligence lies in the stimulus material we used, our emphasis of nonverbal, expressive symbols which are an inevitable part of the total communication matrix. Our research has demonstrated that the nonverbal aspects of a message convey specific meanings, and if intelligence involves symbolic ability, certainly the capacity to deal with these kinds of nonverbal symbols is a significant part of intellectual functioning. The nonverbal stimuli we have studied, therefore, might represent an important addition to the repertoire of symbolic tasks which could profitably be included in a general measure of intellectual ability.

The Nonverbal Stimulus

The emphasis of nonverbal stimuli in our research reflects our view that the nonverbal aspects of any communication, even in the highly verbal culture in which we live, are of prime importance in understanding the message expressed and thus adapting effectively to one's environment. It is possible, for example, that some problems in interpersonal and intrapsychic adjustment might be accounted for in terms of an intellectual dysfunction or inability related to nonverbal communication. We have reported some research concerned with the extreme psychological problems represented by schizophrenia, but even more important, perhaps, are problems of everyday interpersonal relationships that involve nonverbal modes of communication. Our research along this line is only beginning, but we have enough data to suggest that common-sense notions about the relation between high sensitivity and interpersonal compatibility probably are not valid. Just as intrapsychic repression seems to be a necessary ingredient of normal psychological functioning, some sort of interpersonal repression of information might well be a requisite of functionally satisfying interpersonal relations.

Sensitivity to nonverbal stimuli is not only important in interpersonal relations; almost all of life is influenced by nonverbal stimuli which impinge upon us with or without our awareness. I suspect it is the nonverbal, or formal characteristics of one's environment, the "style" of people and things that surround us that primarily determine the emotional meaning of one's world.

In the verbal, problem-solving orientation of Western civilization, response to the nonverbal aspects of one's world in terms of emotional meaning sometimes is regarded as unhealthy or undesirable, sometimes even childish or neurotic. Yet the nonverbal style of all communication probably conveys some emotional meaning. Regardless of whether or not we are conscious of the style or its emotional import, the emotional meanings conveyed inevitably influence our behavior. Perhaps presidents are elected, mates are chosen, psychological theories become popular largely as a function of the emotional meanings they convey, for no matter what verbal or logico-mathematical meanings are expressed, the very modes by which these meanings are communicated also contain stylistic, nonverbal elements which have emotional meaning.

FUTURE RESEARCH

Like most researchers, we have occasionally been set off by our data on flights of fancy that have resolved most of the problems of this world.

But in our more frequent tough-minded moments, we recognize the pristine nature of what has been accomplished thus far, and we return from speculative fancy to the reality of research.

In the preceding chapters, innumerable questions for further research have been raised; many of them remain unanswered because of our own limitations of time, our lack of practical resources or ingenuity. But we are currently engaged in several lines of investigation that stem from the studies already reported. As noted earlier, we are returning to two practical issues that were apparent at the very beginning of our work: (1) the relation of emotional sensitivity to clinical effectiveness as a psychotherapist; and (2) the development of effective training procedures to increase sensitivity. Along a more general, theoretical line, we are studying the relation between simultaneous verbal and nonverbal communication, focusing on the information communicated by congruent and incongruent verbal-vocal expressions. Following Blau's study of the blind, we are essentially replicating his study with a sample of deaf subjects, using visual, rather than vocal, stimuli. And in several parallel studies, we are continuing to explore the relation between emotional sensitivity and interpersonal compatibility in various situations.

An important area of research neglected both in our previous work and in our current studies concerns the process of receiving emotional messages. We have identified some correlates of the end result of this process, but a major step will be taken with experimentally controlled investigations of specific variables involved in the process itself.

BIBLIOGRAPHY

Abel, Georgie Lee. Education of blind children. In W. M. Cruickshank & G. O. Johnson (Eds.), *Education of exceptional children and youth.* Englewood Cliffs, N.J.: Prentice-Hall, 1958. Pp. 295–334.

Allport, F. H. *Social psychology.* Boston: Houghton Mifflin, 1924.

Arnold, Magda B. *Emotion and personality.* Vol. 1. *Psychological aspects.* New York: Columbia Univer. Press, 1960.

Asch, S. E. *Social psychology.* Englewood Cliffs, N.J.: Prentice-Hall, 1952.

Ax, A. F. Physiological differentiation of emotional states. *Psychosom. Med.,* 1953, **15,** 433–442.

Axelrod, S. *Effects of early blindness.* New York: Amer. Found. for the Blind, 1959.

Barbara, D. A. The value of nonverbal communication in personality understanding. *J. nerv. ment. Dis.,* 1956, **123,** 286–291.

Bateson, G., Jackson, D., Haley, J., & Weakland, J. Toward a theory of schizophrenia. *Behav. Sci.,* 1956, **1,** 251–264.

Black, J. W., & Dreher, J. J. Nonverbal messages in voice communication. *USN Sch. Aviat. Med. Res. Rep.,* 1955, No. NM 001 104 500, 45. Cited by E. Kramer. *The judgment of personal characteristics and emotions from nonverbal properties of speech.* Ann Arbor: Univer. of Michigan Office of Research Administration, Report 04411-2-P, 1962. P. 32.

Boring, E. G., & Titchener, E. B. A model for the demonstration of facial expression. *Amer. J. Psychol.,* 1923, **34,** 471–486.

Bossard, J. H. Family modes of expression. *Amer. sociol. Rev.,* 1945, **10,** 226–237.

Brigham, C. C. *A study of error.* New York: College Entrance Examination Board, 1932.

Brody, M. W. Neurotic manifestations of the voice. *Psychoanal. Quart.,* 1943, **12,** 371–380.

Bruner, J. S., & Tagiuri, R. The perception of people. In Gardner Lindzey (Ed.), *Handbook of social psychology.* Vol. 2. *Special fields and applications.* Cambridge, Mass.: Addison-Wesley, 1954. Pp. 634–654.

Brunswik, E. *Systematic and representative design of psychological experiments, with results in physical and social perception.* Berkeley: Univer. of California, 1947.

Buhler, Charlotte, & Hetzer, H. *Testing children's development from birth to school age.* New York: Farrar & Rinehart, 1935.

Buzby, D. E. The interpretation of facial expressions. *Amer. J. Psychol.*, 1924, **35**, 602–604.

Cameron, N. *The psychology of behavior disorders.* Boston: Houghton Mifflin, 1947.

Cantril, H., & Allport, G. *The psychology of radio.* New York: Harper, 1938.

Chevigny, S., & Braverman, S. *The adjustment of the blind.* New Haven: Yale Univer. Press, 1950.

Cline, M. G. The influence of social context on the perception of faces. *J. Pers.*, 1956, **25**, 142–158.

Coleman, J. C. Facial expressions of emotions. *Psychol. Monogr.*, 1949, **63** (No. 1, Whole No. 296).

Cronbach, L. J. Further evidence on response sets and test design. *Educ. Psychol. Measmt.*, 1950, **10**, 30–31.

Cronbach, L. J. Processes and affecting scores on "understanding of others' assumed similarity." *Psychol. Bull.*, 1955, **52**, 177–193.

Cutsforth, T. D. *The blind in school and society.* (2d ed.) New York: Amer. Found. for the Blind, 1951.

Darwin, C. *The expression of the emotions in men and animals.* New York: Appleton, 1896.

Dashiell, J. F. A new method of measuring reaction to facial expression of emotion. *Psychol. Bull.*, 1927, **24**, 174–175. (Abstract)

Davis, E. A. The development of linguistic skill in twins, singletons with siblings, and only children from age five to ten years. *Inst. Child Welfare Monogr. Serv.*, 1937, No. 14.

Davis, I. P. The speech aspects of reading readiness. In *Newer practices in reading in the elementary school. Seventeenth Yearb. Dept. Elem. Sch. Prins.* Washington, D.C.: 1938.

Davis, R. C. The specificity of facial expression. *J. gen. Psychol.*, 1934, **10**, 42–58.

Davitz, J., & Davitz, Lois. The communication of feelings by content-free speech. *J. Communication,* 1959a, 9, 6–13.

Davitz, J., & Davitz, Lois. Correlates of accuracy in the communication of feelings. *J. Communication,* 1959b, 9, 110–117.

Diamond, S. *Personality and temperament.* New York: Harper, 1957.

Dickey, Elizabeth C., & Knower, F. H. A note on some ethological differences in recognition of simulated expressions of the emotions. *Amer. J. Sociol.*, 1941, **47**, 190–193.

Dittman, A. T., & Wynne, C. Linguistic techniques and the analysis of emotionality in interviews. *J. Abnorm. Soc. Psychol.*, 1961, **63**, 201–204.

Dollard, J., & Miller, N. *Personality and psychotherapy.* New York: McGraw-Hill, 1950.

Doran, E. W. A study of vocabularies. *Pedagog. Sem.*, 1907, **14**, 401–438.

Duffy, Elizabeth. *Activation and behavior.* New York: Wiley, 1962.

Dumas, G. La mimique des aveugles. *Bull. Acad. Med.*, 1932, **107**, 607–610. Cited by F. H. Lund, *Emotions: their psychological, physiological, and educative implications.* New York: Ronald, 1939. P. 17.

Dunlap, K. Role of eye-muscles and mouth-muscles in the expressions of the emotions. *Genet. Psychol. Monogr.*, 1927, **2**(3), 197–233.

Dusenberry, D., & Knower, F. H. Experimental studies of the symbolism of action and voice. I. A study of the specificity of meaning in facial expression. *Quart. J. Speech,* 1938, **24**, 424–435.

Dusenberry, D., & Knower, F. H. Experimental studies of the symbolism of action and voice. II. A study of the specificity of meaning in abstract tonal symbols. *Quart. J. Speech,* 1939, **25**, 67–75.

Eldred, S. H., & Price, D. B. A linguistic evaluation of feeling states in psychotherapy. *Psychiatry,* 1958, **21**, 115–121.

Engen, T., & Levy, N. Constant-sum judgments of facial expressions. *J. exp. Psychol.,* 1956, **51**, 396–398.

Engen, T., Levy, N., & Schlosberg, H. A new series of facial expressions. *Amer. Psychologist,* 1957, **12**, 264–266.

Engen, T., Levy, N., & Schlosberg, H. The dimensional analysis of a new series of facial expressions. *J. exp. Psychol.,* 1958, **55**, 454–458.

Fairbanks, G., & Hoaglin, L. W. An experimental study of the durational characteristics of the voice during expression of emotion. *Speech Monogr.,* 1941, **8**, 85–90.

Fairbanks, G., & Provenost, W. An experimental study of the pitch characteristics of the voice during the expression of emotion. *Speech Monogr.,* 1939, **6**, 87–104.

Fay, P. J. & Middleton, W. C. The ability to judge the rested or tired condition of a speaker from his voice as transmitted over a public address system. *J. Appl. Psychol.,* 1940, **24**, 645–650.

Feleky, Antoinette M. The expression of the emotions. *Psychol. Rev.,* 1914, **21**, 33–41.

Feleky, Antoinette M. *Feelings and emotions.* New York: Pioneer, 1922.

Fernberger, S. W. Six more Piderit faces. *Amer. J. Psychol.,* 1927, **39**, 162–166.

Fernberger, S. W. False suggestion and the Piderit model. *Amer. J. Psychol.,* 1928, **40**, 562–568.

French, R. S. *From Homer to Helen Keller.* New York: Amer. Found. for the Blind, 1932.

Frijda, N. H. Facial expression and situational cues. *J. abnorm. soc. Psychol.,* 1958, **57**, 149–153.

Frois-Wittman, J. The judgment of facial expression. *J. exp. Psychol.,* 1930, **13**, 113–151.

Fulcher, J. S. "Voluntary" facial expressions in blind and seeing children. *Arch. Psychol.,* 1942, **38**, No. 272.

Gage, N. L., & Cronbach, L. J. Conceptual and methodological problems in interpersonal perception. *Psychol. Rev.,* 1955, **62**, 411–422.

Gates, Georgina S. An experimental study of the growth of social perception. *J. educ. Psychol.,* 1923, **14,** 449–461.

Gates, Georgina S. The role of the auditory element in the interpretation of emotions. *Psychol. Bull.* 1927, **24,** 175. (Abstract)

Goodenough, Florence L. The expression of the emotions in infancy. *Child Develop.,* 1931, **2,** 96–101.

Goodenough, Florence L. Expression of the emotions in a blind-deaf child. *J. abnorm. soc. Psychol.,* 1932, **27,** 328–333.

Goodenough, Florence L., & Tinker, M. A. The relative potency of facial expression and verbal description of stimulus in the judgment of emotion. *J. comp. Psychol.,* 1931, **12,** 365–370.

Guilford, J. F. An experiment in learning to read facial expressions. *J. abnorm. soc. Psychol.,* 1929, **24,** 191–202.

Guilford, J. F., & Wilke, M. A new model for the demonstration of facial expressions. *Amer. J. Psychol.,* 1930, **42,** 436–439.

Haley, J. An interactional description of schizophrenia. *Psychiatry,* 1959a, **22,** 321–322.

Haley, J. The family of the schizophrenic: a model system. *J. nerv. ment. Dis.,* 1959b, **129,** 357–374.

Halkides, G. An experimental study of four conditions necessary for therapeutic change. Unpublished doctoral dissertation, Univer. of Chicago, 1958. Cited in Carl R. Rogers, *On becoming a person.* Boston: Houghton Mifflin, 1961. Pp. 47–49.

Hanawalt, N. G. The role of the upper and lower parts of the face as a basis for judging facial expressions. I. In painting and sculpture. *J. gen. Psychol.,* 1942, **27,** 331–346.

Hanawalt, N. G. The role of the upper and the lower parts of the face as a basis for judging facial expressions. II. In posed expressions and "candid camera" pictures. *J. gen. Psychol.,* 1944, **31,** 23–36.

Hanford, J. H. *John Milton, Englishman.* New York: Crown, 1949.

Hargreaves, W. A., & Starkweather, J. A. Vocal behavior: an illustrative case study. Paper read at West. Psychol. Ass., Seattle, June, 1961.

Hayes, S. P. *Contributions to a psychology of blindness.* New York: Amer. Found. for the Blind, 1941.

Hebb, D. O. Emotion in man and animal: an analysis of the intuitive processes of recognition. *Psychol. Rev.,* 1946, **53,** 88–106.

Holt, R. R., & Luborsky, L. *Personality patterns of psychiatrists.* New York: Basic Books, 1958.

Hulin, W. S., & Katz, D. The Frois-Wittman pictures of facial expression. *J. exp. Psychol.,* 1935, **18,** 482–498.

Hunt, J. McV., Cole, Marie-Louise W., & Reis, Eva, E. S. Situational cues distinguishing anger, fear, and sorrow. *Amer. J. Psychol.,* 1958, **71,** 136–151.

Jarden, Ellen, & Fernberger, S. W. The effect of suggestion on the judgment of facial expression of emotion. *Amer. J. Psychol.,* 1926, **37,** 565–570.

Jenness, A. F. Differences in the recognition of facial expressions. *J. gen. Psychol.*, 1932a, **7,** 192–196.

Jenness, A. F. The effect of coaching subjects in the recognition of facial expressions. *J. gen. Psychol.*, 1932b, **7,** 163–178.

Jenness, A. F. The recognition of facial expressions of emotion. *Psychol. Bull.*, 1932c, **29,** 324–350.

Kanner, L. Judging emotions from facial expressions. *Psychol. Monogr.*, 1931, **41** (No. 3, Whole No. 186).

Kauffman, P. E. An investigation of some psychological stimulus properties of speech behavior. Unpublished doctoral dissertation, Univer. of Chicago, 1954.

Kellogg, W. N., & Eagleson, B. M. The growth of social perception in different racial groups. *J. educ. Psychol.*, 1931, **22,** 367–375.

Klein, G. S. Cognitive control and motivation. In G. Lindzey (Ed.), *Assessment of human motives.* New York: Grove, 1960. Pp. 87–118.

Kline, L. W., & Johannsen, Dorothea E. Comparative role of the face and of the face-body-hands as aids in identifying emotions. *J. abnorm. soc. Psychol.*, 1935, **29,** 415–426.

Klineberg, O. *Race differences.* New York: Harper, 1935.

Klineberg, O. Unpublished study. Cited in G. Murphy, Lois B. Murphy, and T. M. Newcomb, *Experimental social psychology.* (2d ed.) New York: Harper, 1937. P. 236.

Klineberg, O. Emotional expression in Chinese literature. *J. abnorm. soc. Psychol.*, 1938, **33,** 517–520.

Klineberg, O. *Social psychology.* New York: Holt, 1940.

Klineberg, O. *Social psychology.* (2d ed.) New York: Holt, 1954.

Knower, F. H. Analysis of some experimental variations of simulated vocal expressions of the emotions. *J. soc. Psychol.*, 1941, **14,** 369–372.

Knower, F. H. Studies in the symbolism of voice and action: V. The use of behavioral and tonal symbols as tests of speaking achievement. *J. Appl. Psychol.*, 1945, **29,** 229–235.

Kramer, E. *The judgment of personal characteristics and emotions from nonverbal properties of speech.* Ann Arbor: Univer. of Michigan Office of Research Administration, Report 04411-2-P, 1962a.

Kramer, E. *Personality stereotypes in voice: a reconsideration of the data.* Ann Arbor: Univer. of Michigan Office of Research Administration, Report 04411-2-P, 1962b.

Krause, M. S. Anxiety in verbal behavior: an intercorrelational study. *J. consult. Psychol.*, 1961, **25,** 272.

Landis, C. Studies in emotional reactions. I. A preliminary study of facial expression. *J. exp. Psychol.*, 1924a, **7,** 325–341.

Landis, C. Studies of emotional reactions. II. General behavior and facial expression. *J. comp. Psychol.*, 1924b, **4,** 447–509.

Landis, C. The expression of emotions. In C. Murchison (Ed.), *The foundations of experimental psychology.* Worcester, Mass.: Clark Univer. Press, 1929a. Pp. 488–523.

Landis, C. The interpretation of facial expression in emotion. *J. gen. Psychol.*, 1929b, **2**, 59–72.

Langer, Susanne K. *Philosophy in a new key.* Cambridge: Harvard Univer. Press, 1942.

Langer, Susanne K. Feeling and form. New York: Scribners, 1953.

Langfeld, H. S. The judgment of emotions from facial expression. *J. abnorm. soc. Psychol.*, 1918a, **13**, 173–184.

Langfeld, H. S. Judgments of facial expression and suggestion. *Psychol. Rev.*, 1918b, **25**, 488–494.

Levy, L., Orr, T. B., & Rosenzweig, S. Judgments of emotion from facial expressions by college students, mental retardates, and mental hospital patients. *J. Pers.*, 1960, **28**, 342–349.

Levy, N., & Schlosberg, H. Woodworth scale values of the Lightfoot pictures of facial expression. *J. exp. Psychol.*, 1960, **60**, 121–125.

Lewis, M. M. *Infant speech: a study of the beginnings of language.* New York: Harcourt, Brace, 1936.

Licklider, J. C. R., & Miller, G. A. The perception of speech. In S. S. Stevens (Ed.), *Handbook of experimental psychology.* New York: Wiley, 1951. Pp. 1040–1074.

Lowenfeld, B. Psychological aspects of blindness. *Outlook for the Blind*, 1947, **41**(2), 31–36.

Lowenfeld, B. Psychological problems of children with impaired vision. In W. M. Cruickshank (Ed.), *Psychology of exceptional children and youth.* Englewood Cliffs, N.J.: Prentice-Hall, 1955. Pp. 214–283.

Lund, F. H. *Emotions: their psychological, physiological, and educative implications.* New York: Ronald, 1939.

Lynn, J. G. An apparatus and method for stimulating, recording, and measuring facial expression. *J. Exp. Psychol.*, 1940, **27**, 81–88.

Malmo, R. B. Activation: a neurophysiological dimension. *Psychol. Rev.*, 1959, **66**, 367–386.

May, Helen S. A study of emotional expression among Chinese and Americans. Unpublished master's essay, Columbia Univer., 1938.

McCarthy, Dorothea. The language development of the preschool child. *Inst. Child Welfare Monogr. Ser.*, 1930, No. 4.

Moss, F. A., Hunt, T., Omwake, K. T., & Ronning, M. M. *Social intelligence test.* Washington: Center for Psychological Service, 1927.

Munn, N. L. The effect of the knowledge of the situation upon judgment of emotion from facial expressions. *J. abnorm. soc. Psychol.*, 1940, **35**, 324–338.

Murphy, G., Murphy, Lois B., & Newcomb, T. M. *Experimental social psychology.* (2d ed.) New York: Harper, 1937.

Myklebust, H. Toward a new understanding of the deaf. *Amer. Ann. Deaf*, 1953, **98**, 345–357.

Norris, M., Spaulding, P. J., & Brodie, F. H. *Blindness in children.* Chicago: Univer. of Chicago Press, 1957.

Ortleb, Ruth. An objective study of emphasis in oral reading of emotional and unemotional material. *Speech Monogr.*, 1937, **3**, 56–68.

Osgood, E. C., Suci, G. J., & Tannenbaum, P. H. *The Measurement of meaning.* Urbana: Univer. of Illinois Press, 1957.

Osgood, G. E. Fidelity and reliability. In H. Quastler (Ed.), *Information theory in psychology.* Glencoe, Ill.: Free Press, 1955. Pp. 374–386.

Pfaff, P. L. An experimental study of the communication of feeling without contextual material. Unpublished doctoral dissertation, Univer. of California, 1953. Abstracted in *Speech Monogr.*, 1954, **21**, 155–156.

Pittenger, R. E. Linguistic analysis of tone of voice in communication of affect. *Psychiat. res. Rep.*, 1957, **8**, 41–54.

Pittenger, R. E., & Smith, H. L., Jr. A basis for some contributions of linguistics to psychiatry. *Psychiatry*, 1957, **20**, 61–78.

Pollack, I., Rubenstein, H., & Horowitz, A. Communication of verbal modes of expression. *Lang. Speech*, 1960, **3**, 121–130.

Rapaport, D., Schafer, R., & Gill, M. *Diagnostic psychological testing.* Vol. I. Chicago: Year Book Publishers, 1945.

Raven, J. C. *Progressive matrices, sets I and II.* Dumfries: Crichton Royal, 1947.

Rogers, C. R. The necessary and sufficient conditions of psychotherapeutic personality change. *J. Consult. Psychol.*, 1957, **21**, 95–103.

Rogers, C. R. *On becoming a person.* Boston: Houghton Mifflin, 1961.

Rokeach, M. *The open and closed mind.* New York: Basic Books, 1960.

Ruckmick, C. A. A preliminary study of the emotions. *Psychol. Monogr.*, 1921, **30**, No. 3, 30–35.

Ruckmick, C. A. *The psychology of feeling and emotion.* New York: McGraw-Hill, 1936.

Ruesch, J., & Prestwood, A. R. Anxiety: its initiation, communication, and interpersonal management. *A.M.A. Arch. Neurology Psychiat.*, 1949, **62**, 527–550.

Rump, E. E. Facial expression and situational cues: demonstration of logical error in Frijda's report. *Act. Psychol.*, 1960, **17**, 31–38.

Sakoda, J. N., Cohen, B. H., & Beall, G. Test of significance of a series of statistical tests. *Psychol. Bull.*, 1954, **51**, 172–175.

Sauer, R. E., & Marcuse, F. L. Overt and covert recording. *J. proj. Tech.*, 1957, **21**, 391–395.

Schachter, J. Pain, fear, and anger in hypertensives and normotensives: a psychophysiologic study. *Psychosom. Med.*, 1957, **19**, 17–29.

Schachter, S., & Singer, J. Cognitive, social, and physiological determinants of emotional state. *Psychol. Rev.*, 1962, **69**, 379–399.

Schachter, S., & Wheeler, L. Epinephrine, chlorpromazine, and amusement. *J. abnorm. soc. Psychol.*, 1962, **65**, 121–128.

Schlosberg, H. A scale for judgment of facial expressions. *J. exp. Psychol.*, 1941, **29**, 497–510.

Schlosberg, H. The description of facial expression in terms of two dimensions. *J. exp. Psychol.*, 1952, **44**, 229–237.

Schlosberg, H. Three dimensions of emotion. *Psychol. Rev.,* 1954, **61,** 81–88.

Schulze, R. *Experimental psychology and pedagogy.* New York: Macmillan, 1912.

Scott, W. C. M. Noise, speech, and technique. *Int. J. Psycho-Anal.,* 1958, **39,** 108–111.

Shaffer, L. F., & Shoben, E. J., Jr. The psychology of adjustment. (2d ed.) Boston: Houghton Mifflin, 1956.

Sherman, M. The differentiation of emotional responses in infants. I. Judgments of emotional responses from motion picture views and from actual observation. *J. comp. Psychol.,* 1927a, **7,** 265–284.

Sherman, M. The differentiation of emotional responses in infants. II. The ability of observers to judge emotional characteristics of the crying infants and of the voice of an adult. *J. comp. Psychol.,* 1927b, **7,** 335–351.

Shirley, M. M. The first two years: a study of twenty-five babies. Vol. II. Intellectual development. *Inst. Child Welfare Monogr. Ser.,* 1933a, No. 7.

Shirley, M. M. The first two years: a study of twenty-five babies: Vol. III. Personality manifestations. *Inst. Child Welfare Monogr. Ser.,* 1933b, No. 8.

Skinner, E. R. A calibrated recording and analysis of the pitch, force, and quality of vocal tones expressing happiness and sadness; and a determination of the pitch and force of the subjective concepts of ordinary, soft, and loud tones. *Speech Monogr.,* 1935, **2,** 81–137.

Smith, H. C. *Personality adjustment.* New York: McGraw-Hill, 1961.

Sommers, Vita S. *The influence of parental attitudes and social environment on the personality development of the adolescent blind.* New York: Amer. Found. for the Blind, 1944.

Soskin, W. F. Some aspects of communication and interpretation in psychotherapy. Paper read at Amer. Psychol. Ass., Cleveland, Sept., 1953.

Soskin, W. F., & Kauffman, P. E. Intelligibility of varying samples of spontaneous utterances filtered to suppress frequencies above 550 cps. Unpublished paper, Univer. of Chicago, 1954a.

Soskin, W. F., & Kauffman, P. E. Some psychological characteristics of filtered speech. Paper read at Midwest. Psychol. Ass., Columbus, Ohio, 1954b.

Soskin, W. F., & Kauffman, P. E. Judgment of emotion in word-free voice samples. *J. Commun.,* 1961, **11,** 73–80.

Starkweather, J. A. The communication-value of content-free speech. *Amer. J. Psychol.,* 1956, **69,** 121–123.

Starkweather, J. A. Vocal communication of personality and human feelings. *J. Commun.,* 1961, **11,** 63–72.

Terry, Dorothy. The use of a rating scale of level of response in TAT stories. *J. abnorm. soc. Psychol.,* 1952, **15,** 173–184.

Thompson, Clare W., & Bradway, Katherine. The teaching of psychotherapy through content-free interviews. *J. consult. Psychol.,* 1950, **14,** 321–323.

Thompson, Jane. Development of facial expression of emotion in blind and seeing children. *Arch. Psychol.*, 1941, **37**, No. 264.

Thorndike, R. L. Two screening tests of verbal intelligence. *J. appl. Psychol.*, 1942, **26**, 128–135.

Triandis, H. G., Lambert, W. W. A restatement and test of Schlosberg's theory of emotions, with two kinds of subjects from Greece. *J. abnorm. soc. Psychol.*, 1958, **56**, 321–328.

Vinacke, W. E. The judgment of facial expression by three national-racial groups in Hawaii. I. *J. Pers.*, 1949, **17**, 407–429.

Voorhees, A. L. Attitudes of the blind toward blindness. Boston: *Proc. 23d Conv. Amer. Ass. Workers for the Blind*, 1949, 65–67.

Wechsler, D. *Wechsler intelligence scale for children*. New York: Psychol. Corp., 1949.

Weisberger, C. A. Accuracy in judging emotional expressions as related to college entrance. *J. Psychol.*, 1956, **44**, 233–239.

Woodworth, R. S. *Experimental psychology*. New York: Holt, 1938.

Woodworth, R. S., & Schlosberg, H. Experimental psychology. (2d ed.) New York: Holt, 1954.

Young, F. M. An analysis of certain variables in a development study of language. *Genet. Psychol. Monogr.*, 1941, **23**, 3–141.

Young, P. T. *Emotion in man and animal*. New York: Wiley, 1943.

INDEX

DAT
N